In Recognition of
WILLIAM GADDIS

In Recognition of
WILLIAM GADDIS

Edited with an Introduction by

John Kuehl and Steven Moore

SYRACUSE UNIVERSITY PRESS
1984

Excerpts from *The Recognitions,* copyright © 1955 by William Gaddis, are reprinted by permission of William Gaddis.

Excerpts from *J R,* copyright © 1975 by William Gaddis, are reprinted by permission of Alfred A. Knopf, Inc.

Excerpts from *The Diary of Anais Nin,* Vol. Four, copyright © 1971 by Anais Nin, are reprinted by permission of Harcourt Brace Jovanovich, Inc.

"Gaddis Anagnorisis" reprinted with permission of *Itinerary.* Copyright © 1977 by the *Itinerary* Series.

"To Soar in Atonement: Art as Expiation in Gaddis' *The Recognitions*" reprinted with permission of *Novel.* Copyright © 1977 by *Novel* Corp.

"Disclosing Time: William Gaddis' *J R*" reprinted with permission of *The Journal of Narrative Technique.* Copyright © 1982 by *The Journal of Narrative Technique.*

"Paper Currencies: Reading William Gaddis" reprinted with permission of *The Review of
Contemporary Fiction.* Copyright © 1982 by John O'Brien.

"The Paper Empires and Empirical Fictions of William Gaddis" reprinted with permission
of *The Review of Contemporary Fiction.* Copyright © 1982 by John O'Brien.

Excerpts from *American Fictions,* copyright © 1983 by Frederick R. Karl, are reprinted by
permission of Harper & Row, Publishers, Inc.

Library of Congress Cataloging in Publication Data
Main entry under title:

In recognition of William Gaddis.

Bibliography: p.
1. Gaddis, William, 1922– —Criticism and
interpretation—Addresses, essays, lectures. I. Kuehl,
John Richard, 1928– . II. Moore, Steven, 1951–
PS3557.A28Z74 1984   813'.54   84-159
ISBN 0-8156-2306-2

Manufactured in the United States of America

For Jack Green

Contents

Preface

Like *Ulysses, Finnegans Wake, The Waste Land,* and *The Cantos,* William Gaddis' *The Recognitions* and *J R* are among those twentieth-century texts that demand and deserve close attention: "demand" because of their complex nature; "deserve" because of their undeniable stature. *In Recognition of William Gaddis* attempts to remedy past neglect, affirming what many have known all along—that the creator of these two remarkable novels will inevitably join Herman Melville as a major force in the history of American letters.

We are all familiar with the history of *Moby-Dick:* how the novel received mixed reviews; how Melville stopped writing imaginative prose; how his masterpiece was not revived until the 1920s. Virtually the identical thing happened to Gaddis' first book. This should surprise no one, for the two novels have so much in common that *Moby-Dick* even recurs in *The Recognitions* as a work written by the counterfeit Melville, Mr. Feddle. Though published nearly one hundred years apart (1851 and 1955), both are encyclopedic, crammed with abstruse information and literary, historical, and religious allusions. Their form and content, which bear striking resemblances, made the earlier book a precursor of modernism, the later a templet of postmodernism. Consequently, they suffered the same fate: neglect.

Recently called "the indispensable novel of the last thirty years in America" by Frank McConnell, *The Recognitions* initially encountered reviewers dismayed at its length and complexity. So too were the critics, for ten years passed before the first academic article appeared. And, like Melville, who published no fiction between *The Confidence-Man* and *Billy Budd,* Gaddis, admitting, "I've been posthumous for 20 years," experienced a protracted hiatus between *The Recognitions* and *J R.* However, there is one crucial difference in this pattern. Whereas Melville died in obscurity in 1891, Gaddis has begun to acquire a reputation. The turning point was 1976, when he won the National Book Award for *JR* (1975). During 1982,

The Review of Contemporary Fiction devoted a special issue to Gaddis;
the University of Nebraska Press published Steven Moore's *A Reader's
Guide to William Gaddis's "The Recognitions"*; and Gaddis became a Mac
Arthur Prize Fellow. This generous five-year grant will help him complete
his third novel, tentatively entitled, "That Time of Year," a work tersely
described by the author in *The New York Times Book Review* of 6 June
1982:

> I am engaged in a novel of which for the moment there's little more to say
> than that, to assist the unwary, it will have proportionately more commas
> than its predecessor, fewer characters and locales than the book before that,
> be prudently shorter than either and, if the characters behave themselves,
> be labled "a romance."

It would seem, then, that twenty-nine years after the publication of *The
Recognitions* the time is propitious for a collection of essays illuminating
and evaluating Gaddis' achievement. By 1983, when he was finally the subject of a special session at the MLA convention, Gaddis criticism had grown
so extensive a separation of the wheat from the chaff became necessary.
Our criteria were simple: we decided to include only essays that made an
original contribution to the field (eliminating otherwise fine general in-
troductions) and that were relatively free of factual errors, the bane of this
criticism. Several essays qualified, but only thirteen survived the winnow-
ing process, seven unpublished, five published, and one specially adapted
from a newly printed book.

Biographical information on Gaddis is scarce and scattered, yet the introduction preceding these essays supplements the available data with many
unpublished facts contained largely in the author's letters to various cor-
respondents. Thus, the Introduction — which also addresses the reception
and history of *The Recognitions* — dispels several rumors and sets the record straight.

The first seven essays deal with the earlier novel, the next three, the later, and the last three, both. In the opening essay, David Koenig, who had
access to the Gaddis notes and manuscripts, investigates how *The Recognitions* was conceived, revised, and edited. We learn about the original love
story; the impact of the Faust legend, *The Golden Bough,* and the *Recognitions of Clement;* the abortive epilogue/prologue; and the deleted Munich section.

John Leverence's "Gaddis Anagnorisis" follows "The Writing of *The Recognitions.*" After analyzing the novel's loose baroque style and postmodern
design, Mr. Leverence demonstrates the relation of alchemy to its form and

content and discusses the ouroboros adorning the Harcourt and Meridian title pages.

The complex connection between art and religion constitutes the subject of "To Soar in Atonement: Art as Expiation in Gaddis' *The Recognitions*," by Joseph S. Salemi, and "Flemish Art and Wyatt's Quest for Redemption in William Gaddis' *The Recognitions*," by Christopher Knight. Whereas Mr. Salemi believes that genuine art atones for falsity, Mr. Knight feels that salvation may be achieved only through love. Mr. Salemi makes some interesting comments on the novel's self-reflective and anti-modern aspects, while Mr. Knight's detailed exploration of Flemish painting is particularly rewarding.

There ensues "Dryad in a Dead Oak Tree: The Incognito in *The Recognitions*," an essay which considers Gaddis the literary heir of Melville and Hawthorne. According to Mr. Seelye, the author's fundamentally evil world is dominated by male homosexuals who reflect contemporary sterility. Effeminate art critic and Devil, Basil Valentine, tempts saintly Wyatt during an action that inverts Christian rituals.

John Seelye emphasizes the pursuit of the father, but Steven Moore's "*Peer Gynt* and *The Recognitions*" focuses on the exorcism of the mother. Gaddis uses the Ibsen play as an opportune analogue, since both works are preoccupied with attaining selfhood. However, Mr. Moore points out that Peer remains stunted through an unhealthy attachment to Aasa-Solveig, whereas Wyatt finally triumphs over his Stabat-Mater, Camilla-Esme.

Miriam Fuchs, in "'*il miglior fabbro*': Gaddis' Debt to T. S. Eliot," also examines a literary influence. This debt includes shifting points of view, juxtaposition of past and present, spatialization of events, arid landscapes, mourning women, questers, imposters, fertility figures, chapels, bells, burials, and resurrections. Wyatt's progress toward integration mirrors the harmony of the *Four Quartets*, as civilization's regression toward disintegration echoes the cacophony of *The Waste Land*.

With Stephen H. Matanle's "Love and Strife in William Gaddis' *J R*," the collection shifts from the 1955 to the 1975 novel. Mr. Matanle argues that *J R*, like *The Recognitions*, enacts what the author has termed, "the separating of things today without love." Three interrelated topics are then presented: "The Problem of Chaos"; "The Rule of Strife"; and "The Plurality of Discourse." Especially effective is the discussion centering on Empedocles, whose name recurs in *J R* and whose Love vs. Strife conflict parallels the tension Ms. Fuchs found between the two Eliot poems.

Another version of this dichotomy inspired "Disclosing Time: William Gaddis' *J R*," where Susan Strehle poses successive or public time against durational or private time. Victimized by the former, the characters own broken clocks, grow forgetful, repeat themselves, and quote each other. Contrariwise, the narrator regards time as a fluid process and so abandons conventional linear storytelling while replacing clocks and calendar with seasonal and solar cycles. The novel's fragmented matter is paradoxically conveyed through its unified manner. All this Ms. Strehle asserts in the context of Bergson and Heidegger.

"Art as Redemption of Trash: Bast and Friends in Gaddis' *J R*" contends that the later book continues the polarity between art and money introduced during the earlier. Thus, the Belgian scholar Johan Thielemans traces the unhappy lives led by the various artists (composer, painter, writers) who populate *J R,* revealing that despite personal failure, works of art remain important.

The first two essays treating both texts bear the imprint of structural semiotics. In "Paper Currencies: Reading William Gaddis," Steven Weisenburger is also concerned about artists as they face modern counterfeiters, plagiarists, and usurers. Mr. Weisenburger applies Gide's notion "that sexual, monetary, and literary exchanges form a startling homology" to *The Recognitions* and *J R,* satires "against institutionalized exchange rates." Weisenburger's observations on onomastics, which culminate when Wyatt becomes Stephen to redeem himself, are especially illuminating.

Joel Dana Black, whose "The Paper Empires and Empirical Fictions of William Gaddis" follows, would probably agree with the Gide formulation, since he sees "a vast corporate-political structure" determining both non-fictional and fictional discourse in contemporary Alexandrian novels. For Mr. Black, *The Recognitions* and *J R* function dialectically, the former treating originality vs. imitation, genuineness vs. forgery, the sacred vs. the profane, and the latter, money vs. paper, value vs. worthlessness, meaning vs. nonsense. But whereas *The Recognitions* is an encyclopedic work, *J R*—in which Gaddis tacitly admits encyclopedic endeavors must fail—is a paper empire or playground. Black believes that this evolution freed the author's fiction "from the nemesis of narrative, the Western mania for order and control."

Succeeding these essentially structuralist approaches is the essentially historical approach of Frederick R. Karl, who places the two novels in the tradition of American and modern literature. "Gaddis: A Tribune of the Fifties" concludes the collection because it represents the fullest exegetical evaluation available. Exploring the major themes and techniques, Mr. Karl argues that form and content are inseparable, so that, for example, in *The Recognitions,* one may uncover "narrative under layers of disguise and deception, finding there in plot line the equivalent of counterfeiting."

The most comprehensive Gaddis bibliography to date comes after the Karl essay. It has been formally arranged and briefly annotated.

A few words must be said about our editorial procedures. All articles were edited to conform in format and documentation. As Gaddis often uses ellipses, those employed by the contributors were bracketed. Misquotations, typographical errors, inaccuracies, and minor stylistic infelicities were corrected. Except in block quotations, quotation marks were substituted for the dash Gaddis characteristically uses to indicate dialogue. If more substantial changes were made, these were acknowledged on the essay's opening page in the permission note.

Finally, we would like to thank several people who furnished material on Jack Green: Jane B. Necol, Miriam Rodgers, Zoë Sherwood and John O'Brien of *The Review of Contemporary Fiction*. We would also like to thank Vincent Livelli for sharing reminiscences of his and Gaddis' Greenwich Village days; John Devlin, at Harcourt Brace Jovanovich, for details on *The Recognitions'* rocky publishing history; Thomas Mirkowicz for information on critical activity in Poland; Tom Sawyer and Steven Weisenburger for sharing their Gaddis letters with us; and Thomas Hill and Margaret M. Williams of the Harvard *Lampoon* for answering questions and sending copies of the Gaddis selections we lacked. Our greatest debts of gratitude, however, must be paid to Clifford S. Mead, Rare Books Librarian at Mason Library (Keene State College), who provided us with most of the unpublished material that appears in the introduction and drew our attention to several items on Gaddis that we would otherwise have missed, and to Linda Kandel Kuehl (Delaware Valley College), who gave us sound editorial advice.

Autumn 1983   JK
                                                                         SM

Introduction

"*L'homme c'est rien — l'oeuvre c'est tout,*" Flaubert wrote George Sand, a dictum with which one feels Gaddis would agree. Curiosity about the man who produced the work, though natural and all too human, Gaddis considers irrelevant and impertinent; as he once explained, "I have generally shied from parading personal details partly for their being just that, partly from the sense that one thing said leaves others equally significant unsaid, and the sense in those lines to the effect that we are never as unlike others as we can be unlike ourselves."[1] In a rare interview, he elaborated further:

> The question of autobiographical sources in fiction has always seemed to me one of the more tiresome going, usually what simply amounts to gossip and about as reliable, not that we don't all relish gossip. But it can be as inviting a trap for the bounty hunters as tracing down literary sources. A lot of it seems to spring from this urge to scrimp and ice[2] the creative act, the creative personality, you get the extremes in nonsensically detailed questionnaires that show up in the mail, what is your favourite colour? on which side of the paper do you write? Because finally the work itself is going to stand or fall uniquely on its own. Does knowing Dreiser's intimate biographical details make his writing any the less clumsy? or knowing Butler's finally have much to do with an appreciation of THE WAY OF ALL FLESH? And how do you search out the "portrait of the artist" in a really great novel, is it Dmitri rather than Ivan? or Alyosha? even Smerdyakov? No, characters all draw on some contradictory level of their author's life, as sure as Basil Seal lurked close as thieves under all that houndstooth suiting near to Tony Last.[3]

Characters in both of Gaddis' novels echo their author's disdain for biographical curiosity. "What did you want of him that you didn't get from his work?" Wyatt asks Esther when he learns of her desire to meet a fa-

1

mous poet. "What is it they want from a man that they didn't get from his work?" he continues, realizing Esther's misplaced interest is hardly unique. "What do they expect? What is there left of him when he's done his work? What's any artist, but the dregs of his work? the human shambles that follows it around. What's left of the man when the work's done but a shambles of apology."[4] This social pressure on the artist to be as interesting as his work likewise exasperates Edward Bast in Gaddis' second novel: "Well why should I be interesting!" he answers Rhoda. "I mean, I mean I want my work to be interesting but why do I have to be interesting! I mean everybody's trying to be interesting let them I'm just, I'm just doing something I have to do so I can try to do what I hope I . . ."[5]

Yet such curiosity is to be condemned only when it takes the place of (rather than contributes to) the study of the work itself; the example readiest at hand is the critic in *The Recognitions,* identified always by his green wool shirt, who is mocked for being able to write an essay on "Rilke the man", but unable to recognize the opening lines of Rilke's most famous poem. Even Gaddis has not been averse to writing himself into his novels — just as Wyatt painted himself into his forgeries — and consequently several grounds can be given for a short excursion into those aspects of Gaddis' biography relevant to his work. The first is simply to set the record straight. During the twenty years between publications a variety of ludicrous rumors were rife: that he paid to have *The Recognitions* published; that he wrote a defense of his novel and castigated his critics under the pseudonym of Jack Green, and paid for a full-page ad in the *Village Voice* under the same name; that he was Joyce alive in America or, later, writing under the pseudonym of Thomas Pynchon; that he was so discouraged by the reception of *The Recognitions* that he more than once announced his intention of abandoning writing altogether; that the same discouragement led him to buy up all the remaining copies and burn them; that he was dead; and, a final absurdity, that he was once employed as a floorwalker at Bloomingdale's. "There was an air of legend and mystery about you even then, Wyatt," says a character in *The Recognitions* (115), and we would do well to dispel the air of legend and mystery that has surrounded Gaddis ever since that novel. But more important, Gaddis has drawn extensively upon his own biography for many characters, incidents, and themes in his novels, an understanding of which, while certainly not causing the novels to stand or fall, enhances them with an auxiliary interest. Ideally, then, an investigation of these autobiographical elements and his adaptation of them should vary from an examination of any other field of reference operative in his work only in the tact and circumspection enjoined by private, as opposed to published, sources.

Gaddis admitted indirectly the possible significance of biography to literary study in the one-sentence *vita* he furnished the reference book, *World Authors:*

> Born in Manhattan, boarding school in Connecticut age five till about thirteen, public school on Long Island, Harvard College 1941–1945, a year or so on a New York magazine and the next five in Central America and the Caribbean, Europe mainly Spain, and briefly North Africa before returning to complete the partially written novel finally published in 1955, later issued in paper, and ground for a National Institute of Arts and Letters award in 1963, a sequence, significant only in any transmutations its details may find in my work, which has offered too many temptations to take myself instead of my work seriously, one of concern only to those whose good faith goes long unrewarded, and possibly of some eventual uncontrollable meaning to the son and daughter by whom I set such store, even as they prosper from beginnings that have redeemed more recent years unproductive of any accomplishment but getting a living, and groping in the tangle of apparently disparate projects which continue their struggle to devour, and develop, and illuminate one another, to escape whole the limitations of my own mind.[6]

"A sequence," he emphasizes, "significant only in any transmutations its details may find in my work," and consequently what follows will concern itself with those transmutations alone.

Born on 29 December 1922, William Thomas Gaddis lived in New York City and on Long Island until the age of five. At that time his family owned property in the Long Island village of Massapequa, the location and deterioration of which provided the setting for the Basts' Long Island residence in *J R*. His fifth through thirteenth years were spent at a boarding school in Berlin, Connecticut. In *J R* Jack Gibbs describes his own boarding school as "A place up, small school nobody's ever heard of in Connecticut up near Hartford, probably not even there any . . ." (506). Indeed Gaddis' boarding school is no longer standing; and Gibbs no doubt speaks for the author when he confesses to Amy his loneliness at that time:

> —End of the day alone on that train, lights coming on in those little Connecticut towns stop and stare out at an empty street corner dry cheese sandwich charge you a dollar wouldn't even put butter on it, finally pull into that desolate station scared to get off scared to stay on [. . .] school car waiting there like a, black Reo touring car waiting there like a God damned open hearse think anybody expect to grow up . . . (119)

Like both Gibbs (268) and Otto, Gaddis too grew up without a father;
in a letter to John Seelye (who had written an excellent review of the Meridian *Recognitions* for the *Berkeley Gazette*) he described Otto's unsuccessful reunion with Mr. Pivner as "a try at redoing my own experience
with my father, transmuted, as seemed permissible, with trivia."

Gaddis entered public school in the eighth grade and went on to attend
high school on Long Island. During high school he suffered from the same
illness that Wyatt does in the first chapter of *The Recognitions: erythema
grave,* a tropical disease. Gaddis was cured in less dramatic fashion than
Wyatt is, but the cure would later result in unforeseen side effects. He entered Harvard in September 1941; several characters in both novels attend
Harvard and display the traditional animosity toward those attending rivals
Yale and Princeton. Shortly after the bombing of Pearl Harbor, Gaddis
developed a kidney disorder, the unexpected result of treating the earlier
illness, and the ailment prevented his joining the army (one reason—if not
a justification—for the scorn shown toward physicians in *The Recognitions*). He recuperated away from Harvard, returning a year later to find
it desolated by the war.

His first published writings date from this period. With the suspension
of Harvard's official student literary magazine, *The Advocate,* because of
the war, Gaddis joined the staff of the *Lampoon* in the fall of 1943 and
became its president in the spring of the following year. The most striking
aspect of the *Lampoon* writings is the variety of forms: In the first issue
alone to which he contributed (1 October 1943) there is a story, a brief
essay, a playlet, and brief theater and film reviews. In succeeding issues
he published verse (some parodying such poems as "The Walrus and the
Carpenter" and "Ozymandias," others with titles such as "Tripanosomiasis in B Flat"), mock record and book reviews,[7] a Christmas list, a pastiche
in biblical English, a verse play in Elizabethan English, essays on such topics as perpetual calendars and the christening of ships, crib notes for psychology and French students (the latter purporting to be a translation from
Putains Que J'ai Connues, par Guillaume Ravenkill), a report on the Harvard dining hall entitled "A Psychometric Study of the Effects of Nourishment" by "Dr. H. H. Rumpôt-DuBille and Dr. Gudge," and even a silly
crossword puzzle. In addition there are a number of short stories in a variety
of styles: O. Henry is mentioned in one, and many read like O. Henry laced
with weak Saki. A few have a slight chill to them and anticipate the dark
humor of *The Recognitions,* but the majority of Gaddis' *Lampoon* contributions are merely clever, collegiate pieces that give little indication of
the immense talent that was to unfold after he left college.

A stanza from one of his *Lampoon* poems foreshadowed his leaving Harvard in 1945 without a degree:

> I'll escape the alma mater,
> Rise above the madding throng;
> Join a band of vulgar gypsies,
> And make my sordid song.[8]

In his senior year, Gaddis' name and that of a drinking companion appeared in the local paper as a result of a fracas with the Cambridge police, and they were asked by the dean to resign from the college.

His life for the next few years is closely paralleled in *The Recognitions* by Otto's, who likewise leaves Harvard to become a writer in New York. Gaddis was employed by the *New Yorker* as a "checker"—and the *New Yorker* is the recipient of some rather harsh remarks in *J R* (517)—examining articles for factual accuracy, but he soon felt the need for a change of place, away from the "madding throng" of Greenwich Village. He left New York toward the end of 1947, and his travels over the next five years are not only reflected in the travels of his characters but provide the novel's international scope. He went first to Mexico City, where one aspect of *The Recognitions* was begun, then to Panama City, initially to launch an "international news career" but eventually to work on the Canal as a machinist's assistant, adding to the novel in his spare time. (Thirty years later, when American control of the Canal Zone was under debate, Gaddis would write a brief memoir of his days there.[9]) He soon left the zone for a war in nearby Costa Rica, where he "was handed over to a young captain named Madero and issued a banged-up Springfield that was stolen from me the same day." He finally returned on a Honduran banana boat (as does Otto from his first trip to Central America) to New York again, staying at his family's summer house on Long Island.   *sermons and soda water*

The Greenwich Village characters and incidents in *The Recognitions* were largely drawn from that summer of 1948: like Otto, Gaddis continued to wear a white Panama suit in the Village and kept his unimpaired right arm in a sling—"so that he would write explosively when it was released from its bandage like a bird from a cage," a friend from his Village days remembers him saying.[10] "Willie, by Village standards in the '40s, was something of an English gentleman," the same friend recalls, "but very cunning and madly in love." The object of his affections was Sheri Martinelli, a well-bred, well-educated poet and painter on whom Gaddis would model Esme for his novel. A few years earlier she had met Anaïs

Nin, who included in her *Diary* an intriguing description of Sheri that reveals how closely Gaddis patterned his Esme after her.

> Gonzalo tells me there is a romantic-looking girl who sits near [his] press, reading *Under a Glass Bell,* and wants to know me. But at the same time, she is frightened, so he suggested she meet me when I lecture at the Mills School. At the end of the lecture, she appeared. I recognized her. She was like a ghost of a younger me, a dreaming woman, with very soft, burning eyes, long hair streaming over her shoulders, ready at any moment to vanish if the atmosphere was not propitious.
>
> [. . .] She did not say a word. She merely stared at me, and then handed me a music box mechanism, without its box. She finally told me in a whisper that she always carries it in her pocket and listens to it in the street. She wound it up for me, and placed it against my ear, as if we were alone and not in a busy school hall, filled with bustling students and professors waiting for me. A strand of her long hair had caught in the mechanism and it seemed as if the music came from it.
>
> She came to see me, blue eyes dissolved in moisture, slender, orphaned child of poverty, speaking softly and exaltedly. Pleading, hurt, vulnerable, breathless. Her voice touches the heart. She came because she felt lost. I had found the words which made her life clearer. She talks as I write, as if I had created a language for her feelings. She walks out of my books and confronts me. She is without strength and without defenses, as I was when I first met Henry [Miller] and Gonzalo.
>
> Her name is Sherry [*sic*] Martinelli. She lives with a painter, Enrique Zanarte. She tells me: "Enrique says I am mad, because sometimes I ask him: 'Are you feeling blue or purple today?' as I believe our moods have colors. Also, I prefer to break a dish after I eat, rather than wash it. Do you think there might be, somewhere, a man who feels as I do? When we went to the zoo together, I was angry because he loved the rhinoceros, who has a carapace against feeling, whereas I liked the kangaroo, who carries its young as I would like to carry my three-year-old daughter with me all the time."
>
> She is twenty-seven,[11] but she belongs with Pablo, Marshall, and Charles Duits. "There are phrases one picks up in the street and lives with." She is pure poetry walking and breathing, inside and outside of my books, so I feel I am not lying, I am not inventing, I am not far from the truth. "Oh God, all the books one reads which don't bring you near the truth. Only yours, Anaïs."
>
> Her eyes become immense when she asks questions. Blue, with the pupil very dark and dilated. She looks mischievous and fragile. She wears rough, ugly clothes, like an orphan. She is part Jewish, part Irish. Her voice sings, changes: low, gay, sad, heavy, trailing, dreaming.[12]

Again like Otto, Gaddis had to compete with rivals for this woman's affection: first with littérateur Anatole Broyard,[13] who advantageously lived
around the corner from Sheri, and later with a jazz musician named Ed-
die Shoe. The model for Chaby Sinisterra, Shoe took painting lessons from
her, lived in the same apartment building on Jones Street (Esme's address
on page 522 of *The Recognitions*), and unfortunately introduced her to
drugs, to "that world not world where the needle took her" (300). Gaddis'
affair with Sheri was as frustrating as Otto's with Esme: she too attempted
suicide many times (once in the same manner as Esme [476 ff.]) and eventually took to pinning notes to the outside world on her locked door. The
romance was hopeless, so Gaddis decided to leave New York City in 1948
for Spain to travel and to continue working on his novel. His parting challenge to his Village companions was: "I will be the first one to publish."

Gaddis stayed in Spain for two years; in Madrid he read Robert Graves'
newly published *The White Goddess* and, he relates in a letter, "hurried
up to Deya to talk to Graves and ask for suggestions regarding what religion might a Protestant minister becoming unhinged turn to. He came up
with something about Salem witchcraft (I later dug up the Mithras solution elsewhere) but was such a fine and generous man that we had numerous talks and, in fact, he was to become somewhat the physical model for
Rev Gwyon."[14] Afterward, Gaddis traveled as both Reverend Gwyon and
Wyatt do throughout the peninsula and likewise retreated to a monastery
for a while. In the novel, the Real Monasterio de Nuestra Señora de la
Otra Vez that father and son stay at is based on the Real Monasterio de
Guadalupe in Estremadura,[15] which Gaddis entered in much the same spirit
as Ludy does in the novel, also to be given a comfortable room and meals
at a modest price and kept at arm's length from the monk's devotions.[16]
He stayed about a week, then moved on.

Gaddis left Spain in 1950 and went to Paris for a year, setting the novel
aside and writing short radio programs for UNESCO. At this time he also
wrote an amusing article on player pianos entitled "'Stop Player. Joke No.
4'" for the *Atlantic Monthly.*[17] (Twenty-five years later Gaddis was reported
as still having "a few important obsessions, one of them involving the player
piano as symbolic of the triumph of technology over art"[18] — as *J R* well
attests. Coincidentally, Kurt Vonnegut's novel *Player Piano*, reflecting the
same concern, appeared shortly after Gaddis' article.) He left Paris in the
spring of 1951 and made a short trip to North Africa (as does Wyatt) before returning to America. He published a draft of the second chapter of
his novel in the first issue of *New World Writing* (April 1952) and worked
briefly in New York for the government, writing pieces for a cultural maga-

zine sent to Russia until a contract with Harcourt, Brace and Company—negotiated by his agent Bernice Baumgarten (Mrs. James Gould Cozzens)—was signed 11 December 1952, and the publisher's advance allowed him to isolate himself and work full time on the novel.

In a farmhouse outside a small town called Montgomery, west of Newburgh, New York, Gaddis worked through the winter of 1952–53 to complete the work.

> I worked there daily & well into the nights with my usual stack of notes, 2nd thoughts, outlines &c till finally very late one night, having intended only to try to get through the sequence of Stanley at the organ to my satisfaction—& with still outlined notes at hand for spinning out the novel's conclusion—I sat back to look at that last "still spoken of, when it is noted, with high regard, though seldom played" (anticipating, of course, the fate of the novel itself: for played read read) & abruptly realized, both appalled & elated, that I'd reached the end of the book; that no matter my planning & intentions, & even that sense of loss overreaching any of fulfillment, there was no arguing it: the book ended right there.[19]

Ironically, just as Gaddis finished turning the proto-Beats of his Greenwich Village days into fictional characters, he himself was turned into a literary character by none other than the "King of the Beats." *The Subterraneans* chronicles Jack Kerouac's two-month affair with an exotic young black woman called Mardou Fox in August and September of 1953.[20] One Friday night toward the end of the affair, Leo Percepied (Kerouac) and Mardou are drinking with Yuri Gligoric (Gregory Corso) in the Black Mask—that is, the notorious San Remo, the same bar that figures in *The Recognitions* as the Viareggio and in Chandler Brossard's *Who Walk in Darkness* (1952) as the Sporting Club. In walks "a kid called Harold Sand," as Kerouac calls Gaddis, "a chance acquaintance of Mardou's from a year ago, a young novelist looking like Leslie Howard who'd just had a manuscript accepted and so acquired a strange grace in my eyes I wanted to devour."[21] Corso also knew Gaddis "from before, so he, Sand, walking into the Mask, flushed successful young author but 'ironic' looking and with a big parking ticket sticking out of his coat lapel, was set upon by the three of us with avidity, made to sit at our table—made to talk." Eventually Kerouac, Mardou, and "polite dignified Sand" decide with some reluctance to drive down to visit Austin Bromberg (poet Alan Ansen), a mutual acquaintance. But Kerouac and Mardou have quarreled over Corso, and so "Sand having anticipated a gay talkative weekend now finds himself with a couple of grim lover worriers, hears in fact the fragment 'But I didn't mean you to think that baby' so obviously hearkening to his mind the Yuri incident—finds himself with this pair of bores and has to drive all the way down to Los Altos,[22] and so with the same grit that made him write the half million words of his novel bends to it and pushes the car through the Peninsula night and on into the dawn." The rest of the sequence takes place at Bromberg's house, where Sand and Bromberg discuss "every tom dick and harry in art" in what Kerouac describes as a "brilliant conversation," "the likes of which cannot be surpassed anywhere in the world." Sand finally drives them to a bus stop to return to the city, but in a bar across the street "Bromberg go[es] right on with big booming burbling comments on art and literature and even in fact by God queer anecdotes as sullen Santa Clara Valley farmers guzzle at rail, Bromberg doesn't even have consciousness of his fantastic impact on the ordinary—and Sand enjoying, himself in fact also weird."

In November 1953 Ansen left for Europe, and Gaddis occupied his house for a nominal rent, spending yet another winter alone revising the novel. By the time Ansen returned the following April, *The Recognitions* was finished; Gaddis remembers Ansen "sitting down barely off the boat in that ghastly diningroom & reading it straight through in a day and a half," and shortly thereafter the manuscript was delivered to the publisher.

Robert Giroux, editor in chief of the trade division of Harcourt at the time, was responsible for publishing *The Recognitions*. "I had a hell of a time getting it through the Harcourt hierarchy," he later recalled, "but Donald Brace okayed it."[23] The novel was copyedited first by David Chandler, a college summer trainee, but principally by Catharine Carver (managing editor of *Partisan Review* then), who likewise fought for the book and worked not so much to reduce its length, as has been suggested, as to increase its cohesion.[24]

A curious prepublication contretemps foreshadowed the novel's impact on an outraged book-reviewing industry. As the story goes, the man setting type for the book, a good Catholic, was sufficiently troubled at what he considered sacrilege and obscenity to consult his priest, who advised him to refuse to set it. Quinn & Boden, the printers, notified the publishers accordingly but were curtly told to set it or it would be the last job they received from them. They finished setting it, and, ironically enough, the only award *The Recognitions* received was for its typographical and physical format.[25]

The novel was published on 10 March 1955, the leading controversial literary title on Harcourt's spring list.[26] Unfortunately, 1955, as one critic would put it seven years later, was "one of American criticism's weakest hours."[27] The novel merited as many as fifty-five reviews, an impressive number for a first novel by an unknown writer, but with two or three exceptions all were, at best, inadequate. The names of some of the worst offenders are parodied in *J R* (515–16), following the "trade list comments" (on anagrammatic versions of *The Recognitions*) "from your topflight name critics and all, noses a little out of joint when they trip over topflight talent but that's par for the course."[28] The inadequacies, misreadings, factual errors, and outright plagiarisms of the original notices would later come under heavy attack from "Jack Green," the pseudonym of an amateur journalist who wrote, mimeographed, and distributed an eclectic magazine called *newspaper* in Greenwich Village in the late fifties and early sixties. He devoted three long issues to an exhaustive examination of the book-reviewing industry's irresponsible reaction to Gaddis' novel; his "constructive suggestion: fire the bastards!"[29] One aspect of the problem, as Green pointed out, was simple:

> its again that the critics dont do the job theyre paid for, they dont read the whole book with even a minimum of attention   of course most of the *recognitions* reviewers are mediocre untalented people   even doing their best they couldnt produce an interesting review of a great novel on publication date   they cant tell a great novel from an ordinary one, or they prefer the ordinary   but they dont even try to do a good job   they fake it, & the result is *amateurish* and *incompetent* – the 2 words that describe the review racket[30]

Green's argument was seconded by the avant-garde editors of *Writers in Revolt,* who reprinted the first part of the third chapter of *The Recognitions* in their 1963 anthology. They isolate Gaddis' alleged literary ambition as the red flag waved before the bovine critics:

> The author, it was said, was obviously trying to create a "work of art" or a "masterpiece"—this put them off. What they really said was that the author was trying to give the *impression* of having created a work of art or a masterpiece. This is because American "literary criticism" is not equipped to deal with work on any other level than that of the author's intentions. American critics—and this is true of no other contemporary culture—are themselves so far removed from the creative process, and from all imaginative thought, that their response to a work can never be on the basis of what the work is, but on what it seems to represent. It is psychologically untenable for such a person to admit the possibility of direct contact, or experience with a "work of art" or a "masterpiece"—other, of course, than those so certified and still smelling of the grave.[31]

Equally obtuse reviews have buried any number of fine novels in the past, but *The Recognitions* managed to attract enough notice to stay alive in spite of the publishers who, embarrassed by the negative reviews and having little faith in the book itself, remaindered *The Recognitions* some time afterward and kept it only intermittently in print thereafter. (Robert Giroux had resigned from Harcourt a few weeks after the novel's publication, and Donald Brace died later that year, apparently leaving no one with an active interest in the novel.) John W. Aldridge was one of the first to argue that *The Recognitions* had been slighted. In an essay entitled "The Function of the Book Critic," he too castigated the book-reviewing industry, using as cases in point Gaddis' novel and Alan Harrington's *The Revelations of Doctor Modesto* (also 1955):

> Both of these novels possess merits and idiosyncrasies remarkable enough to have aroused a storm of critical controversy and to have won them a fair public following had they been published ten or fifteen years ago, when an Edmund Wilson might have performed for them the service he performed for the younger Hemingway or a Malcolm Cowley for the neglected older Faulkner. Instead, they were allowed to pass from publication to oblivion with nothing in between to arrest their passage.[32]

The oblivion, fortunately, was only temporary—at least for *The Recognitions*. The years immediately following saw occasional references to the novel, all favorable. In 1957, Anthony West called it "the most interesting and remarkable novel written by a young American in the last twenty-five years" and predicted that it would "one day take a place in classic American literature beside the work of Thomas Wolfe as an expression of the developing American spirit."[33] Other references, all giving the novel greater due than did the first reviewers, were made by Gerald Walker, Eugene McNamara, Gilbert Highet (reversing his 1955 position), and even Norman Mailer, who condescendingly "tipped his hat" to Gaddis and other "men and boys of good repute" in *Advertisements for Myself* (1959).

The 1962 publication of the Meridian paperback edition with corrections (many supplied by Jack Green, a free-lance proofreader by profession) drew fewer reviews but more positive response. A full-page advertisement, written and paid for by Green (partly as a protest against publishers' meager advertising budgets), appeared in the *Village Voice* for 29 March 1962 to draw attention to both *The Recognitions* and the first installment of his "fire the bastards!" and strong sales were reported for the reprint. (Indeed the Meridian edition would eventually sell 8,469 copies, as opposed to 4,722 copies of Harcourt's cloth edition and 1,926 of their Harvest paperback edition.) The novel was also published (from the corrected Meridian edition) for the first time in England in September of the same year by MacGibbon & Kee,[34] but it annoyed many British critics in much the same way as it did its American reviewers, and largely for the same wrong reasons. The capstone of this sudden rediscovery of Gaddis' novel was a grant from the National Institute of Arts and Letters, presented by Malcolm Cowley on 22 May 1963:

> To WILLIAM GADDIS, novelist, born in New York City, whose novel *Recognitions* exhibits breadth and subtlety of imagination, a sense of fictional architecture with a remarkable effectiveness in the rendering of details, and unflagging stylistic verve.[35]

But all this momentum, sad to say, dissipated quickly; symptomatic was the abandonment of a special issue of *Prairie Schooner* that was to be devoted to *The Recognitions*. Karl Shapiro, then editor, later wrote, "Writers, critics, and scholars from all over the world were going to contribute to the resurrection of this gigantic, all but unknown American masterpiece of a novel."[36] "There was so much material that I thought of two issues," he remarked (and one wonders what became of all that material),[37] but an unrelated problem with censorship resulted in Shapiro's resignation, and the special issue never materialized.

Gaddis was engaged in a variety of writing projects by this time. They were inventoried in a 1962 letter as follows: "a novel on business begun and dropped in about "57; a novel begun, rebuilt into an impossibly long play (very rear guard, Socrates in the US Civil War), shelved 1960; current obsession with expanding prospects of programmed society & automation in the arts which may bring an advance, a commitment, even an escape from the tomb of the 9–to–5." These projects would eventually be subsumed into *J R*, and just as Gaddis split himself into the playwright Otto and the novelist Willie in *The Recognitions*, he did so again in the persons of Jack Gibbs and Thomas Eigen in the second novel. The latter, employed in the same corporate capacity as Gaddis was in those days, is at work on a play that another character describes as "undigested Plato" (282). A fragment of the play appears on pages 262–63 and is apparently from Gaddis' own unpublished Civil War play, *Once at Antietam*. Jack Gibbs, representing another contradictory level of his author's life, revives a sixteen-year-old project that he describes as "more of a book about order and disorder more of a, sort of a social history of mechanization and the arts, the destructive element . . ." (244). The opening pages of this book, including a page of Gaddis' notes, are scattered through the novel (288–89, 571–87, 594–95, 603–5) and represent the unfinished state of Gaddis' own study *Agapē Agape*.

Gaddis packs into *J R*'s one or two months most of his occupations in the sixties: A writing project on school television for the Ford Foundation in 1963 fell through after the expenditure of much time and energy, but it was salvaged for an early sequence in *J R,* as was his public-relations work for Pfizer International, a pharmaceutical firm represented in the novel by Nobili. Eigen's trip to Germany is based on Gaddis' own trip there in the summer of 1964, and while in Belgium to make a film for the army on the Battle of the Bulge, he met two generals—one American, one German—who were still arguing over which side had displayed the most brilliant strategy during the Ardennes offensive (cf. *J R*, 390–91). And one certainly need not look far for a parallel to Eigen's important novel, or for his "fatuous bastard" of a publisher, "sitting on that book for how many years? blubbering about his loyalty to it pretending it was what did he tell Tom? very much in print? when the only God damned place you could find it was a rare book dealer's for twenty dollars a copy after they'd remaindered practically the whole first edition?" (269).[38]

Meanwhile, *The Recognitions* had gone underground,[39] and references to it became few and far between. The first academic essay on it appeared in 1965, but unfortunately this proved to be an inaccurate demonstration of the novel's nonexistent debt to Joyce's *Ulysses.*[40] Richard Kostelanetz, in the same spirit as the 1955 reviewers, complained that its "surface discontinuity pushes the novel over the line of effectiveness into outright, thorough incoherence,"[41] but mercifully such misjudgments were becoming rarer. In his 1966 review of Joseph McElroy's *A Smuggler's Bible,* for example, J. R. Frakes used Gaddis' novel as a chastizing reminder of this sort of critical neglect: "'A Smuggler's Bible' is a remarkable novel," he wrote. "To ignore it would be as shameful an act of blind self-deprivation as that which so many of us performed when 'The Recognitions' and 'Under the Volcano' were first published,"[42] but the academic community remained for the most part self-deprived. The novel appeared in an Italian translation in 1967 and received more than twenty long and largely favorable reviews, including one by Mario Praz. (A German translation was also planned at this time, and the publishing firm of Rowolt went through two or three translators, but nothing ever came of it; a reference to the aborted translation seems to occur on page 578 of *J R*).

There appeared in the 2 June 1968 issue of *Book World* a feature entitled "Ten Neglected American Writers Who Deserve to Be Better Known" with a profile of Gaddis brief and interesting enough to be quoted in full:

William Gaddis, forty-five, with only one book under his belt, remains a novelist by trade. *Recognitions,* which appeared in 1955, came close in the opinion of many critics to being an American *Ulysses*. "It still sells a little despite the publisher," said Gaddis, "who didn't publish it; he privated it." Gaddis lives in Croton-on-Hudson, N.Y., supports himself, "however feebly," with industrial and corporate writing. He has received grants from the National Institute of Arts and Letters and from the National Endowment, and is working away steadily at his second novel, to appear he doesn't know when. "I try to remember that most reviews are just absurd; whether good or bad they're plain silly. All the same, almost any kind of attention is flattering." He avoids publicity, parties, interviews "Anything I might say outside of my work, someone who works in a bank could say too. Of course, among friends, literary gossip and money are pretty much all we do talk about." Gaddis has always been self-reliant, indifferent to outside opinion ("not so bad as Salinger, though"). As editor of the Harvard *Lampoon,* he once leaped out a window into a net, completely sauced, without suffering a scratch. Now, his full attention goes into his work: "You just have to decide—or have it forced on you—whether you're a craftsman or a commercial writer. I wouldn't want to compete with Leon Uris if it should come to that."[43]

"Though I weep for order I live still in a world of scrawled notes on the backs of envelops," he lamented elsewhere, and during these difficult years of critical neglect—not to mention a failing marriage and a series of frustrating jobs—Gaddis no doubt took to heart the poem by Yeats drunkenly misquoted by Gibbs on occasion in *J R,* "To a Friend Whose Work Has Come to Nothing."

Momentum began gathering again in the early seventies with the appearance of selections from Gaddis' forthcoming novel, the first dissertation on *The Recognitions,* articles by critics of the caliber of Tony Tanner and David Madden, and, abroad, an excellent French translation of *The Recognitions.* Gaddis' brilliant second novel, *J R*—nominally edited by Robert Gottlieb but this time free from editorial intervention—was published on 29 October 1975 in simultaneous cloth and paper editions, in the United States by Alfred A. Knopf and in Britain by Jonathan Cape the following year, and sales were strong enough for three printings in its first five months. In marked contrast to the churlish reception of his first novel, the reviews of *J R* were for the most part favorable and thoughtful. There were, of course, a few reviews Jack Green would have excoriated: reviewing *J R* in a jumble of other books for the *Hudson Review* (which had panned *The Recognitions*), William H. Pritchard brazenly admitted he did not even finish the book, then, not surprisingly, proceeded to misname an important character. Pearl K. Bell, in the *New Leader* (which Green had taken to task for not even bothering to review Gaddis' first novel), began with literary cocktail party chitchat and seldom rose above that level:

clearly unsympathetic to the novel, she gave the reader a jaundiced, misleading view based on her evident inability to comprehend it. The *New Leader* should have followed the *New Republic*'s lead: after Alfred Kazin's incompetent review in their 6 December 1975 issue, they turned the novel over to Elizabeth Fox-Genovese, who produced a splendid review for their 7 February 1976 issue. George Steiner pronounced the novel "unreadable," then he proceeded to give a reading of it, apparently untroubled by the contradiction. And Green would certainly have had something to say about John Gardner's review of *J R* in the *New York Review of Books* as seen through the rose-colored glasses of his "moral fiction." [44] But whereas *The Recognitions* received only two competent reviews by Green's count, *J R* garnered a large number of positive reactions: particularly outstanding were the commentaries by John W. Aldridge (*Saturday Review*), George Stade (*New York Times Book Review*), Thomas LeClair (*Commonweal*), and J. D. O'Hara (*Virginia Quarterly Review*). Gilbert Sorrentino, whose excellent review appeared in *Partisan Review,* singled out Gaddis' masterful use of dialogue for special praise and then went on to write a novel also constructed almost entirely from dialogue (*Crystal Vision,* dated 1975–76, published 1981). William H. Gass, one of Gaddis' few artistic peers, called *J R* "perhaps the supreme masterpiece of acoustical collage" and later, "a culmination of the oral tradition." [45]

J R won the prestigious National Book Award for the best novel of 1975; the judges for the fiction award (Gass and Mary McCarthy) selected Gaddis' novel over Bellow's *Humboldt's Gift,* Calisher's *Collected Stories,* Kaplan's *Other People's Lives,* Nabokov's *Tyrants Destroyed and Other Stories,* and Woiwode's *Beyond the Bedroom Wall.* [46] In his acceptance speech, Gaddis reiterated his opposition to the cult of personality:

> To list every one I owe a lasting debt in relation to the occasion for this award would go back a good many years, and keep us here all evening. I have simply got to trust in their awareness of my gratitude. At the very least though, I must of course thank the judges who have given *J R* this distinction.
>
> After that, I feel like part of the vanishing breed that thinks a writer should be read and not heard, let alone seen. I think this is because there seems so often today to be a tendency to put the person in the place of his or her work, to turn the creative artist into a performing one, to find what a writer says about writing somehow more valid, or more real, than the writing itself.
>
> In this regard, I was struck by something I read recently in a preface to a novel of Gorky's. "Before 1880," this editor noted—his name is F. D. Reeve—"before 1880, roughly, the main problem about being a writer was to keep writing well. By the end of the century, the main problem was to write well enough to establish or to maintain the position of being a writer."

If that provides a glimpse of a current dilemma, it seems to me the only way to keep writers writing well, or trying to write well, is to read what we write.

And if this reeks of a truism, we're back where we started, which may recommend it as a good place to stop.[47]

Now that the sequence of Gaddis' life—"significant only in any transmutations its details may find in my work"—has been explored, this, likewise, is "a good place to stop" and turn, as Flaubert recommended, from *l'homme* to *l'œuvre*.

Notes

1. James M. Ethridge, Barbara Kopala, and Carolyn Riley, eds., *Contemporary Authors: A Bio-Bibliographical Guide to Current Authors and Their Works* (Detroit: Gale Research, 1968), 19/20: 135. "Those lines," quoted in both *The Recognitions* and *J R*, are Pascal's.

2. From John Boyle O'Reilly's (1844–1890) poem "In Bohemia": "The organized charity, scrimped and iced, / In the name of a cautious, statistical Christ."

3. John Kuehl and Steven Moore, "An Interview with William Gaddis," *The Review of Contemporary Fiction* 2, no. 2 (Summer 1982): 4. The Russian characters are, of course, from *The Brothers Karamazov*; Basil Seal and Tony Last are from Waugh's *Black Mischief* and *A Handful of Dust*, respectively.

4. *The Recognitions* (1955; reprint with corrections, Cleveland and New York: World Publishing Co., Meridian Fiction, 1962), 95, 95–96. Subsequent references will be cited parenthetically in the text.

5. *J R* (New York: Alfred A. Knopf, 1975), 561; subsequent references will likewise be cited parenthetically in the text. Gaddis himself drew the attention of journalist Helen Dudar to this passage for her "Book and Author" column on him that appeared in the *New York Post,* 6 December 1975, 33.

6. John Wakeman, ed., *World Authors: 1950–1970,* (New York: H. W. Wilson, 1975), 517.

7. Here, for example, is his capsule review of *Lady Chatterly's Lover:* "A terrifically uninteresting work on the very earthy banal subjects so familiar to all of us. It is the sort of book that will always have a following among people who are interested in other peoples' [*sic*] lives, and who are convinced that love (in its illicit mundane states) is the most wonderful thing in the world.

"Widener Library has no copy, and it is not on sale in the United States. We will pay any sum for an unexpurgated copy in any condition" (11 February 1944, 40).

8. Untitled poem, 14 January 1944, 6.

9. "In the Zone," *New York Times,* 13 March 1978, 21; reprinted in Steven Moore, *A Reader's Guide to William Gaddis's "The Recognitions"* (Lincoln: University of Nebraska Press, 1982), 301–4. The quotations are from this memoir.

10. From one of a series of letters from Vincent Livelli to Steven Moore, February 1982. Mr. Livelli's recollections furnished all the material in this paragraph.

11. In December 1945, the date of the diary entry; in 1948, she was thirty (as is Esme (*The Recognitions,* [276]), five years Gaddis' senior.

12. *The Diary of Anaïs Nin: 1944–1947,* ed. Gunther Stuhlmann (New York: Harcourt Brace Jovanovich, 1971), 4:107–8. (Mr. Livelli, who called attention to the *Diary,* appears as Vincent on 180–83 of the same volume.) Later, Nin adds: "Half of her body is heavy and animal, and the upper half is childlike and fragile, tied by threads of sensuality to many" (144). Miss Martinelli later became a protégé of Ezra Pound, who wrote an introduction to her book of paintings *La Martinelli* (Milan: Vanni Scheiwiller, 1956) and wrote much of the Rock-Drill section of *The Cantos*—especially Canto 90—with her in mind. A shadowy photograph of her appears in Eustace Mullins's *This Difficult Individual, Ezra Pound* (New York: Fleet, 1961), 292.

13. Otto loses an easy pickup to a rival named Anatole on 513 of *The Recognitions.*

14. Gaddis to Steven Moore, 23 July 1982. See the dust jacket photograph of Robert Graves on the Farrar, Straus and Cudahy edition of *The White Goddess.*

15. An instructive description of the monastery can be found in Baedeker's *Spain and Portugal* (Leipsic: Karl Baedeker, 1913), 461 (the same edition Sinisterra consults [*The Recognitions* 775]).

16. Ludy and his pious article are based on novelist A. J. Cronin's "What I Learned at La Grande Chartreuse," *Reader's Digest,* February 1953, 73–77.

17. July 1951, 92–93; reprinted in Moore, *Reader's Guide,* 299–301.

18. Dudar, "Book and Author," *New York Post,* 6 December 1975, 33.

19. Gaddis to Steven Moore, 7 April 1983.

20. Kerouac wrote the novel a month later during "three full moon nights of October" on benzedrine. The biographical background to *The Subterraneans* (published five years later in 1958) is given in all the Kerouac biographies, but Gaddis' appearance in the novel was first noted in *Jack's Book* by Barry Gifford and Lawrence Lee (New York: St. Martin's Press, 1978), 176.

21. The Harold Sand episode occupies pp. 113–27 of all recent Grove/Ballantine editions of *The Subterraneans.*

22. Though set in San Francisco and environs, the novel is based on events that took place in New York. Ansen's home was in Woodmere, Long Island.

23. Quoted in Tom Morgan's "Feeding the Stream," *Saturday Review,* 1 September 1979, 43. Elsewhere, Giroux included Gaddis on a list of the ten authors whose first books he is proudest to have discovered and published (see Donald Hall's "Robert Giroux: Looking for Masterpieces," *New York Times Book Review,* 6 January 1980, 3, 22–24).

24. In a letter to John Seelye, 21 August 1964, Gaddis gave this account of the editing process: "As I recall, I did the original cutting in one of the first rewrites (though this is imprecise since some parts were rewritten a number of times, some scarcely at all), the next following a list of suggestions (but *not* demands) from an editor [Carver], the final and most thorough (as, a dropped prefatory chapter) myself for reasons I felt convincing and would most probably find even more convincing now." Cf. this account (and that in Kuehl and Moore, "An Interview with William Gaddis," 5) with that by David Koenig in his essay included in this volume.

25. See *Fifty Books of the Year: 1955* (New York: American Institute of Graphic Arts, 1956), no. 35.

26. Or so the first of Harcourt's few advertisements suggests: see *Publisher's Weekly,* 5 February 1955, facing 869.

27. Maurice Dolbier, review of the Meridian edition in the *New York Herald Tribune,*
14 April 1962, 6.

28. The reviewers are Granville Hicks (*New York Times Book Review,* 13 March 1955),
Maxwell Geismar (*Saturday Review,* 12 March 1955), Sterling North (*New York World
Telegram and Sun,* 10 March 1955 — probably the most vicious review), Brendan Gill (*New
Yorker,* 9 April 1955 — though, of course, he does not describe it as "a delicately evocative
novel"), *Newsweek* (14 March 1955), Milton Rugoff (*New York Herald Tribune Book Review,* 13 March 1955), Frances Burnette (*Baltimore Sun,* 13 March 1955), Kirkus' Service
(1 February 1955), and Maurice Dolbier, who confused Gaddis with writer William Gibson
in "The Summing-Up in Books for 1955," *Saturday Review* (24 December 1955, 11) and made
further elementary errors in his review of the Meridian edition seven years later (see n. 27).
For Dolbier's reception of *J R,* see n. 45.

29. "fire the bastards!" (parts 1–3), *newspaper,* nos. 12–14 (24 February, 25 August,
10 November 1962), 1–76. (It should be noted that *newspaper* was typed in lowercase and
unpunctuated.) *newspaper* no. 11 (3 June 1961) had announced, "the quoteprecis (#10) was
the 1st of at least 5 long issues on Gaddis the articles on references & crossreferences in
the recognitions & attacking the reviews that prevented the book from being accepted as
the masterpiece it is are far from finished & there will again be a long delay between issues" (6), but the articles on references and cross-references never appeared. Green continued to work on this material until about 1980, but he finally decided it "would never be
satisfactory and I threw it out" (Green to Steven Moore, 19 December 1981). For an account
of Green's career up to 1962, see Jerome Beatty, Jr.'s "Trade Winds" column in *Saturday Review* for 21 April 1962 (8–9) — or, better yet, Green's own autobiographical essay, "insurance
company days," in *newspaper* no. 15 — and for an assessment of *newspaper* in general, see
Donald Phelps' "Obit of a Sort," in *Covering Ground: Essays for Now* (New York: Croton,
1969), 208–12.

30. "fire the bastards!" 10–11. Green originally planned to publish his essay in book form;
the 50,000-word manuscript was sent to Grove and Putnam's, but neither was interested.
Twenty years later, however, when permission was sought to reprint the work in this collection, Green refused, giving as his reason the revised opinion that *newspaper* was "poorly
written."

31. Richard Seaver, Terry Southern, and Alexander Trocchi, eds., *Writers in Revolt* (New
York: Frederick Fell, 1963), 225.

32. The essay appears in both his *In Search of Heresy* (New York: McGraw-Hill, 1956)
and *The Devil in the Fire* (New York: Harper's Magazine Press, 1972).

33. "The Pleasures of Reading," *Woman's Day,* July 1957; quoted in "fire the bastards!" 68.

34. The book was originally to be published by Secker & Warburg in 1955, but Warburg, alarmed by its poor reception, backed out with the excuse of being unable to find a
printer in England who would set it because of the obscenity laws. The dissemblance was
taken seriously by some (see Norman St. John-Stevas, "Printers' Censorship," *The Spectator,*
9 December 1955, 792, 794).

35. Gaddis writes that Cowley "did indeed hand me the envelop but I'm sure he hadn't
a clue who or what either I or the book was & don't recall his reading the citation."

36. "A *Malebolge* of Fourteen Hundred Books," in Karl Shapiro, *To Abolish the Children and Other Essays* (Chicago: Quadrangle, 1968), 231.

37. John Seelye's essay in this volume was commissioned for the Gaddis issue, but none
of the others have come to light. Shapiro intended to reprint "fire the bastards!" complete,
then asked Green for an abridged edition: "so i prepared a ½ length version but came to my

senses at last moment, didn't send it   few months more, shapiro out as editor" (*newspaper,* no. 16 [n.d., probably late 1964], 16).

38. First editions of *The Recognitions* now command prices as high as $200, while the black paper-covered advance-reading copies of the same (some 220 copies were printed) have been advertised for as high as $400.

39. Victor S. Navasky discussed "The Pure Underground Book" with special reference to *The Recognitions* in "Notes on the Underground," *New York Times Book Review,* 5 June 1966, 2.

40. For the record, Gaddis read Joyce's *Dubliners* and Molly Bloom's monologue at the end of *Ulysses* while at college (but never read the rest of the novel), and later, parts of Stuart Gilbert's edition of Joyce's *Letters.* All that can be said on the similarities between *Ulysses* and *The Recognitions* is contained in one of Green's footnotes ("fire the bastards!" 36): "*ulysses & the recognitions* are very '20thcentury' & have a number of technical resemblances: both are long & closely organized; sharp contrast between humorous & nonhumorous passages; lots of blasphemy; modeling/parodies on classics & extensive crossreferences (*ulysses* having much more of former, *recognitions* of latter); 'timegrowth' in rereading; many nonfictional references (miscalled 'erudition') to give desired tones to the fiction; passion for other books; importance of ideas of major characters (dedalus, wyatt); delight in carrying humorous situations to extremes; <u>restraint as basic technique of style</u> but the worlds of the 2 books arent alike, nor are the characters   the 2 have little resemblance in the essential   ie artistic   sense[.]"

41. "The Point Is That Life Doesn't Have Any Point," *New York Times Book Review,* 6 June 1965, 30. Kostelanetz later reversed his judgment and included Gaddis "among my choices for revived novelists" (*The End of Intelligent Writing: Literary Politics in America* [New York: Sheed & Ward, 1974], 33).

42. *New York Times Book Review,* 2 October 1966, 48. McElroy expresses his contentment with this comparison in "Neural Neighborhoods and Other Concrete Abstracts," *Tri-Quarterly* 34 (Fall 1975): 205.

43. Lois Cantor, *Book World* (Washington *Post*/Chicago *Tribune*), 6.

44. Gaddis is likewise condemned (along with most of our better writers) in Gardner's *On Moral Fiction* (New York: Basic Books, 1978), 65–66, 93–94, and 192.

45. "Authors' Authors," *New York Times Book Review,* 5 December 1976, 102; and "Immortal Nominations," ibid., 3 June 1979, 13.

46. Maurice Dolbier, the third member of the fiction committee, stayed true to form by dissenting and went so far as to disassociate himself from the award.

47. "Acceptance Speech for the National Book Award in Fiction for *J R,*" National Institute of Arts and Letters, 21 April 1976.

1

The Writing of *The Recognitions*

David Koenig

Discovering the Novel

> Toward dawn he dreamt that he had hidden himself in one
> of the naves of the Clementine Library. A librarian wearing
> dark glasses asked him: *What are you looking for?* Hladik
> answered: *God.* The Librarian told him: *God is in one of the
> letters on one of the pages of one of the 400,000 volumes
> of the Clementine.*
> —Jorge Luis Borges, "The Secret Miracle"

Creation begins in the dark, for the artist himself is not certain of the
origins of his art. But what we can learn of the artistic process holds
great fascination. In the case of literature, we would like to know where
an author got his ideas, how he first set them down, whether he rearranged
them, and why he chose to leave them precisely as he did. Naturally, the
more remarkable the novel, the more interesting will be the story of its
writing. *The Recognitions* inevitably prompts the question, how was it written? because of its eccentric subjects, its vast fund of obscure knowledge,
and sprawling yet minutely complex structure. Fortunately, Gaddis in both
his notes and manuscript versions provides an extensive record of how he
wrote *The Recognitions.* _talented_
   Gaddis left Harvard in 1945 a young man of intense spiritual concerns.
He was preoccupied with redeeming American reality from its banal, ma-
terialistic ambience at the end of World War II. Gaddis came to New York,
where he wrote a story that was the primitive core of his novel of redemption. It simply described a love triangle in which a young man breaks up
an already disintegrating marriage. This triangle makes its appearance in

David Koenig was formerly known as Peter W. Koenig.—Eds.

the third chapter of the published *Recognitions*. Gaddis did not actually begin fashioning his 1945 sketch into a novel until 1947 when he began traveling abroad. He lived as a young writer in New York, supporting himself as a trainee at *New Yorker* magazine. He checked articles for factual accuracy, a job well suited to his encyclopedic interests, if not to his artistic abilities. But thanks to this job, his Harvard connections, and his inclinations as a writer, Gaddis seems to have penetrated the social life of artists and critics, both in the fashionable upper East Side and in Greenwich Village. Here he gathered the "party" material that he brilliantly transposed into *The Recognitions*. He did not however merely transcribe this material for use in his novel. The art life of New York also suggested to him theoretical ideas about the plight of the artist in America.

This plight, which Gaddis saw and which completely fascinated him, was the Faustian spectacle of enormous artistic talent that could find no inspiration worthy of its powers. He wrote: "When I started this thing . . . it was to be a good deal shorter, and quite explicitly a parody on the FAUST story, except the artist taking the place of the learned doctor."[1] Gaddis added a Faust legend to his original concept of the degenerating marriage and farcical love triangle. Here we have the first important stage of *The Recognitions,* a parody of Goethe's *Faust,* which Gaddis later summed up in the following way:

> It began with the Otto-Wyatt-Esther triangle, and progressed openly as it does here, in the first part; though the original intention, closely following the FAUST, was Wyatt-Esme as Faust-Gretchen, and Esme's damnation through Wyatt's negation of her (as a model in forgeries; and his refusal to love her) . . . (Notes)

Wyatt is the man of Faustian ambition and nearly unlimited talent who can find no meaningful activity as an artist and so turns to forgery, damning himself and corrupting the female innocence of his model whose love might have saved him. Gaddis retained the Faust parody in *The Recognitions* but later reduced it to one of many myths of redemption. The Faust myth centers around Wyatt and Esme, whom Wyatt meets after he has broken off with Esther. Finally, we shall see that all the characters, including Esme, became subordinate to Wyatt when the novel developed into a parody of *Recognitions of Clement.*

The Faust parody was uppermost in Gaddis' mind when he left New York and traveled to Mexico City and Panama in 1947 and after that through Central America. Gaddis left Puerto Limon, Costa Rica, for New York, then went to Spain in 1948, taking with him as he did throughout his travels large sacks of newspaper clippings and notes. All the while he read voraciously and sent home to friends for books that he could not obtain abroad. At this time, he discovered a book that can now be seen as a turning point in *The Recognitions'* history. Gaddis became immensely excited over Sir James Frazer's *The Golden Bough.* Frazer's book, first published in 1890, is a pioneering work in anthropology, showing how civilization evolved from myths, taboos, magic, and superstition. It greatly influenced such thinkers as Freud and such artists as the poet Robert Graves, whom Gaddis met in Spain in 1948. He was particularly excited by Frazer's demonstration of how Christianity derived from pagan antecedents. This fit in perfectly with Gaddis' search for counterfeits, which he had begun by this time.

One passage from *The Golden Bough* actually went verbatim into *The Recognitions.* Gaddis quotes a half page of Frazer to show what Wyatt's father, Reverend Gwyon, is reading. Gaddis introduces the quotation, "But the book open before him was not the Bible, nor the words Saint Paul's." [2] The point of using this quotation is to show the departure of the minister from the Christian text and his delving into the sources of Christianity. Specifically, Wyatt at this point in the novel is ill, and Reverend Gwyon is seeking ways to cure him—not from the Bible, but from *The Golden Bough*—after the doctors have failed. Gwyon eventually performs the rite of killing his barbary ape, a ceremony for healing that he got from reading Sir James Frazer.

More important than specific borrowing was the basic notion of Christianity as a copy or counterfeit, which Gaddis derived from *The Golden Bough.* He went from there into the early history of the Christian church, where he found ample evidence of counterfeits and frauds, as well as of things genuine. One book of early Christian writing coincided perfectly with his idea of counterfeits, since it was an original of the Faust legend! This was the third-century *Recognitions of Clement.*

Recognitions of Clement is an early Christian theological romance, authorship unknown, which tells the story of Clement's travels and his search for salvation. In the course of his travels, with the help of Saint Peter, he recognizes that salvation lies in God, but first he makes the mistake of thinking that magicians in Egypt can disclose the secret of salvation. In this error, he resembles Faust and his pact with Mephistopheles. *Recognitions of Clement* came to be known, therefore, as the first Faust legend.

Gaddis adapted the title and made it his own. He also changed the entire conception of his novel in accordance with the format of *Recognitions of Clement.* The Clementine *Recognitions* is the story of a wandering hero who travels across much of the then-known world in search of salvation.

Thus, it has a large range that Gaddis was coming to see as appropriate for his novel. "I think this book will have to be a voyaging, all the myth & metaphor of that in modern times" (Notes). With this expansion of scope and the new concept of "recognition," he continued to travel throughout Europe and Africa, recognizing counterfeits and seeking to recognize authentic values. With the discovery of Frazer's encyclopedic *Golden Bough* (and the fact that Christianity was a "counterfeit"), and with the discovery of *Recognitions of Clement* (and the fact that Faust was in a sense a counterfeit of Clement), the novel entered its second major stage of development. From a limited Faust parody, it expanded into an epical, theoretically limitless pilgrimage of satirical "recognitions" parodying the religious *Recognitions of Clement*. Gaddis was later to say that the decision to expand the novel was never formally made. It simply grew in every direction, and the need for a decision came only when the expansion had to end.[3]

Gaddis lived in Spain for more than a year, traveling from place to place as Reverend Gwyon and Wyatt do, in search of something spiritual that he could not seem to find. Spain disappointed him, for as he traveled in 1948 from Algeciras and Gibralter to Madrid, and out again across the countryside to El Escorial, Gaddis realized that Spain was full of counterfeits too. He considered making the little town of San Zwingli in *The Recognitions* "an open parody on Escorial." He wrote:

> A town being enamoured of its Foreign past: v[ide] Granada & the Moors: produces parody of anomalies. But what with the weight of monuments apparently everywhere today the present is thoroughly unsatisfactory: has any rising civilization spent so much time preserving & exhibiting things from the past, testimony to its legitimacy? Did the Elizabethans make sightseeing trips to Stonehenge? (Notes)

In 1949 Gaddis visited and stayed at the Real Monasterio de Guadalupe in Estremadura, Spain. This monastery became the Real Monasterio de Nuestra Señora de la Otra Vez (Royal Monastery of Our Lady of Another [a second] Time). The title he chose for the monastery in the novel is ironically appropriate, since Reverend Gwyon visits this monastery at the beginning of the novel, and his cremated ashes return here (another time!) at the end. Here also Wyatt has his epiphany on the hillside.

Gaddis stayed at the Monastery of Guadalupe through 1949 and part of 1950. In 1950 he left Spain and went to Paris, which accounts for the matching Paris chapters in *The Recognitions*. He returned to Spain, then traveled through the countries of North Africa, where his travels produced a section of *The Recognitions* that was later deleted almost entirely. In the final version, we hear only in one of Wyatt's deranged monologues near the end that he has been in Africa. Wyatt says of Africa: "I was only there because I wasn't anywhere else" (895). This seems to have been the conclusion Gaddis was coming to about all his travels, because in 1952 he returned to America, apparently convinced that after the Second World War, America *was* the world. Along with this discovery, he had also unearthed the basic elements of *The Recognitions* and would show, through a parody of *Faust* and of *Recognitions of Clement,* the counterfeit spirituality of the modern world.

Revising the Novel

. . . When Wyatt is redeemed through love, it must be personified in the love of a child, that is, in freely given love . . .
—William Gaddis, Notes

Having returned permanently to America in 1952, Gaddis began the process of shaping *The Recognitions* into a consistent piece of dramatization. His spiritual search had led him to the conclusion that Wyatt must be redeemed through "freely given love." *The Recognitions* originally was to have a chapter in which this occurred, but during the period of revision it was eliminated. Later, when Gaddis worked with his editor on bringing the novel to completion, he left only hints of Wyatt's possible redemption and made Wyatt more a symbol of redemption for the other characters.

Gaddis isolated himself in the New York farmhouse of a deceased friend. Here he lived alone, seeing people only when he went to town for groceries, and, in a burst of intense enthusiasm and labor, revised *The Recognitions.* He had come to think of it as a voyaging epic to end with a homecoming for Wyatt. Like Clement and Faust, Wyatt was to be nearly damned at the beginning but saved at the end. Gaddis later decided that a simple homecoming, after all the obstacles to it that he had described, would be dishonest. But in the process of working out the problem of homecoming, or redemption, he expanded the novel at both ends.

Gaddis initially planned a final chapter in which Wyatt would be "at last redeemed through love" (Notes). This redemption took several possible forms, but in the main one Wyatt was to have a child by a Spanish prostitute, Pastora. Wyatt would be seen at last on a Spanish beach, beginning to draw a picture of his little illegitimate Spanish daughter:

> I say I don't want the end to seem trite, an easy way out; because I don't
> want it to sound as though Wyatt has finally found his place in company
> with a simple stupid and comparatively unattractive woman who loves him
> . . . I simply want the intimation that, in starting a drawing of his daughter,
> Wyatt, seeing her in her trust and faith (love), is *beginning*. He may not yet
> understand, but the least we can do is start him, after all this, on the right
> way, where the things that mattered, not simply no longer matter, but no
> longer exist. (Notes)

He says that there is no reason Wyatt must stay where he is, "nor marry
Pastora and live happily ever after, nor even bring up the child, for whether
it's actually his hasn't even been stated" (Notes). In this scene on the beach,
Wyatt's little daughter was to wear gold earrings, which were to recall Camilla's gold earrings. Camilla, Wyatt's mother, had died of appendicitis
when Wyatt was three. His little girl was also to be three. Gaddis explains
that, "in an implicit way I want her (the child) to be Camilla's innocence
reincarnated . . ." (Notes).

The fact that Camilla had a pair of gold earrings, that she died, and
that Wyatt was three when she died, all appear in part 1, chapter 1 of the
published version. It describes Camilla's death and Wyatt's childhood. This
chapter was written after the initial core of the novel was conceived and
shows Reverend Gwyon burying Camilla in Spain and Aunt May raising
Wyatt in New England. Since America could never be home to Wyatt after
the disastrous experiences he suffered there, and since Camilla and Spain
represent purity to Reverend Gwyon and Wyatt, Camilla's resting place
served as a "home" to which Wyatt could return. So the homecoming that
Gaddis saw as the final chapter or epilogue also led him to put a chapter
with Spain and Wyatt's childhood "home" at the beginning of the novel
in front of the love triangle.

However, at some point in the revisions, a plan for a prologue or chapter to go in front of the first chapter replaced the idea of an epilogue. Up
to then the order consisted of a description of Wyatt's early life and Camilla's death, followed by Wyatt's broken marriage and his pact with the
Devil, and finally his redemption in the epilogue through recognizing the
little girl. But Gaddis began to feel that an epilogue was structurally un-
sound in so long and difficult a novel.

> But here, on the one hand, is a simple time element; since love will be rep-
> resented by the child, it must be three or so years since she was conceived;
> and I believe that presenting her, and the household where he ends, and works,
> and is loved, for a gap between a long novel which has in time extended

a few months, and its last chapter three years later, is worse than a preface, especially in a novel of bound up fragments such as this one. (Notes)

He contemplated having Wyatt appear briefly as the grown man he would become in a prologue before his story is told. We were to see Wyatt redeemed, with his little girl, then begin to hear the story behind this strange young man sitting on the beach in Spain.

Specifically, the preface was to be related by an unidentified "I" narrator, who would afterward disappear. Herman Hesse uses a similar device in *Steppenwolf,* having someone come on the scene after the events and relate his own brief meeting with the hero and the story he subsequently heard. Gaddis' partially written preface began, "I stayed on another month or so in Oran after our road accident, in which D____ was killed." In the first paragraph we were to learn that the narrator had recently been the driver in an auto accident that killed his passenger and friend, D____. This first paragraph concludes, "It took a long time for me to work through the guilt of that accident, and after all, if that were worked out, was it time lost?" Gaddis explained why this basic situation for the narrator suited his purposes:

> It at once sets Guilt in view, in a most obvious circumstance, which never intrudes again, the guilt of the "I" that is, over the road accident. Then guilt goes on, in the body of the thing, being built up from the bottom (and Sigismundo's "the greatest sin of man is being born"), in all of which such a thing as a road accident outside Sidi-bel-Abbes is quite foreign, but still there. (Notes)

The narrator's guilt was to prepare the reader for Wyatt's guilt, but, more important, the thirty-three-year old hero was to prepare and reassure the reader about the young Wyatt. Wyatt might be warped in childhood, sell his soul to the Devil, and be under every conceivable illusion, but his soul would ultimately be redeemed.

Wyatt's name changes to "Stephen" at the end of the published version, and this ending links directly with what was to have been the preface in which Wyatt is referred to as Stephen. In the preface, the narrator leaves Africa (after the accident) and takes a boat to Barcelona. He meets on board the "distinguished novelist" who is with Stephen in the last chapter. On shore in Spain the novelist of the preface introduces the "I" narrator to Stephen. Here we get a physical description of him:

> Stephen was a man about my own height and rather more slightly built. The only thing curious about him was the way he squinted his eyes, and he looked

a good deal older than he was, not yet forty then. There was an alertness, and a look of mild surprise about him, which I liked immediately. (Notes)

The narrator is fascinated with Stephen: "For there was that about him which suggested one's self, not the daily utilitarian self, nor certainly not some ethereal image, but a working self which understood its challenges and met them without question, without comparison to others or fear of one's own inadequacy, and humility only in accomplishment" (Notes). Gaddis in the final version never allows himself anything this explicit about Wyatt-Stephen.

The narrator, seeing these things in Stephen, accompanies him and the novelist to Palamos, where he witnesses the scene with Stephen and the little girl on the beach.

> Now, if we've got the reassurance of the preface, that is, that Stephen, as the hero resurrected, comes out all right, that, in a long novel, is far enough behind not to be obvious and conscious. To leave him, then at the moment of his emergence, and go on to the last stages of collapse of all those things he has emerged from, is I think far more effective. (Notes)

The explicit assurance that Gaddis thought to give the reader of Wyatt's triumphal reappearance somewhere beyond his great trial and near insanity did not materialize. Gaddis finally decided that this reassurance was impossible and dishonest whether it occurred at the beginning of the novel or at the end. He eventually removed the preface and began the novel where it now starts, with Camilla's death and Wyatt's unfortunate upbringing by Aunt May.

Wyatt is not redeemed by his daughter in the published version, for although he does have the affair with Pastora, the Spanish prostitute, no child seems to have resulted from it. In Wyatt's mad scene at the end, just before his final epiphany, he does make one reference to his daughter, unrecognizable to anyone unfamiliar with the unpublished preface: "A daughter, yes! and born out of, not love but borne out of love, when it happened, the bearing, the present reshaped the past" (897–98). (Gaddis retained other unrecognizable or merely suggestive fragments for the sake of making the novel spill over endlessly into life.) But the child as a visible means of Wyatt's redemption is gone. Gaddis chose to end *The Recognitions* as he chose to begin it, not with assurances, but with the fall of innocence and truth on all sides. *The Recognitions,* therefore, concludes with an unnumbered chapter or coda in which Wyatt does not appear at all. Instead, all the minor characters, having failed to recognize the suggestion of their better selves in Wyatt, are killed or disposed of one by one.

Editing the Novel

> . . . the body of the novel has not been squarely about
> [Wyatt], it has been about the others, and he only insofar as
> he was the spirit they lost.   —William Gaddis, Notes

The daughter who was to redeem Wyatt in an epilogue or prologue is
not the only character who disappeared from *The Recognitions*. Since the
novel was published, rumors have circulated that *The Recognitions* was
originally longer than it is and was cut down to its present 956 pages. These
rumors are correct, for Gaddis and his editor cut much documentation
and several minor characters. They also made Wyatt less explicit and more
a symbol suggestive of what the others had lost.

When William Gaddis left the New York farmhouse and delivered the
manuscript to Harcourt, Brace's editors, he had made the major structural
revision, removing the epilogue-prologue and hence any explicit assurances
about Wyatt's fate. In 1953 *The Recognitions* went to the editors, the job
of writing and revising finished, but with a crucial task still to come. *The
Recognitions,* unlike some books, required a great deal of editing, for in
seven or more years of writing it, Gaddis had been largely alone. He finished it alone in the isolated farmhouse. During all this time, he had allowed virtually no one to read it. Now it would have to be read by people
who had no idea of its history as a novel and who did not necessarily share
Gaddis' concern with redemption. Only the fiction as fiction could insure
the public's attention.

The editors proceeded to cut down the inordinate size and make the
complex novel easier to follow. Their difficulty from the very beginning
was that comprehensiveness and intricate structure were the unique vir-
tues of the novel and were faults only in their excesses. The reader first
assigned to *The Recognitions* wrote this comment in 1954:

> [In this section,] what I expect to be the ultimate problem of the book ex-
> poses itself thoroughly. This problem, which is at once the force and flaw
> of the novel, arises from the thoroughness with which Gaddis feels obliged
> to recreate his atmosphere.[4]

Catharine Carver, the competent young woman who became Gaddis' editor, worked along the same lines. In the course of her editing, whole sections and characters were deleted, always with his consent. It is this period
in 1954 when the cutting took place that gave rise to the rumors of a much
longer book.

The Recognitions was so heavily documented when Gaddis submitted the manuscript for editing that it even had footnotes! From the start Carver sought to eliminate the footnotes, and eventually this was done. She also found that the internal documentation was excessive and wrote, "This catalogue somewhat too much, full in the face as it is. Just the reading list seems fulsome, all that follows which proves the point OK. You have to show his somewhat erratic fields of interest, not document them."[5] This suggestion was repeated in substance throughout, and Gaddis often eliminated lists and documentation. On the other hand, Carver sometimes pointed to "a place where a catalogue of learned references goes exactly right, and makes the tone precisely what it ought to be." While reading part 2, Carver was again forced to comment, "Esme is quite submerged under this tide of saintly information. Help!" On the next page she writes, "Again, much overloaded — cut all from bracket 283 to bracket 289. (I am beginning to believe again in an appendix!)." The appendix was never made, and much of the documentation was left in. To many of Carver's cuts, as to the one above, Gaddis replied in the margin, "disagree."

Like John Dos Passos, Gaddis wished to record the times in his art, and many of the conversations and incidents, although they expanded the novel, did seem to him perfect as documents of the period. As far as the learned documentation was concerned, Gaddis felt he had to retain most of it because it was pertinent to his central themes. Many deletions of documentation, as well as some much more crucial ones, were agreed to. The first of these was a large section after the first chapter on Wyatt's childhood, which finds Wyatt a young artist in Paris. Carver wrote, "I feel very strongly that the whole Munich section of this chapter ought to be cut." Gaddis deleted the Munich section and left only Wyatt's fleeting memory in Paris of "a Munich which had known spring and summer only in the irretrievable childhood of the Middle Ages" (68).

We have the Munich section preserved in Gaddis' manuscript. It deals with Wyatt's art-school days in Munich, his teacher, Herr Koppel, and his so-called friend, Han. Herr Koppel remains in Wyatt's thoughts, as does Han, although Han is reduced to several isolated references. We learn from *The Recognitions* that Herr Koppel was an art teacher in Munich who instructed Wyatt, then sold one of his paintings as an original Memling. Koppel is mentioned again in Wyatt's mad ramblings at the Spanish monastery, where he also speaks briefly about Han. We learn, if this passage is carefully read, that Han was also a student of Koppel. Wyatt recalls that Han approached him in a café in Africa, thinking that Wyatt had come there to join him in the Foreign Legion. When he finds that Wyatt had not been thinking of him at all, Han becomes violent with an unexplained, old hatred, and Wyatt shoots him to death.

What we cannot get from the published version is that Han was a totally brutalized and brutal companion of Wyatt in Germany. A homosexual, he was to be the first of many characters who would try to use Wyatt. Han, like the others, was not interested in what Wyatt could do, but what "they" could do, or what Wyatt could do for Han. In the deleted section, Wyatt and Han travel from Munich on an excursion to the Jungfrau in Switzerland, where Han attempts to make love to Wyatt. Wyatt leaves Han and goes on to Paris, where we actually find him in the published version of the novel. The Munich and Jungfrau scenes with Han were cut.

Carver and Gaddis eliminated other scenes as well. On the whole, they cut party scenes, such as a party at Don Bildow's, and consolidated others. Carver (the pun that her name suggests is one that Gaddis is likely to have appreciated) worked also to pare down the minor characters. Wyatt's seminary friend, John; the waiters in the Flamenco restaurant; Agnes Deigh and her husband, Harry; Agnes' dentist; and Esther's demented sister, Rose; were reduced to almost nothing. These characters originally had larger parts, but for the sake of dramatic unity they were drastically reduced.

Not only were the minor characters reduced, but the hero himself became less explicit. This was done not so much for the sake of economy as to make Wyatt the shadowy kind of character they wanted him to be. Following along these lines, Carver wrote:

> I think this whole soliloquy ought to be cut. W[yatt] G[wyon] is too explicit, trying too hard. He really does seem labored and false. I think better to have him simply drinking & writing, with the dog there, before Brown enters. I am now convinced that you are telling too much about him in this chapter, it will be hard to see him in some of the later scenes, he will not be the "he" you want him to be, unless some of this explication is cut now.

The soliloquy was deleted, as well as much of Wyatt's garrulousness. He became the silent character whom others refer to simply as "he." Wyatt is not named directly throughout the whole middle part of the book. Carver helped Gaddis to cut his speeches, arguing from a definite conception of Wyatt's characterization. For example, she wrote, "W[yatt] G[wyon] relating Brown's exploits, seems wrong. He might be aware of, but would hardly recount, such information." Thus, Wyatt grew more reticent as the incidental characters practically vanished.

The net result was that Wyatt's counterparts took on increased importance in the middle part of *The Recognitions*. Gaddis intended Otto, Anselm, Valentine, Stanley, Esther, Chaby Sinisterra, and so forth, to represent facets of Wyatt. They were all to be one, or one-and-a-half dimensional versions of Wyatt's shortcomings, just as he would represent their possibilities.

If the daughter whose love was to have redeemed Wyatt disappeared, and if Wyatt represents what all the other characters have lost, then is there no one who is redeemed in *The Recognitions?* The answer is that Wyatt still has at least the possibility of finding redemption. He realizes in the final epiphany that life is sin that must be lived through, not lied about in counterfeit terms of redemption. But Gaddis deliberately reduced Wyatt's visible means of salvation, as well as the reader's means of identification with the hero. Instead, he made Wyatt the symbol of what all the others had lost, so that his sin and their loss would be mutually instructive to the reader. These artistic decisions with which Gaddis concluded the creation of *The Recognitions* brought from some readers the charge of nihilism. However, the hope that Gaddis extinguished in his plot he rekindled through parody.

Notes

1. William Gaddis, Notes for *The Recognitions,* 1945–1951. Gaddis has in his possession a multiplicity of notes, largely unpaginated, undated, and arranged in no systematized fashion. In addition, there are newspaper and magazine clippings to which Gaddis did not affix dates or pages. Reference to these materials will be indicated by the word "Notes" in parentheses in the text.

2. William Gaddis, *The Recognitions* (1955; reprint with corrections, Cleveland and New York: World Publishing Co., Meridian Fiction, 1962), 49. Subsequent references will be cited parenthetically in the text.

3. William Gaddis, unpublished interview with Peter W. Koenig, Piermont, New York, 28 April, 1970.

4. David Chandler, notes on Gaddis' *The Recognitions,* Harcourt, Brace, 1953.

5. Notes exchanged by Gaddis and his editor, Catharine Carver, at Harcourt, Brace, 1953–54. Subsequent quotations from this source will be self-evident.

2

Gaddis Anagnorisis

John Leverence

Harcourt, Brace & Co. presented *The Recognitions,* a first novel by
William Gaddis, in their spring trade list for 1955. The novel's
956 tightly printed pages of unclear plot lines; unpunctuated dialogue;
arcane references to occult, pagan, and Christian practices; a multitude
of characters who appeared and reappeared but were rarely identified by
name; and a brace of disparaging reviews were enough to remainder its
mainly unsold copies. The author had predicted as much. Appearing as
"Willie," a writer discussing his work-in-progress under the din of a crowded
bar, Gaddis steps briefly into his own novel to say something about his
book's audience:

—Scatological?
—Eschatological, the doctrine of last things . . .
—Good lord, Willie, you are drunk. Either that or you're writing for
a very small audience.
—So . . . ? how many people were there in Plato's Republic? [1]

Supporters and critics alike have mulled over the notion that Gaddis,
with pride and prejudice, wrote *The Recognitions* with a mind to exclud-
ing the riffraff from his novelistic republic. This essay will argue that Gaddis is not an elite obscurantist; rather, he is a novelist who wrote a book
to accomplish complex purposes—to dramatize his recognition that the
"last things" of modern life are drear deceptions, and the life that is full
and significant is spiritually derived from the resources of our deepest and
purest humanity. Through a look at its form and design (loose baroque
and postmodern), content (alchemy) and intent (recognition), this essay

Reprinted, with changes, from *Itinerary,* no. 3 (Summer 1977):49–62, by permission of the
author and publisher.

will attempt to show that Gaddis drew heavily on established literary form and philosophical content to construct a sturdy harmony of tradition and individual talent that, on its own terms, is a straightforward solution to the novelistic problems he confronted.

In its purpose and design, syntax, grammatical constructions, and meditative reflections the prose style of *The Recognitions* often parallels seventeenth-century loose baroque prose. As described by Morris W. Croll in his classic essay on the subject, loose baroque shows "a mind discovering truth as it goes, thinking while it writes." [2] The loose baroque sentence begins

> without premeditation, stating its idea in the first form that occurs; the second member [clause] is determined by the situation in which the mind finds itself after the first has been spoken; and so on throughout the period [sentence], each member being an emergency of the situation [since each is suddenly called for by what preceded it]. The period—in theory at least—is not made; it becomes. It completes itself and takes on form in the course of the motion of mind which it expresses. [3]

The following passage from *The Recognitions* describing the hero's indecision exemplifies Croll's observations about how a prose style takes form "in the course of the motion of mind which it expresses":

> He had become increasingly reluctant wherever decisions were concerned; and the more he knew, the less inclined to commit himself. Not that this was an exceptional state: whole systems of philosophy have been erected upon it. On the other hand, the more he refused to commit himself, the more submerged, and the more insistent from those depths, became the necessity to do so: a plight which has formed the cornerstone for whole schools of psychology. So it may be that his decision to marry simply made one decision the less that he must eventually face; or it is equally possible that his decision to marry was indecision crystallized, insofar as he was not deciding against it. (79) *angst*

Croll found loose baroque syntax to have three recurring elements: coordinating conjunctions, absolute constructions, and parentheses. The syntax of Gaddis' prose style is marked by the frequent appearance of these elements, as well as apposition, conjunctive adverbs and relative clauses, all appearing in compound-complex sentences. An example is found in Gaddis' description of a group of outcast Spanish monks:

> They chose Homoiousian, of *like* substance, as a happier word than its tubular alternative Homoousian (no one gave them a chance at Heteroousian),

and were forthwith put into quiet dungeons which proved such havens of
self-indulgence, unfurnished with any means of vexing the natural processes,
that they died of very shame, unable even to summon such pornographic
phantasms as had kept Saint Anthony rattling in the desert (for to tell the
truth none of these excellent fellows knew for certain what a woman looked
like, and each could, without divinely inspired effort, banish that image enhanced by centuries of currency among them, in which She watched All with
inflamed eyes fixed in the substantial antennae on Her chest). (9–10)

Sir Thomas Browne, a seventeenth-century English physician and author, is cited by Croll as a paradigmatic stylist of loose baroque. Here is
a passage from Browne's *Religio Medici* that demonstrates the elements
of that style:

As there were many Reformers, so likewise many reformations; every Coun-
trey proceeding in a particular way and Method, according as their nation-
all interest together with their constitution and clime inclined them, some
angrily and with extremitie, others calmely, and with mediocrity, not rend-
ing, but easily dividing the community, and leaving an honest possibility
of a reconciliation, which though peaceable Spirits doe desire, and may conceive that revolution of time, and the mercies of God may effect; yet that
judgement that shall consider the present antipathies between the two ex-
treames, their contrarieties in condition, affection and opinion, may with
the same hopes expect an union in the poles of Heaven.[4]

Browne's sentence develops in associative reflections on the broad topic
of reformers and reformations. The first two clauses do not restrictively
direct what follows; rather, they provide a loose basis for a variety of sub-
topics, each following the other, although they follow neither as logical
necessity or as non sequitur, but as an associative response to a prior
thought.

Gaddis uses the same associative development in his sentence about the
heretical Spanish monks. He begins with an explanation of their heretical
error, which is followed by a description of their punishment, which leads
to a contrast of the monks and Saint Anthony, followed by a long paren-
thetical discussion of the order's traditional misconceptions about female
anatomy. Gaddis does not seem to be recording what he has already thought
out so much as he is describing his imaginative associations as they occur
to him.

The loose baroque style gives the novel a sense of unfolding possibilities, but it is less well understood as a progressive, sequential narrative
that lays out one plot ingredient after another than as an inventional clus-

tering of linear narrative segments that are properly perceived in patterns. A painterly analogy to this construction is pointillism. Another is television, which projects its pictures in a manner similar to the constructions/ distributions used by Gaddis. In the cathode-ray tube a scanning finger electronically distributes a screen full of lines that compose the shades of the picture. Even as this moving finger contours a whole-screen complex of shades, the shades are redistributed in a rapid progression of images. The viewer's perception of television is one of total pattern recognition — a perception unlike the fragmented, marching-dot construction of the conventional novel.

reaching!

The Recognitions contains explanations of these postmodern constructions/distributions. In the following long passage, the novel's protagonist, Wyatt Gwyon, discusses writing:

> —How . . . how fragile situations are. But not tenuous. Delicate, but not flimsy, not indulgent. Delicate, that's why they keep breaking, they must break and you must get the pieces together and show it before it breaks again, or put them aside for a moment when something else breaks and turn to that, and all this keeps going on. That's why most writing now, if you read it they go on one two three four and tell you what happened like newspaper accounts. [. . .] They write for people who read with the surface of their minds, people with reading habits that make the smallest demands on them, people brought up reading for facts, who know what's going to come next and want to know what's coming next, and get angry at surprises. [. . .] Why, all this around us is for people who can keep their balance only in the light, where they move as though nothing were fragile, nothing tempered by possibility, and all of a sudden bang! something breaks. Then you have to stop and put the pieces together again. But you never can put them back together quite the same way. You stop when you can and expose things, and leave them within reach, and others come on by themselves, and they break, and even then you may put the pieces aside just out of reach until you can bring them back and show them, put together slightly different, maybe a little more enduring, until you've broken it and picked up the pieces enough times, and you have the whole thing in all its dimensions. (113–14)

The "situations" that "keep breaking" are also the "pieces" that are put together again and again, although never in "quite the same way." These situations/pieces are the recurring characters, descriptions, dialogue fragments, and events of the novel. The patterns they cluster into are not permanent but are constantly breaking and then being "put together slightly different, maybe a little more enduring." The progress of the novel is not "one two three four," but complex after complex of configurations being exposed, left within reach, and brought back to be shown again. The end of this construction and reconstruction comes when "you've broken it and picked up the pieces enough times, and you have the whole thing in all its dimensions."

An example of Gaddis' manipulation of the pieces of his fiction can be noted in the comparison and contrast of two passages.

> The letter he had torn in pieces lay on the moving air for an instant, was caught, spread up over the ground and blew away from him like a handful of white birds startled into the sky. (62)

Almost eight hundred pages later, Gaddis reworks the pieces into another pattern.

> Down below, the white birds, finding nothing, startled by the clap of the hull, fled coming up all together, and away, like the fragments of a letter torn up and released into the wind. (846)

The basic ingredients of diction and image in the first passage are "put together slightly different" in the second passage. Each description is a dimension of the possibilities for the words and images that comprise it, while each functions independently of the other within its particular context.

Another area of reconstruction is dialogue. Characters in *The Recognitions* have a tendency to repeat what others, or they themselves, have said at another time. Sometimes these recurrences come after several decades. Reverend Gwyon, Wyatt's father, makes the following statement when Wyatt is only a small child:

> —Spain . . . Gwyon said, —the self-continence, and still I have a sense of ownership here, but even now . . . to outsiders, it seems to return their love at the moment, but once outside they find themselves shut out forever, their emptiness facing a void, a ragged surface that refuses to admit . . . (16)

Some twenty years later, and four hundred pages into the novel, Gwyon makes a similar observation:

> —Damned, empty land, you're part of it when you're there. Part of it, that self-continent land, and when you're out, outside, shut out, and look back on it, you look back on its emptiness from your own, look over its ragged edges to its . . . its hard face, refuses to admit you've ever touched it. (429)

In a traditional novel, the linear sequence of events increases the reader's understanding of plot, character, and theme. In *The Recognitions*, the sequence of arrival of information is not scheduled to further the reader's understanding of those conventionally important story elements. The best possible arrangement of "fragile situations" is toward the end of showing "the whole thing in all its dimensions." Gaddis' commentator, Wyatt, indicates that there comes a time when the writer cannot proceed further without restructuring the patterns he has developed by arranging the patterns in a new way. A linear construction selects the proper plot direction and pursues it. Gaddis' novel does not progress in a direct, plot-unfolding manner; its progression is not "one two three four" but is directed toward the breaking and restructuring of the patterns—a larger application of the loose baroque technique. This progression allows Gaddis a structural framework in which to experiment with ideas, patterns, characterizations, language, and the form of the novel itself. Not being restricted by conventional linear development, Gaddis can create partial, tentative, and "delicate" configurations, move on to new patterns, and then return to the former configurations afterwards. Gaddis' construction implies that traditional logical development is not the only way to deal with the perplexing, "fragile situations" of life and art.

Gaddis' use of the unfolding loose baroque within a patterned structure is supplemented by his distribution of recurring motifs into variable configurations. This interplay of the familiar and the strange creates a feeling of déjà vu. For example, Wyatt once falls asleep in the afternoon, wakes at twilight, and thinks he has slept through until dawn. This occurs in Paris when he is a young artist and precedes his first serious confrontation with dishonesty in the art world. Years later he experiences the same confusion of dusk and dawn—this time before his *last* involvement with dishonest art manipulation. The pattern of criminal involvement is reversed from the first incident to the second, but the basic incident remains the same.

Another type of motif distribution begins early in the novel, after Reverend Gwyon has buried his wife and almost died himself during an interlude in a Spanish monastery. He spends a troubled night in Madrid, concluded by a walk in Retiro Park. As the morning approaches, the narrator describes the sky:

False dawn past, the sun prepared the sky for its appearance, and there, a shred of perfection abandoned unsuspecting at the earth's rim, lay the curve of the old moon, before the blaze which would rise behind it to extinguish the cold quiet of its reign. (15)

The narrator then comments on Gwyon's sudden "feeling of liberation":

He felt that a decision had been made somewhere beyond his own consciousness: that he must follow its bent now, and discover its import later. There
would be time. (ibid.)

One Sunday morning, many years later, Gwyon makes manifest the import of the Madrid decision when he, a Christian minister, turned Mith-
raic priest, ritually sacrifices a neighbor's bull. The bizarre events of that
day begin with a description of the morning sky:

In the false dawn, the sun prepared the sky for its appearance: but even now
the horned moon hung unsuspecting at the earth's rim, before the blaze which
rose behind it to extinguish the cold quiet of its reign. (700)

Gaddis uses the motif of dawn, described in parallel passages, to introduce Gwyon's sense of decision in Madrid and the end result of that decision in his parish yard. In the first passage, the eminently reliable narrator
indicates that the import of the decision will be discovered later, noting
in a Prufrock phrase, "There would be time." The narrator's judgment—
more an explicit prediction than an implicit foreshadowing—is supplemented by a cuing device—the description of the sky. Rather than reversing a pattern of action, as in Wyatt's second confusion of twilight and dawn,
Gaddis here uses the descriptive cue to complete a pattern of action.

A further component of the novel's interlocking system is its epistemological theme:

—Who can tell what happened? Why, we have movement and surprise, movement and surprise and recognition, over and over again but . . . who knows
what happened? (543)

"Fragile situations" are not only the contents of time and possibility, they
are also the functions of "Every moment reshaping the past" (547). Situations are necessarily fragile, necessarily must continue breaking, if the present is to exist in its Janus-faced role of reshaping the past by living through
the present.

The notion of every moment reshaping the past is metaphoric of the
construction peculiar to the loose baroque sentence. Every member of the
sentence is both "an emergency of the situation," the situation being the
member that has preceded it, and another piece of context which the
prior member is a part of. As the loose baroque sentence breaks with every
turn of the associative reflections of the mind creating it, *The Recognitions* progresses by breaking and then rearranging the situations already
presented. Gaddis does this by providing new contexts (a conventional de-

vice used to reconstruct the crime in the classical detective novel that is appropriate to the mysteries and potboiled intrigues of *The Recognitions* and by actually rearranging the diction, image, and pattern of action from one section to another. The epistemological theme that one can never know what happened because the present has the power to reshape the past is a denial of stable contexts and an affirmation of "fragile situations." The loose baroque sentence reshapes prior members by the simple device of not recording them as fully developed thoughts, but as aspects of thoughts that introduce other aspects until the whole is seen in all its dimensions. The loose baroque sentence is potentially greater than the sum of its parts, because its parts are shaped and reshaped by the contexts provided by the various reflective turns of the sentence. This is also the case with the whole of *The Recognitions*.

Such matters are further linked to the aesthetic theme of recognition, that is, originality is not invention but a sense of recall, a recognition of patterns that are already there: "Cicero gives Praxiteles no credit for anything of his own in his work, but just for removing the excess marble until he reached the real form that was there all the time" (124). These a priori forms are not only important touchstones of personal identity in a world of counterfeit identities, posturing, and interchangeable poses, but they are the substance of the works of art that redeem time by recognizing the forms—the archetypes—that are the content of time. The same thing that redeems is that which is redeemable, and art redeems time as the present reshapes the past. A symbol of these complex functions is the ouroboros, a serpent biting its tail, which is symbolic of a self-contained system of recurring form and motif. Although Gaddis does not mention the ouroboros in his novel, there is one stamped on the cloth cover and another printed on the title page of the Harcourt edition. They stand as a visual introduction to the idea of wholeness-through-return, which is a significant part of the novel's theme and aesthetic.

Aesthetic recognition, containing the possibility of artistic perfection, is hampered by corruption. The world of *The Recognitions* is one of fraud, falsification, and disintegrated values. Wyatt's opportunity to sell his early paintings is ruined because he will not bribe an art critic; Wyatt's art teacher, Herr Koppel, passes off one of Wyatt's pictures as an authentic German masterpiece; Wyatt's mother dies of an appendectomy because the surgeon attending her is really a counterfeiter posing as a physician; an art dealer places glassware in manure to "age" into high-priced antiques; a literary critic reviews new books by reading the flap notes; and an advertising agency promotes "Necrostyle," a sleeping pill in the design of a Eucharistic wafer.

Aesthetic recognition requires a penetration of the layers of corruption

until the underlying forms of beauty are exposed and recognized. Because
the archetypes of form cannot penetrate completely the matter of corrupti-
ble things, these forms of beauty are looked into corruption by corruption.

A historical group of individuals who sought to free the ideal human
spirit, of which beauty is a component part, were the alchemists, of whom
Gaddis writes with erudition. They tried to find an alchemical gold, as
much a spiritual as a physical substance, that would free the potential of
perfection and ideal "from the conspiracy of earth, air, fire and water bind-
ing it here in baseness. 'For me an image slumbers in the stone,' said Zarathustra" (149). Zarathustra's philosopher's stone, like Praxiteles' sculp-
ture, was obscured and bound away.

The alchemist and the artist both seek to free the hidden form, to recognize that which is already there but exists in corruption only as a potential. The alchemist's identity was linked to his philosopher's stone and was
the apotheosis of his work. Gaddis writes that in this world "the things
worth being were so easily exchanged for the things worth having" (131).
To the alchemists, being and having the stone were the same thing; the
material and spiritual aspects of their work were not mutually exclusive.
Even as the identity of the true artist is linked to his recognition of pre-
existing forms, so was the identity of the alchemist linked to his redemptive work with spirit and matter. Although Wyatt forges masterpieces, his
sense of what he does is not the sense of a forger.

> —It's not. It's not, damn it, I . . . when I'm working, I . . . Do you think
> I do these the way all other forging has been done? Pulling the fragments
> of ten paintings together and making one, or taking a . . . a Dürer and re-
> versing the composition so that the man looks to the right instead of left,
> putting a beard on him from another portrait, and a hat, a different hat from
> another, so that they look at it and recognize Dürer there? No, it's . . . the
> recognitions go much deeper, much further back, and I . . . this . . . the X-
> ray tests, and ultra-violet and infra-red, the experts with their photomicrogra-
> phy and . . . macro-photography, do you think that's all there is to it? Some
> of them aren't fools, they don't just look for a hat or a beard, or a style they
> can recognize, they look with memories that . . . go beyond themselves, that
> go back to . . . where mine goes. (250)

When Gaddis asks if the great alchemists have been transcended by
modern technology that can, at the cost of $10,000 an ounce, transmute
base metal into gold, he is being more or less ironic: more ironic because
true alchemists were concerned with universal redemption, not making
common gold; less ironic because, in *The Recognitions*, the modern world
is so constricted by reason, so atrophied by demystification, that technol-

ogy seems to have shown its enlightened superiority to the alchemists'
dreams.

> Once chemistry had established itself as true and legitimate son and heir,
> alchemy was turned out like a drunken parent, to stagger away, babbling
> fantasies to fewer and fewer ears, to less and less impressive derelicts of lone-
> liness, while the child grew up serious, dignified, and eminently pleased with
> its own limitations, to indulge that parental memory with no doubt but that
> it had found what the old fool and his cronies were after all the time. (132)

But Wyatt is not satisfied with the slick surface of our enlightened age.
He sees modernity as thin ice over the fathomless past. His duty as a true
artist is to scratch through the surface of things and recognize their aw-
ful depths.

At times, Wyatt makes his living as an art forger. Yet he does not care
anything for money; he does his work of copying as an homage to the old
masters. Modernity has so successfully obscured the artist's recognition
of the spiritual essences of God and man, as well as the ideal forms of
beauty, that he must reorient himself to those essences and forms by meticulous copying:

> —There was nothing God did not watch over, nothing, and so this . . . and
> so in the painting every detail reflects . . . God's concern with the most in-
> significant objects in life, with everything, because God did not relax for
> an instant then, and neither could the painter then. (251)

Wyatt's belief that spiritual and formal ideals are locked in corruption
and can be freed only by an intuitive recognition of them has an alchemical parallel. The fundamental alchemical premise is that all metals gestate
toward the perfect state of gold. Being an impatient, heroic sort, the alchemist sought to bring fruition to the metals by means of chemical manipulation rather than by waiting for them to mature naturally. Perhaps
their critics could accuse them of usurping God's work, but the alchemists
did not think so. Since they did not have the luxury of divine immortality,
they had to devise and apply chemical procedures that would achieve the
same results as time. The athanor, the alchemical oven, was but a metaphor for time; the procuring of the philosopher's stone was equated with
seeking knowledge of God. Imitation of God's work was but an act of
recognition.

Wyatt's forgeries are illegal in the secular world of art marketing, but
they are, to him, only attempts to cut through the false and obscured world

of the present. His forgeries, like the alchemist's manipulations, are not secular blasphemies but quests of spiritual recognition. When technology transmutes lead to gold, it creates a new substance. Creation, Wyatt was taught as a child, is not man's right or privilege — originality is a usurpation of God's work. It is a falsification of something in the divine order, and it is therefore a sin. The greatest reverence Wyatt can pay to God is to imitate Him, not to attempt to outdo Him with anything original. And so he copies the old masters rather than creating "new" paintings. If Wyatt and the alchemists are heroes as well as true artists, it is because they share an uncompromising devotion to something higher than themselves by means of acts of recognition.

Wyatt's father, Reverend Gwyon, provides another kind of spiritual link with alchemy. It was the alchemist Michael Maier who had seen in gold an image of the sun when the sun could still be taken as the image of God (132). It is Reverend Gwyon who rejects Christianity for the sun worship of Mithraism. Gwyon's apostasy is predicated on his belief that the microcosmic salvation of Christ, who saved mankind, pales before the macrocosmic salvation of Mithra, who saved the universe. Such beliefs were shared by the alchemists. True alchemists were not magical dilettantes but religious philosophers who sought to go beyond the limitations of religion as an ethical system or means of microcosmic redemption.

Gaddis not only uses alchemical ideas, but he also structures some of the novel as a parallel of the minor opus, the alchemical progression from lead to silver. On page 839, during a confused narration of events on a trans-Atlantic ship crossing, there is indication that Wyatt is rescued from a shipwreck. When he is pulled from the sea, near death, he is covered with black oil slime. The first step of the minor opus (lead changed to silver) is the *calcination* of lead, which involves a *melanosis* or blackening of the *materia prima,* the physical and spiritual essence to be purified, during which all interest in the profane world is killed. Wyatt's oily *melanosis* is followed by an extreme unction — certainly a putting off of worldly matters. The ceremony is conducted by a priest whom one of the characters on board ship refers to as a "black androgyne" (851). The priest as androgyne is significant in an alchemical way: *Mercurius,* the element of direction and control within this "black" stage of the opus, is an androgyne.

When we find Wyatt later, he has given up the world and plans to simplify his life. The conclusion of the minor opus is the *solution,* or purification of matter. The alchemical parallel is that Wyatt has found wisdom through simplicity, even as the minor opus finds its completion with the simple purity and symbolic wisdom of silver.

Iconography provides a further reference to alchemy. The alchemical possibility of a mysterious conjunction of opposites is based on the belief that the world is unfinished and in a constant state of gestation. The alchemists believed that human experience was not linear, each moment abandoning the past, but that experience was circular, each moment reshaping the past. Their symbol of the continuous, repetitive, and unified world was the ouroboros, often with the Greek for "All Is One" lettered within its coil.

The philosophy, progression of the minor opus, and iconography of alchemy are not merely coincidental to *The Recognitions*. Gaddis' novel is explicitly and implicitly alchemical in theme, structure, and motif. Alchemy, with its mythical, eternally returning patterns, points to the depths of possibility below the surface of rational consciousness in the modern world. It does not propose definitive answers to the contemporary novelist or his heroes, but it suggests possibilities for investigation. It rejects the enlightenment notion that the modern world is a unique transformation of man and society, that what we have come to is a superior synthesis of mind and matter. Instead, alchemy proposes that the better understanding of man is the recognition of his dualities, oppositions of good and evil, and delicate balances. Modern man knows something is wrong, that something is lost, but he is ignorant of a means of recognizing the loss or the solution. All he can do is look for the possibilities that are components of truth. And that is all the alchemists or Wyatt are trying to do.

In *The Recognitions* the search for possibilities is carried on in an ouroboric world of continuous, repetitive, and unified experience. The numerous chance meetings, seeming coincidences, sense of déjà vu, crossed paths, ships passing and colliding in the night are part of Gaddis' use of chance as a component of his novel's structure. Aristotle's comments on the element of chance in tragedy are apropos to Gaddis' plot:

> . . . for even coincidences are most striking when they have an air of design. We may instance the status of Mitys at Argos, which fell upon his murderer while he was a spectator at a festival and killed him. Such events seem not to be due to mere chance. Plots, therefore, constructed on these principles are necessarily the best.[5]

S. H. Butcher notes that chance is usually antithetical to the artist's job of getting at the "central meaning of facts" by transforming them "into truths by supplying vital connexions and causal links, to set the seal of reason upon the outward semblances of art."[6] In *The Recognitions*, this is the process of putting together "fragile situations" until "you have the whole thing in all its dimensions." This is what Gaddis does to give chance a design.

The sphere of chance, Butcher's second category, "is that wide domain of human life which baffles foresight, defies reason, abounds in surprises: and also those regions of Nature where we meet the abortive efforts, mistakes, strange and monstrous growths."[7] It is very much a part of Gaddis' plot content. Those things that dwell in the sphere of chance are the chaos of events appearing in *The Recognitions*. As an artist, Gaddis works to provide "vital connexions and causal links" to the essence of chance; as a novelist of contemporary life, he describes the dimensions of falsity and the atmosphere of corruption in the modern world's sphere of chance.

This is a place of chaos, but it is also an area which offers possibilities. Wyatt's grandfather offers some advice: "Later on we shall simplify things. Why, all the others are drowning in details. That's what happens to them, you know. That's where we'll outwit them. We must simplify . . ." (411). One means of simplifying is to live deliberately. Rather than drowning in the details of his own mistakes and moral imperfection, Wyatt concludes that it is better to confront the inevitability of temptation, sin, and corruption and deal with it by "living it through":

> —Look back, if once you're started in living you're born into sin, then? And how do you atone? By locking yourself up in remorse for what you might have done? Or by living it through. By locking yourself up in remorse with what you know you have done? Or by going back and living it through. By locking yourself up with your work, until it becomes a gessoed surface, all prepared, clean and smooth as ivory? Or by living it through. By drawing lines in your mind? Or by living it through. If it was sin from the start, and possible all the time, to know it's possible and avoid it? Or by living it through. [. . .] and deliberately go on living it through. (896)

Having been locked out of his monastic sanctuary, Wyatt resolves that it is better to be locked out into deliberate living than be locked into a closed world where details of guilt can be suffocating. Wyatt's plan to simplify his life by living deliberately is not so much a concrete solution to his problems as it is a recognition of the moral integration of good and evil in his own character: something from the past that he was born into, and something of the present that will reshape the past as he deliberately lives it through. If every moment reshapes the past, then every recognition of the past will clarify the possibilities for deliberate living, a life in which the aesthetic principle of picking up and restructuring the pieces until "you have the whole thing in all its dimensions" becomes a moral principle. Wyatt becomes a true artist when his life, not just his work, becomes an act of recognition.

From his special vantage point, Wyatt can see that the fool's gold forgeries of modern life have value insofar as they refer to the auric ideal of "the whole thing in all its dimensions" unfolding deliberately. Plato wanted life to be that way in his Republic, with philosopher-kings showing the way. Gaddis (or "Willie," the writer who was satisfied with a small audience if it was a Republic audience) created Wyatt, the true artist, as his leader. The main course of the novel is Wyatt's long and perilous journey from a childhood of religious terror to a maturity of spiritual recognition, where nothing is empty or without significance that is spiritually derived from one's deepest and purest humanity.

That main course develops from loose baroque sentences and paragraphs, postmodern patterns, cues, and motif reconstructions; these integrate epistemological, aesthetic, and philosophical substance into an occult pattern of spiritual exaltation that operates in a sphere of unfolding possibilities. The sturdy harmony of tradition and individual talent that all the interlocking elements achieve is not a muddle of obscurantism, but a straightforward solution to the novelistic problems Gaddis confronted. *The Recognitions* curves, with scaled torso—tail in teeth—out and around and back on itself like the ouroboros printed on the title page. While it is sometimes difficult to find where one part of its great circle begins, segues into another part (and where that part ends or links with the next part), there is no doubt that the novel is true to its ouroboric emblem, and "All Is One."

Notes

1. William Gaddis, *The Recognitions* (Harcourt, Brace & World, Inc., 1955), 478. Subsequent references to this work will be cited parenthetically in the text.

2. Morris W. Croll, "The Baroque Style in Prose," *Studies in English Philology,* ed. Kemp Malone and Martin Ruud (Minneapolis: University of Minnesota Press, 1929), 442.

3. Ibid., 446.

4. *The Prose of Sir Thomas Browne,* ed. Norman Endicott (New York: New York University Press, 1968), 9–10.

5. *Aristotle's Theory of Poetry and Fine Arts*, trans. S. H. Butcher, 4th ed. (1894; reprint. New York: Dover, 1951), 39.

6. Ibid., 180.

7. Ibid., 181.

3

To Soar in Atonement
Art as Expiation in Gaddis'
The Recognitions

Joseph S. Salemi

Despite the intricacies of structure and design that have gone into the making of *The Recognitions*, there is apparent in the work, as in the flamenco music so loved by Wyatt, "the tremendous tension of violence all enclosed in a framework."[1] Much of what strikes the casual reader as "excessive" in the book—its length, the virulence of its satire, the wide and esoteric range of its allusiveness, the improbability of certain incidents —suggests the extreme lengths to which William Gaddis was prepared to go to create an art commensurate with all reality rather than some limited aspect of it. As with *Moby-Dick,* the novel's implications move in wider and wider circles from the bobbing coffin of Queequeg, or the catastrophic final harmony at Fenestrula.

The Recognitions is an obsessive book, in that both author and characters seem driven to extremities of experience, perception, and thought. Individual figures such as Reverend Gwyon, Stanley, and Anselm are obsessed with the ultimate validity of reality, though their obsessions take different forms: arcane theology and philosophy, Catholicism and baroque music, absurdity and religious despair. Recktall Brown is driven by avarice, Otto by prideful self-esteem, Basil Valentine by his personal variety of embittered fastidiousness. These obsessions jar each other in contrapuntal relationships: Valentine and Brown, Stanley and Anselm, Gwyon and Aunt May, and the quasi protagonist Wyatt in individual relation to each of them. Indeed, it is through the focal character of Wyatt that *The Recognitions* carries on a continual and insistent debate. That debate, which might be

Reprinted from *Novel* 10 (Winter 1977):127–36, by permission of the author and the publisher.

termed the obsession of the novel as a whole, revolves around the following double question: *What is the nature of, and what are the conditions
for, genuine art?*

That in *The Recognitions* "reality" and "art" are interchangeable metaphors for each other is, I think, clear to every thoughtful reader. The cheap
tourist art of Montmartre, the upside-down painting of Max, the distorted
portrait of Recktall Brown—each symbolizes and epitomizes the context
of life that surrounds it. For Gaddis, art is the touchstone by which the
genuineness of life is judged, and the purity of human motives measured.
Wyatt is not only an individual artist, but an Everyman whose concerns
are universal; his art—and art in general—is no mere adornment or addition to life, but life itself in the deepest and truest sense. This is part of
the achievement of the novel: it succeeds in turning the simple analogy
of art and life into a baffling and frightening identity. In *The Recognitions*
questions that ostensibly deal with aesthetics actually are questions that
probe to the very core of the human condition.

The Recognitions is remarkably self-reflective, in that the novel abounds
in authorial comments about itself, its style, its difficulties—even its prob-
able reception by critics. Part of the parody of the book is directed at itself, as if Gaddis were holding up a mirror to his work as it progressed.
The comparison is an apt one, I think, for Wyatt uses mirrors in his work
to obtain deliberate effects, and a sense of "the obscure reveries of the inward gaze" is sustained throughout the novel. This kind of conscious self-
scrutiny, which unlike a conventional prologue or epilogue is intrinsic to
the work itself, indicates that Gaddis' own art as a novelist, as well as Wyatt's
as a painter, is a thematic and structural concern. *The Recognitions* is a
first novel, and as such displays more than its share of self-consciousness,
but the author's insistent scrutiny of his protagonist's aesthetic[2] may well
have served as a personal exorcism of similar demons troubling his own art.

It will be useful, in this regard, to consider the kind of artist Wyatt is,
and the kind of art he recognizes as genuine. His aesthetic is one of precise and severe laws that aim at the creation of such genuine art. I have
used the word *genuine* here deliberately. It must be carefully distinguished
from *original,* which in the lexical context of *The Recognitions* has a
slightly pejorative connotation. The quest for originality is denigrated in
the novel more than once as a misunderstanding of the artistic task. Wyatt
quotes his teacher, Herr Koppel, on the subject:

> —"That romantic disease, originality, all around we see originality of incom-
> petent idiots, they could draw nothing, paint nothing, just so the mess they
> make is original . . . Even two hundred years ago who wanted to be origi-

nal, to be original was to admit that you could not do a thing the right way, so you could only do it your own way." (89)

These sentiments are recalled in the comments of Stanley, who, as I hope to demonstrate, works successfully within the laws of Wyatt's aesthetic. In a discussion of modern painters, Stanley says:

> —Some of them have set out to kill art. [. . .] And some of them are so excited about discovering new mediums and new forms [. . .] that they never have time to work in one that's already established. (186)

Genuine art, on the other hand, respects the achievements of the past and consciously builds upon them. It is concerned not with the vagaries of period style, but with transfigured reality, with that captured moment of luminous significance that Wyatt calls *recognition*.[3] Such art is only secondarily original in the romantic sense, but primarily seeks out, as Stanley puts it, "the origins of design" (322), the archetypes of formal perfection that art can reproduce only in a reflected image.

Wyatt's chosen mode of expression is that of the fifteenth-century masters, in particular the Flemish primitives. Even before his forgeries we see him working in handmade tempera, a medium suited to carefully defined forms and precise detail, and one that demands painstaking discipline and subtlety of the artist who employs it. It is singularly appropriate that Wyatt should choose as his artistic archetypes the works of van der Weyden, Bouts, David, van der Goes, and Memling, all of whom, despite differences, share a peculiar sensitivity and vision. This vision includes themes of pious, almost quietistic devotion, meticulous attention to small objects and fine lines, and above all a consciously architectonic composition, with figures poised in a hieratic manner that suggests to Wyatt "that sense of movement in stillness."[4] All these things comprise more than a mere technique for Wyatt; they are signs of a special religious awareness in an artist that marks his work with *recognition*. We may apply to Wyatt what one critic has said of one of the Flemish primitives: he "paints not so much a visage as a certain disposition of the soul."[5] Throughout *The Recognitions* Wyatt defines his aesthetic in these terms, and when they are finally mocked and denied he is driven to murder.

Curiously enough, it is in some comments on flamenco music that Wyatt most fully and lucidly expounds the artistic impulse that animates him:

> —That's what it is, this arrogance, in this flamenco music this same arrogance of suffering, listen. The strength of it's what's so overpowering, the

self-sufficiency that's so delicate and tender without an instant of sentimentality. With infinite pity but refusing pity, it's a precision of suffering, [. . .]
the tremendous tension of violence all enclosed in a framework, . . . in a
pattern that doesn't pretend to any other level but its own, do you know what
I mean? [. . .] It's the privacy, the exquisite sense of privacy about it [. . .]
it's the sense of privacy that most popular expressions of suffering don't have,
don't dare have, that's what makes it arrogant. (111–12)

This aesthetic of disciplined agony is continued when Otto parrots these
opinions in a talk with Wyatt's wife Esther:

—This kind of stringency of suffering, this severe self-continence of suffering that looks almost peaceful, almost indifferent. But in a way it's the same
thing, this severe quality of line, this severe delicacy and tenderness. (123)

It is easy to see the reality that such art suggests, and which Wyatt desires
to make his own. It is a reality marked by breadth of vision, chaste dignity, and controlled intelligence. Wyatt's aesthetic is typically that of a certain kind of "melancholic" artist, if we might use that term in its full traditional significance as a humor. It is an aesthetic that is extremely conscious
of technique and manner, often to the extent of forcing creativity into a
Procrustean bed of preconceived forms. It sees itself as supremely serious,
tending to a rejection of frivolity and play as inappropriate or unworthy
of the truly artistic. It cherishes a personal piety (whether religious or secular) that invests reality with numinous, even mystical significance. It is an
art of distillation rather than the wide swath, of the delicate jewel rather
than the rough-hewn stone. Moreover, it tends to exalt suffering as the
origin and subject matter of all truly great creation, choosing themes and
motifs reminiscent of Virgil's *Sunt lacrimae rerum, mentem et mortalia
tangunt.*
   At its worst, this art lapses into stiltedness and preciosity; at its best,
it is subtle, refined, and capable of piercing discernment and sensitivity.
By way of illustration, let me suggest that Wyatt's art is in a position analogous to that of Pound at the time of *Hugh Selwyn Mauberley*. It is an art
that has developed a high degree of technical proficiency in small, limited
forms ("medallions" or fine work in "porcelain," as Pound puts it). The
drawback to perfection in small, limited forms (the "separate objects" that
so intrigue Wyatt) is the danger of stagnancy and hyperrefinement, just
as the danger in wide "epic" vision is banality and inflation. A healthy tension between the two modes is ideally desirable, although individual artists and periods lean to one or the other. In *The Recognitions* Gaddis is

acutely conscious of the simultaneous polarity and complementarity of
these two modes, and it may be a useful point of departure for structural
criticism to consider the novel as a continuing counterpoint between them.
Gaddis shows his love for (and skill with) fine detail and suggestion in the
finely woven texture of his description and the labyrinth of his allusions;
he reveals an impulse to epic scope in his effort to tie a welter of plots,
characters, places, and conflicting and parallel levels of meaning into a coherent symphony.

What concerns us here, however, is the manner in which Wyatt's work
has shaped his actions and attitudes in ways that isolate him from other
persons. The tense rigidity of his art is mirrored in uncongenial withdrawal,
even from his wife, who complains that "this restraint, this pose, this control you've cultivated, Wyatt, it becomes inhuman . . ." (97). Like a human simulacrum of Flemish saints and Madonnas, he maintains a silent
privacy, becoming more and more sparing of words, refusing "to make explicit things that should be implicit" (121). In spite of her deep love for
Wyatt, Esther sees—and suffers from—the indifference and arrogance of
her husband's almost hierophantic solitude.

Wyatt, not very much at ease with others by nature, grows intolerant
of the bland stupidity of those he meets. It is often difficult to tell where
a satiric authorial voice chastising the foibles of the literary-artistic world
ends, and where a misanthropic Wyatt begins:

> —It's suffocating. Right this minute, she's talking. They're down there right
> this minute and that woman with the granulated eyelids is talking. [. . .] the
> instant you look at them they begin to talk, automatically, they take it for
> granted you understand them, that you recognize them, that they have some-
> thing to say to you, and you have to wait, you have to pretend to listen, pre-
> tend you don't know what's coming next while they go right on talking with
> no idea what they're talking about. [. . .] Who are they, to presume such
> intimacy, to . . . go right on talking. And they really believe that they're talk-
> ing to me! (107–8)

The woman in question represents the world of shallow art and intellectual falsity that throughout *The Recognitions* is parodied and attacked,
mostly through the devastating technique of quoting its representatives verbatim. Cliques of dishonest critics, backbiting literati, the entire rout of
cocktail-party intellectuals and pen pushers—all are mercilessly exposed.
In its form and structure *The Recognitions* is thoroughly modern, but in
its cumulative judgment of these representatives of modernity, it is
profoundly antimodern. Like Pound's *Cantos* or Eliot's *Waste Land,* the

novel betrays bitterness over a world gone rotten with oversimplification, facile moral relativism, glib, hucksterized psychology, latitudinarian religion, and amorphous, undisciplined art. This is a world where the equally pompous dogmas of Establishment and Anti-Establishment are indifferent or hostile to the labor of genuine creation, and where *Invidia, Ira,* and *Avaritia* are as virulent as ever. Above all it is a world of clichés, publicity, pretentious faddism in thought, and fatuous posturings by both the great and the small.

What this world lacks most, from the vantage point of Wyatt's art, is dignity. The self-possessed privacy of genuine *recognition,* the chastened and awed silence in the face of a significance deeper than the merely human, is absent, and the absence renders characters trivial and clownish. What makes Otto so ridiculous, for example, is the lack of such inner dignity and self-possession. His art, like his life, is a wretched patchwork of fraudulent playacting and stilted monologues. Otto senses something of what the genuine artist must be in Wyatt, but he remains enamored of the surface appearances of profundity, sophistication, and posturing masculinity. His lust for the social approbation that the honorific title of "artist" carries is more fatal to his art than the prodigious lack of talent he displays.

In a real sense, Wyatt's forgeries are more genuine than the products of romantic originality. When Basil Valentine accuses him of calumniating the old masters with counterfeits, Wyatt refutes the charge vigorously:

> —Do you think I do these the way all other forging has been done? [. . .]
> No, it's . . . the recognitions go much deeper, much further back [. . .] the
> experts with their photomicrography and . . . macrophotography, do you
> think that's all there is to it? Some of them aren't fools, they don't just look
> for a hat or a beard, or a style they can recognize, they look with memories
> that . . . go beyond themselves, that go back to . . . where mine goes. (250)

Where that memory goes is back to the fifteenth century, not only in regard to the technique but also the spirit of the craft of that time. Wyatt is, literally, a dedicated artisan of Bruges or Ghent:

> —And . . . any knock at the door may be the gold inspectors, come to see
> if I'm using bad materials down there, I . . . I'm master painter in the Guild,
> in Flanders. [. . .] I've taken the Guild oath, not for the critics, the experts,
> the . . . you, you have no more to do with me than if you are my descendants, nothing to do with me, [. . .] the Guild oath, to use pure materials,
> to work in the sight of God . . . (Ibid.)

But wherein does the genuineness of a work of art consist, according to Gaddis? I suggest that these three criteria are involved in the judgment of a work of art in *The Recognitions:* (*a*) Does the work in question adhere to the "origins of design"? (*b*) Is it a faithful reflection of the artist's "recognition" of this design? (*c*) Does it refuse to serve any motive beyond these two? Wyatt's forgeries perhaps fulfill the first two criteria, but they violate the third. Their value is vitiated by the intrusion of avarice and pride; indeed, it is the greed of Recktall Brown and the self-centered isolation of Wyatt that have called them into being. Despite Wyatt's rationalizations, deceit and falsity have riddled his art; his playing at medieval craftsman serves only to cover the continuing and deliberate fraud that he must perpetrate to satisfy his employer. A man of consummate technical proficiency, Wyatt dedicates himself solely to the reduplication of medieval techniques, hoping that through the perfection of such skills alone he will recapture the mysterious *Innigkeit* that gives art its life. Thus, Wyatt calls himself a craftsman, but the very stridency with which he insists upon this self-definition hints at the serious doubts entertained (unconsciously by Wyatt, consciously by Gaddis) concerning the usefulness of deriving the élan of art from craftsmanship alone.

And yet it is by means of such self-definition that Gaddis sets Wyatt — and one other character, I believe — apart from all other figures in the novel. Wyatt is the sensitive and profound soul, living in but not of the world around him. Like his father, who serves in the novel as a kind of emblematic prologue to Wyatt's life and troubles, he is a brooding, complex, self-sequestered person, obsessed with plumbing the depths of an occult truth. Wyatt's designing of bridges relates him, metaphorically, to his father. Each is a *pontifex* ("bridge-builder") or high priest: Reverend Gwyon in terms of divine ceremonies, Wyatt in terms of human art. It will be remembered that Esther complains bitterly of Wyatt's self-contained, priestly solitude and even calls him a priest. Such juxtaposition reinforces the novel's insistence on the intimate connection between art and religion, or more properly, between the secular and sacred attempts to interpret reality, to bridge the gulf between what we see and what we imagine.

It is through the unwitting agency of his father, moreover, that Wyatt has his first chance at forgery. Reverend Gwyon's purchase of the Bosch tabletop painting, *Seven Deadly Sins,* introduces a tangible symbol that appears and is alluded to over and over again in the novel. The metaphoric importance of this table in *The Recognitions* cannot be stressed enough. One is never certain as to the authenticity of the painting; Gaddis carefully confuses the issue. Is it the original Bosch? Is it the copy ordered by the Conte di Brescia? Is it Wyatt's copy? But the real question to be asked and answered is this: To what extent are we oblivious of our enslavement by the sins allegorized on the table, the sins of pride, avarice, envy, and lust that drive us to trickery and deceit? This larger moral question goes beyond the minor issue of the painting's genuineness. Whatever its provenance, the table serves as a stunning emblem throughout the novel of the *unconscious* fraud and falsity of human motives. Gaddis is masterful in his use of the table to bring into high relief the venality of characters who are not even aware of their place and judgment in a wider cosmic framework. Consider this cameo of Recktall Brown, almost medieval in its moral caricature: "'We've wasted half the God damn afternoon as it is, waiting for you.' He turned to Basil Valentine, raising the left hand, with the diamonds, and the cigar which dropped its ash on *Gula,* gluttony, before him" (241).

Wyatt is a divided self whose two warring halves are externalized in other characters. Basil Valentine represents the demands of Wyatt's aesthetic carried to a poisonous, suicidal extreme. Valentine is the waspish, sterile intellect—it is no accident that there are homosexual overtones to his character—cut loose from all human fellowship. Although his appreciation of art is informed and intelligent, he is merely a connoisseur without sympathy or love for the objects he appraises. As a spoiled Jesuit, he is a mirror image of Wyatt's deepest psychological conflicts, and his role as a secret traitor highlights the furtive, repressed nature of that image in relation to Wyatt. The cryptic Gypsy words on his gold cigarette case ("Much I ponder why you ask me questions, and why you should come thither" [255]) suggest a mysterious, riddling quality about Basil Valentine that is often associated with a psychological "shadow" in the Jungian sense. In confrontation with Valentine, Wyatt faces certain dark truths about his own life and art.

Wyatt's other self is revealed in Stanley, who labors exactly as Wyatt does, and according to the same laws. Like Wyatt, he is set apart from others in the novel—and indeed, his death from falling stones in the book's climax is in reality a death by proxy of Wyatt (rechristened Stephen after the first Christian martyr, who died by stoning). That Stanley's aesthetic accords with Wyatt's can be seen in his attitude towards the music he is writing:

> How could Bach have accomplished all that he did? and Palestrina? the Gabrielis? and what of the organ concerti of Corelli? Those were the men whose work he admired beyond all else in this life, for they had touched the origins of design with recognition. And how? with music written for the Church. Not written with obsessions of copyright foremost; not written to be played

by men in worn dinner jackets, sung by girls in sequins, involved in wage disputes and radio rights, recording rights, union rights; not written to be issued through a skull-sized plastic box plugged into the wall as background for seductions and the funnypapers. [. . .] It [the work] must be finished to a thorough perfection, as much as he humbly could perceive that, every note and every bar, every transition and movement in the pattern over and against itself and within itself proof against time: the movement in the Divine Comedy; the pattern in a Requiem Mass; prepared against time as old masters prepared their canvases and their pigments, so that when they were called to appear the work would still hold the perfection they had embraced there. (322–23)

I have quoted at length because the passage illuminates not only the art of Stanley and Wyatt, but also the art of *The Recognitions.* The statement goes to the heart of Gaddis' aesthetic intentions in a rather long and difficult novel, and one which many readers react to with baffled impatience. If one does not appreciate the art of a symphony, with its variations on a theme, improvisations, reminiscenses, and recapitulations, then the novel will be tedious in the extreme. But if one is willing to put into the study of a work of art an effort commensurate with the effort that went into its creation, then the rewards can be great. And it is well to remember that all genuine art demands this kind of attention, for art is meant to be more than an ephemeral amusement, as the length and difficulty of the *Aeneid,* the *Divine Comedy,* the *Faerie Queene,* and *Paradise Lost* indicate.

In Stanley we see the same striving for perfection, the same disdain for the popular, the same sense of *recognition* that motivates Wyatt. Stanley's and Wyatt's shared preference for the controlled "classical" over the chaotic "romantic" lends support to my suggested analogy to Pound, and both exhibit a melancholic piety that makes them solitary figures, qualitatively different from those around them. But what differentiates the composer from the painter is his genuine religious faith. Stanley gladly believes what Wyatt (along with his father) cannot accept: that he is the man for whom Christ died. It is the lack of such faith that drives Reverend Gwyon to a sterile insanity; that makes Anselm a raging, Lear-like figure; and that is the real source of the loveless incommunicability of Wyatt's character. The "privacy of suffering" that is so important to Wyatt betrays a stiff-necked pride that will not stoop to share its feelings with fellow-sufferers, a pride that is almost satanic in its haughty isolation. Esther instinctively senses the cruelty of such pride: "Precision of suffering . . . privacy of suffering . . . if that's what it is, suffering, then you . . . share it" (116). Consider, for example, Wyatt's revulsion at the "vulgarizing" of the Passion.

He rejects the sentimentality of cheapened public emotion: "Has there ever been anything in history so exquisitely private as the Virgin mourning over Her Son?" (127). The irony of such a thought is that the Passion of Christ is specifically directed to all the world—its very raison d'être is "public" in the widest possible sense. The aloof privacy that Wyatt cherishes is esoteric, while the religious significance of Christ's suffering is of its very nature exoteric in its appeal to all men. Wyatt's awareness does not go beyond the beauty of a religious motif to its universal human meaning. Faith for Wyatt—as for his father—is a self-contained niggardliness of the spirit that rejects the one reality that unites the human and the divine: communion.

It is Basil Valentine who shakes the foundations of Wyatt's private aesthetic-religion. Over the corpse of Brown he excoriates Wyatt for a fraud more sinister than forgery:

> —Vulgarity, cupidity, and power. Is that what frightens you? Is that all you see around you, and you think it was different then? Flanders in the fifteenth century, do you think it was all like the Adoration of the Mystic Lamb? [. . .] Yes, I remember your little talk, your insane upside-down apology for these pictures, every figure and every object with its own presence, its own consciousness because it was being looked at by God! Do you know what it was? What it really was? that everything was so afraid, so uncertain God saw it, that it insisted its vanity on His eyes? [. . .] Because maybe God isn't watching. Maybe he doesn't see. [. . .] everything in its own vain shell, everything separate, withdrawn from everything else. Being looked at by God! Is there separation in God? (689–90)

Basil Valentine has put his finger on the question that Wyatt cannot answer without hesitation: How much of his aesthetic is traceable not to a rarefied "medieval" sensibility, but rather to a loveless and tormented childhood? Every tenet in Wyatt's aesthetic can be viewed, psychologically, as a rationalization of early conflicts and guilt. The disparagement of originality finds its roots in the terror of original sin instilled in Wyatt by his aunt when he first began to draw. The love of privacy and "violence all enclosed in a framework" (112) are merely adult versions of the secretive repression and fear of his childhood. And, most symbolically of all, the loving God who solicitously looks at every detail is simply a palatable counterfeit of the stern Christ of the Bosch tabletop, who with the warning *Cave, cave, Dominus videt* (Beware, beware, the Lord sees) stares out in judgment from amidst a host of sins.

I certainly do not mean to write off Wyatt and his aesthetic in a psycho-

logically reductionist manner. This would be to fall into one variety of simplistic narrowness that Gaddis attacks in the modern world. It is crucial
to an understanding of *The Recognitions* to realize that Gaddis uses this
particular falsity in Wyatt's life as an image of the spurious core of human
life *as a whole.* It would be a mistake to look upon Wyatt as an individual
troubled by idiosyncratic mental habits, all the result of a curious upbringing. He, like most of the other characters in the novel, is in many ways
more of an archetype in a moral drama than a person in a realistic story.
Yet he is also unmistakably human, and it is a mark of Gaddis' artistry
that he is able to create characters who are clearly part of the world and
at the same time implicated in a metaphysical scheme of things transcending their own lives. The force of Wyatt's past is as vividly present to the
reader as it is insistently at work in Wyatt's life, but rather than allow Wyatt
to be conveniently pigeonholed as a clinical "case history," the art of *The
Recognitions* forces upon the reader the question that modern psychology
cannot bear to listen to, much less answer: Even if it is so that a man's
ideas and actions stem from sordid or unhappy incidents in his childhood,
why should those ideas and actions not be judged solely on their own merits *as* ideas and actions? The question is not explicit in *The Recognitions,*
but the cumulative force of Gaddis' art raises it, and with it the specter
of those traditional realities of free will, faith, sin, and grace.

   Here indeed is the aesthetic that lies at the core of *The Recognitions,*
both as a work of art and as a statement *about* art. The words of Stanley
that "the Devil is the father of false art" (464) take on ethical, even metaphysical meaning in this light. The creation of art is an act of atonement,
in that it constellates true significance in the midst of falsity, redeeming
that falsity just as the cross redeems sin. In point of fact, Gaddis' position
seems to be that genuine art atones not only for false art, but for false life
as well. Stanley's work expiates the falsity of Wyatt's and that same work
is the instrument of his martyrdom. This martyrdom, as I have mentioned,
is actually that of Stephen-Wyatt, for Gaddis has deliberately created a
"mystical participation" between these two characters, corresponding to
the relationship of Redeemer and redeemed. Art is the ultimate expiation,
for through it not only suffering, but the falsehood that lies at the core
of existence is transfigured beyond the pettiness and sordidness of its context and origins. Thus, as Stanley's music "soared in atonement" (956),
the shaky edifice of falsehood trembles and falls, and this final counterpoint of upward release and triumph and downward collapse and fatality
is art's perfect image of both man's implication in falsehood, and his capacity for redemption.

Notes

1. William Gaddis, *The Recognitions* (New York: Harcourt, Brace & World, 1955), 112. Subsequent references to this work will be cited parenthetically in the text.

2. I use the term "aesthetic" as a noun to indicate the peculiar vision of beauty that a given artist enjoys. One's aesthetic would include not only specific preferences of form (proportion, composition, line, color), but also a less definable sense of psychic satisfaction that is experienced in one work rather than another.

3. Cf. Wyatt's reaction to a Picasso: "It was one of those moments of reality, of near-recognition of reality. [. . .] When I saw it all of a sudden everything was freed into one recognition, really freed into reality that we never see, you never see it" (*Recognitions*, 91–92).

4. Ibid., 96. Here Wyatt is speaking of the arch, but it applies equally, as other quotations show, to the Flemish school.

5. Germain Bazin, *Memling* (New York: French Library of Fine Arts, 1939), 17.

4

Flemish Art and Wyatt's Quest for Redemption in William Gaddis' *The Recognitions*

CHRISTOPHER KNIGHT

In his preparatory notes to *The Recognitions,* William Gaddis writes, "The process of art is the artist's working out of his own redemption."[1] Fittingly, this quest, initially sought by the hero, Wyatt Gwyon, through art, and then later through a denial of the efficacy of art to effect salvation, constitutes the central theme of the novel. In the following essay, I will chart the line of Wyatt's quest and examine how a larger mass of cultural history, early Renaissance painting, is related to it. The two subjects are, I think, inseparable.

In his own work, Wyatt chooses to paint in an idiom distinctly out of date. As he tells Crémer, art critic for *La Macule,* his approach bears a strong resemblance to that of the Flemish painter Roger de la Pasture, better known as Roger van der Weyden. The choice is not made out of ignorance. Wyatt knows what he is about, or more exactly, he knows what midcentury plastic arts are about. For as Wyatt sees things, contemporary painting is little more than a reflection, and in this sense a part, of the modern situation or, as he might describe it, malaise. His contemporaries, Wyatt feels, are unable to distance themselves from what they see. Their art offers neither an effective judgment nor a higher standard by which to measure the events of the age. In this view, Wyatt is not so unlike Gaddis, who, in a note upon the text, says:

> Modern art and music are not comments on current values, soul-lessness, spiritual failure as they pretend to be even to themselves. But they are simply products of it. Painting has no place, most of it [is] more static than Egyptian two-dimensionals.[2]

In working in a style outside the range of modernism, Wyatt is also doing something else. He is trying to work himself free of self-imposed intellectual boundaries that modernism has tended to reinforce. Modern art, in its affirmation of materialism, has disengaged itself from the whole area of metaphysics. Wyatt's refusal to acquiesce in this emasculation necessitates that he discover another idiom. The approach of van der Weyden at first appears as an alternative.

Wyatt is a driven man, one whose desire to understand the universe and his place in it often makes it impossible for him to relate to other people except on the most abstract level. The subject of quiddity, or essence, is among his favorite topics of conversation. It is not really surprising then that Wyatt draws a connection between van der Weyden's artistry and his own. Van der Weyden is known more for his interest in the construction and idea of painting than for the representation of nature, light, or color. His figures are often isolated from their environment, as if to suggest that worldly existence is to be valued only to the extent that it foreshadows the heavenly realm. About van der Weyden's *Triptych* in the Louvre, one critic writes, "Purified and detached from earthly trivialities, here where the task is conceived hieratically, the abstract stylization appears inevitably the only solution, in no sense a defect or a limitation."[3]

It is hard to say how we are to judge Wyatt's paintings at this point. He refuses to pander to a decadent art circle interested in only its own perpetuation, and as a result, his work is roundly lambasted. He is also painting at a time when the mastery of the discipline has fallen off, a time, that is, when even the most talented artists find themselves hamstrung. In *Aesthetics and History,* a book much admired by Gaddis, Bernard Berenson writes, "Nowadays we are in the midst of a decline which, like all cultural declines, ignores its symptoms and euphorically images that it is revolutionizing the world when it is merely playing the infant, kicking, screaming, and smashing, or daubing and kneading with paint and clay."[4]

There is then no hint that Wyatt is deluding himself when he tells Esther that in a time such as their own there is little the artist can creatively accomplish: "Looking around us today, [. . .] there doesn't seem to be . . . much that's worth doing."[5] Wyatt has talent but no worthy artistic milieu, and in judging him, it is perhaps necessary to keep in mind the words on Pope Hadrian VI's tomb: "How much the genius of even the most gifted depends for its effectiveness on the time in which it appears."[6]

The age is particularly weak because it has estranged itself from the past. Past assumptions, including the belief that if an artist were to make a mark he would have to take a "problem of form and design further than it has yet been carried,"[7] have lost their edge. No longer are artists mind-

ful of Saint Luke's dictum, "The disciple is not above his master: but every
one that is perfect shall be as his master" (6:40). Instead, originality is
the disease of the age. Traditional paths of direction and development are
eschewed in favor of fads and reactions. Wyatt knows this and is maddened
by it:

> —It's as though . . . there's no direction to act in now.
> —People react. That's all they do now, react, they've reacted until it's the
> only thing they can do, and it's . . . finally there's no room for anyone to
> do anything but react. (156)

With no tradition, and originality the only guide, artists begin to cater
to the public's wish that each work be as unlike that which has come before as those works that follow will be unlike their own. Works of art are
produced for public consumption, to be thrown away once they outlive
their fashion. Esther's plea to Wyatt, "If you could finish something original" (99), typifies the admonishment of the age to its artists.

It's all a bit strange, for the notion of originality itself goes back no
further than the romantic period. Certainly, Dürer did not think himself
original, nor did Leonardo. In fact, rightly considered, as Berenson points
out, originality may even be considered a trait of a decaying civilization.
That is, if civilization is defined as a progressive cultural tradition that includes the arts, sciences, and statesmanship, then the more it moves in the
direction of the egocentric and the private the greater will be the strains
upon its fabric. As for Wyatt, he believes that originality is no more than
a euphemism for the degeneration of form and design, an idea first ham-
mered into his head by Herr Koppel:

> "—That romantic disease, originality, all around we see originality of incom-
> petent idiots, they could draw nothing, paint nothing, just so the mess they
> make is original . . . Even two hundred years ago who wanted to be origi-
> nal, to be original was to admit that you could not do a thing the right way,
> so you could only do it your own way. When you paint you do not try to
> be original, only you think about your work, how to make it better, so you
> copy masters, only masters, for with each copy of a copy the form degener-
> ates . . . you do not invent shapes, you know them, *auswendig wissen Sie*,
> by heart . . ." (99)

Gifted but bereft of an artistic tradition in which to work, Wyatt chooses
to abandon his artistic career and turns, after some work as a draftsman
and restorer, to the forging of Flemish masterworks. Wyatt is led on in this
endeavor by what he sees as the spiritual character of the work. A Pla-

tonist by nature, he senses that just beyond the material plane there lies an ideal plane. All men have a recollection of this other plane, but their attachment to the quotidian world weakens their recall. Knowledge is recollection. Until recently, painting was a mode of knowledge that heightened this recollection. Seeing a Picasso for the first time, for example, Wyatt is struck by a sudden sense of recognition, the feeling that he can almost look through the canvas and pick out another reality that has been lying there all along:

—Yes but, when I saw it, it was one of those moments of reality, of near-recognition of reality. [. . .] When I saw it all of a sudden everything was freed into one recognition, really freed into reality that we never see, you never see it. You don't see it in paintings because most of the time you can't see beyond a painting. Most paintings, the instant you see them they become familiar, and then it's too late. (102)

Wyatt consents to Recktall Brown's forgery scheme because his need to realize the underlying pattern beneath the canvas's plane is too great. As Wyatt explains to Brown, "every work of art is a work of perfect necessity," forcing him almost to cry out, "This is mine, this is what I must do, this is my work . . ." (157). Forging Flemish paintings represents a chance for Wyatt to work under the aspect of necessity, an aspect his contemporaries know nothing about. His design then is not to cheapen the work of the Flemish artists but to become one with them, a member of the Flanders Guild, working "in the sight of God." It is by working as "a master in the Guild" that Wyatt hopes to deepen his recollection, to make that which is fleeting sensation in the mind a concrete fact of the understanding. Saint Anselm writes:

For, it is one thing for an object to be in the understanding, and another to understand that the object exists. When a painter first conceives of what he will afterwards perform, he has it in his understanding, but does not yet understand it to be, because he has not yet performed it. But after he has made the painting, he both has it in his understanding, and understands that it exists, because he has made it.[8]

Any discussion of the Flemish masters requires a mention of perspective. Perspective, "a mathematical theory of vision," was originated by the Italian trecento artists Giotto and Duccio. Albert Dürer, the German artist, wrote, "*Perspectiva* is a Latin word and means a 'Durcheshung'" (a view through something).[9] Although not an accurate translation, Dürer's definition typifies the way the early Renaissance painters conceived of the technique. With perspective, Leone Battista Alberti said, the canvas became a "kind of window" opening onto a three-dimensional space.

The Flemish painters were, of course, not as strict as the Italians in their application of perspective. Theirs was not a "correct" perspective, mathematically conceived, but one acquired from a close study of nature. A Flemish painting might have several vanishing points, not just one. Wyatt himself says:

> —There isn't any single perspective, like the camera eye, the one we all look through now and call it realism, there . . . I take five or six or ten . . . the Flemish painter took twenty perspectives if he wished, and even in a small painting you can't include it all in your single vision, your one miserable pair of eyes, like you can a photograph, like you can painting when it . . . when it degenerates, and becomes conscious of being looked at. (270)

What counts, however, as Erwin Panofsky writes, is that perspective, be it mathematical or empirical, generally pushes the painter to a position where he "conceives of light as a quantitative and isolating rather than a qualitative and connective principle, and that he places us before rather than within the picture space. He studies and uses light mainly in terms of rectilinear propagation, employing modeling shadows to characterize the plastic shape of material objects and cast-shadows to clarify their relative positions." [10] When this happened, the canvas ceased to appear flat and artistic naturalism began.

It is this quality of naturalism, advanced not only by perspective but also by the substitution of oils for tempera, that most distinguishes the Flemish painters from their medieval predecessors. Theirs is an art particularly attentive to nature's surfaces. There is, for example, in a van Eyck painting, a noticeable sense of joy, even of exhilaration in the infinite variety of nature. Max J. Friedlaender writes:

> Essential for Jan van Eyck's art is the positive pleasure, the indiscriminate unprejudiced delight in the appearance of things. The illusion itself is the goal, reached in a blaze of triumph. He accepts the whole of the visible world without any preferences. Searching observation and a persistent study of the model suppress subjective invention and sweep tradition aside. [11]

Jan van Eyck is, of course, an important figure for Wyatt. So is his more ghostly brother Hubert, whose work—in the form of an *Annunciation*— Wyatt agrees to forge, even as his, Hubert's, historical actuality remains somewhat in question. [12] Still, even more important for Wyatt than either of these two men is Hugo van der Goes, who in many ways prefigures Wyatt.

A free master at Ghent in 1467, and author of both the Monforte and Portinari altarpieces, van der Goes demonstrated an intensity of character that at least once pushed him to try to take his own life. It was in the hope of subduing this inner tension, many art historians agree, that van der Goes continued to paint, but his mania (he thought he was beyond redemption), helped along by his heavy drinking, did not abate. He died in 1482.

The character similarities (i.e., a single-minded "striving for more than [one] could accomplish" combined with an unusual preoccupation with redemption) and the individual histories (i.e., monomaniacal devotion to artistry leading to both the monastery and madness) linking Wyatt with van der Goes are everywhere to be noticed. So are the artistic parallels. For one, Wyatt shows a particular devotion to van der Goes' work—two of the key paintings that he manages to complete, *Descent from the Cross* and *Death of the Virgin,* are forged under the name of van der Goes. These are intended to be additions to the known van der Goes collection, produced not simply by a mechanical re-creation of van der Goes' techniques but also by an assumption of van der Goes' spiritual and artistic temperament. To paint van der Goes' work authentically, one must become van der Goes, and for awhile Wyatt does, so much so that he forces an unwilling Valentine to say to him, "The face of Christ in your van der Goes, no one could call that a lie" (413).

Not many paintings of the real van der Goes have been spared by time, and part of the temptation for Wyatt here is to restore to the world the canvases of an artist whom the nineteenth-century art historian Scheibler called "equal in quality to every one of van Eyck's successors and as prolific as the majority of them."[13] *The Descent from the Cross* that Wyatt paints, for instance, has only a suppositive predecessor (in the Kaiser Friedrich Museum), and early work, if by van der Goes, that the art world would be happy to see another, preferably later, example of. This is not so much true with the *Death of the Virgin*—there survives a very good one in Bruges—though a later illustration of the subject, that which Wyatt paints, would again be appreciated. (Sir Martin Conway dates the Bruges painting ca. 1472.) In response to Valentine's mention of the Bruges canvas, Wyatt mutters, "Yes, yes, I know it, I know that one. It is splendid, that one. But this one, this one I've done is later, painted later in his life, when the shapes . . ." (260).

What Wyatt starts to explain but does not finish is the degree to which van der Goes' powers of observation (that focus on detail mentioned above in connection with van Eyck) began in the later stages of his career to override his concern for preconceived forms, began, that is, to acclimatize themselves to the differentia of nature. In van der Goes' last canvases, Friedlander writes, "The light in the pictures picks out some forms, represses others, emphasizes, dissolves, loosens, divides and unites. He searches out reflexes that are hostile to form and draws more of the infinite wealth of nature into his picture than is observed by any other painter of his period."[14] And yet there remains a sense of illumination. Not opaque, the facts in van der Goes painting are "facts illumined by imagination."[15] They are, as Valentine notes respecting Wyatt's *Descent from the Cross,* a testimony to the artist's "increased power of eyesight," a statement that evokes Wyatt's own response, "Yes, it gives that sense of projecting illumination, instead of receiving it from outside" (257).

That the facts of van der Goes' world, distinctly pictured as they are, should radiate with a spiritual significance at first seems odd. Normally, our expectations would lead us to draw a connection between the rise of naturalism and the decline of religious belief. Yet there is little evidence in van der Goes or in the other Flemish artists to support such a conclusion. Paradoxically perhaps, the Flemish masters suffused their paintings with an unusual piety. They achieved this effect not only through a careful selection of subject matter, mostly religious, but also through a devotion to a fully developed iconography. Though they did not use symbols without a respect for their naturalistic sense, as did their medieval predecessors, they still managed to transfuse a worldly stage with an otherworldly import. Meaning was less an appendage than an integral aspect of things, reflected in the smallest as well as the largest details. Panofsky states:

> . . . It has been said of the "Annunciation" in the *Merode Altarpiece* that God, no longer present as a visible figure, seems to be diffused in all the visible objects. The naturalism of the Master of Flemalle and his fellow painters was not yet wholly secular. It was still rooted in the conviction that physical objects are, to quote St. Thomas Acquinas (*Summa Theologiae,* I, qu. I, art. 9, C), "corporeal metaphors of things spiritual" (spiritualia sub metaphoris corporalium) and it was not until much, much later that this conviction was rejected or forgotten.[16]

Thematically, then, the Flemish material works several ways in the novel. First, as already mentioned, Flemish technique offers Wyatt an artistic alternative to contemporary art's opacity. In both his originals and his copies, he experiences a sense of recollection, that is, transcendental intuition, not readily achieved through working in the modern idiom. Secondly, the Flemish technique of "disguised symbolism," saturating a natural world with a spiritual presence, also offers a model for Gaddis as novelist. The setting of *The Recognitions* is naturalistic but just about everything else is symbolic. Gaddis writes, "Everything I have observed has been only for its symbolic (simile) value."[17] Thus, like the Flemish masters, Gaddis constructs a symbolic assemblage, the intention being in his words to probe "deeply enough to unfold, not the pattern, but the materials of the pattern, and the necessity of a pattern."[18]

Then, quite apart from the first two explanations, Gaddis also uses the Flemish material to point out the failure of not only Wyatt's but also his own quest for redemption through art. While the Flemish masters' concern for separation (representing things in three-dimensional space) and the accumulation of symbolic detail helped establish their pious reputations, it is necessary to wonder, as Basil Valentine does, whether this accumulation is not really indicative of the disintegration of faith. Can the artist pursue the path of separation and still reach a recognition of transcendental unity? Valentine, for one, rightly perceives the inherent flaw in such an approach:

—Yes, I remember your little talk, your insane upside-down apology for these pictures, every figure and every object with its own presence, its own consciousness because it was being looked at by God! Do you know what it was? What it really was? that everything was so afraid, so uncertain God saw it, that it insisted its vanity on His eyes? Fear, fear, pessimism and fear and depression everywhere, the way it is today, that's why your pictures are so cluttered with detail, this terror of emptiness, this absolute terror of space. Because maybe God isn't watching. Maybe he doesn't see. Oh, this pious cult of the Middle Ages! Being looked at by God! Is there a moment of faith in any of their work, in one centimeter of canvas? or is it vanity and fear, the same decadence that surrounds us now. A profound mistrust in God, and they need every idea out where they can see it, where they can get their hands on it [. . .] all of it cluttered with separation, everything in its own vain shell, everything separate, withdrawn from everything else. Being looked at by God! Is there separation in God? (736)

Wyatt and Gaddis have both been guilty of pursuing the path of separation in their quests for redemption. It is their dedication to "the disciplined recognitions," "the detail," "the algebra of suffering," the fragility of situations, and the "accumulation," which in the end obfuscates their goal.

Belief is, of course, at the center of their problem. Both Wyatt and Gaddis are unsure exactly how to obtain it. Wyatt's nervous questioning points out the problem: "What I mean is, do we believe in order to understand? Or understand in order to be . . . be fished for" (409). Forced to act, Wyatt,

Gaddis, and also Stanley seek belief through art, that is, through the understanding. Yet even as Gaddis affirms in a practical manner the way of reason, he asks his readers to see the folly of pursuing belief through intellection. Valentine is right when he says, "It's true then? We're not supposed to understand?" (399). Instead, belief must in some way precede understanding, reason being able to take us only so far and no farther. It is, as Pascal asserts in *Pensees,* "the heart which perceives God and not the reason," something that Esme realizes even as the others do not. In her suicide note she writes, "Paintings are metaphors for reality, but instead of being an aid to realization obscure the reality which is far more profound" (504).

Wyatt soon confronts the error of his thought. "The devil is," as Stanley remarks, "the father of false art" (495), and Wyatt has been in his active employ. His forgeries have not been an affirmation of belief but a denial. Recalling Saint Anselm's "credo ut intelligam," Wyatt comes to see everything too clearly. He experiences a "crash of reality" and vows to throw over his role as artist, the "exposer of mysteries," for that of the priest, the "guardian of mysteries." Nevertheless, Wyatt remains emotionally wrought. His rush to change situations smacks too much of desperation, as Valentine notices. Valentine compares him to his own childhood friend, Martin:

> —You and Martin. The ones who wake up late. You suddenly realize what is happening around you, the desperate attempts on all sides to reconcile the ideal with reality, you call it corruption and think it new. Some of us have always known it, the others never know. You and Martin are the ones who cause the trouble, waking suddenly, to be surprised. (409)

However, Wyatt does set about to right all the wrong he has done—to renounce his forgeries and to redeem himself in the eyes of Esme. The first matter naturally fails. Nobody wants to believe that already authenticated Flemish masterworks are not just that; and though Wyatt makes a most sincere effort to reveal the fraudulence of his work, boisterously upsetting a Brown Christmas party in the process, no one's mind is turned. Nor does Wyatt fare better in the second matter, for though he madly combs the city looking for Esme, she is not to be found.

There is at this point in the novel a movement reminiscent of Henry James' *The Ambassadors,* for as Chad Newsome and Lambert Strether appear figuratively to change places as that novel moves to its completion, so too in *The Recognitions* do Wyatt and Stanley exchange positions. Stanley and Wyatt are alike in that they both reject artistic modernism for a style associated with a pious age: Stanley imitates the music of Gabrieli, while Wyatt imitates the art of the Flanders Guild. Stanley, however, is the self-conscious artist who even as he works toward the completion of his mass understands that we destroy the thing we love. Unlike Wyatt, he does not consider himself exempt from the modern disease, and he knows that even as he aims for perfection in his music, perfection is no longer possible. It is no more possible to piece together the fragments of modernity than to put Humpty-Dumpty back together again. Stanley says to Agnes:

> —That's what it is, a disease, you can't live like we do without catching it. Because we get time given to us in fragments, that's the only way we know it. Finally we can't even conceive of a continuum of time. Every fragment exists by itself, and that's why we live among palimpsests, because finally all the work should fit into one whole, and express an entire perfect action, as Aristotle says, and it's impossible now, it's impossible, because of the breakage, there are pieces everywhere . . . (657)

Wyatt lacks Stanley's self-consciousness. Unlike Stanley, he does not at first realize that "the devil is the father of false art." Nor is he mindful of the hurt that he causes others, particularly Esme, in the pursuit of his art. Wyatt does, in fact, destroy the one he loves. Lastly, he oddly believes in the possibility of accounting for the accumulation and making it one. But now, after all that has happened, it is Wyatt, even in his madness, who begins to see things more clearly. And at the end, it is Wyatt, not Stanley, who really does try to pass beyond the accumulation.

Exhausted, Wyatt seeks rest at the Real Monasterio de Nuestra Señora de la Otra Vez. Wyatt tells Ludy, "It's a place here to rest, to rest here, finally, a place here to rest" (937). Wyatt's mind has slipped further into madness, but it is a madness intermittently relieved by great lucidity. He sees his past mistakes clearly. He sees that he has pursued the wrong path, that the separation in his work was not a testimony to his faith, but the opposite. "Separateness," Wyatt says, "that's what went wrong" (932).

Had he models, Wyatt now sees, they should have been a Titian or an El Greco, for it is in Titian, the supreme colorist, and his student, El Greco, that the outside world is brought together not as a composition of juxtaposed fragments but as a harmonious whole. Van der Goes and van der Weyden are draftsmen, Titian and El Greco colorists. The difference is that the draftsman sets a high priority on delineating reality, of separating one object from another and seeing that all objects are spatially coordinated. The colorist, on the other hand, is more interested in the harmony of things, the way one object's color will lend itself to another. Color for him is diffused in space; it impresses no clear edge between objects.

The distinction between the two techniques is important for Wyatt. Structure is meaning, and the colorist's style is more supportive of a transcendent unity than the draftsman's, which tends to betray his doubt. Wyatt, now aware of the difference, says:

> —Yes, the El Greco . . . that . . . using carmine for shadows, and . . . the red and yellow ochre for the flesh . . . the flesh, the . . . hematitic . . . painters who weren't afraid of spaces, of . . . cluttering up every space with detail everything vain and separate affirming itself for fear that [. . .] for fear there was no God . . . before the Renaissance. [. . .] Everything vain, asserting itself . . . every vain detail, for fear . . . for fear . . . (933)

Wyatt now knows that he must go past the accumulation of detail and ascertain that simplicity lying beyond. As Esme struggled "through this imposed accumulation of chaos" in order to realize the "simplicity, unmeasurable, residence of perfection, where nothing was created, where originality did not exist; because it was origin; where once she was there work and thought in casual stumbling sequence did not exist, but only transcription" (321), so must Wyatt. He must go beyond art, even the art of a Titian or an El Greco, because "Art couldn't explain it." Scraping the paint off the El Greco canvas in the monastery is symbolic of his recognition of this limitation. Truth must finally be sought beyond art's boundaries.

The Recognitions is one of the most finely wrought books in American letters. Decrying the moral relativism of midcentury modernism, Gaddis defiantly argues for the reality of sin and, in turn, the possibility, through love, of redemption. For him, matter is complemented by essence, an idea thematically made clear in his metaphoric handling of the Flemish painters. The artist, Gaddis says, is often among the first to gain an intimation of the ideal, though, paradoxically, his work ultimately obscures that which he would seek to know. Truth lies beyond the plane of art, even the plane of *The Recognitions*.

Notes

1. Quoted in Peter W. Koenig's "'Splinters from the Yew Tree': A Critical Study of William Gaddis' *The Recognitions*" (Ph.D. diss., New York University, 1971), 90.
2. Quoted in ibid., 113.

3. Max J. Friedlaender, *From Van Eyck to Bruegel,* ed. F. Grossman (1956; reprint New York: Phaidon, 1969), 23.

4. Bernard Berenson, *Aesthetics and History* (1948; reprint, Garden City, N.Y.: Doubleday, 1954), 270.

5. William Gaddis, *The Recognitions* (1955; reprint, New York: Avon Books, 1974), 628. Subsequent references will be cited parenthetically in the text.

6. Berenson, *Aesthetics,* 205.

7. Ibid., 203.

8. Quoted in Alvin Plantinga, *The Nature of Necessity* (Oxford: Clarendon Press, 1974), 197.

9. Erwin Panofsky, *Early Netherland Paintings: Its Origins and Character* (Cambridge: Harvard University Press, 1966), I:3.

10. Ibid., I:7.

11. Friedlaender, *Van Eyck to Bruegel,* 4.

12. The existence or nonexistence of Hubert van Eyck is a crucial question for Wyatt. He thinks the relation of his fraudulent *Annunciation* to Hubert van Eyck's original work as a variant of the ontological argument, for Wyatt is able, more than 400 years after the master's death, to paint a fresh van Eyck because his "recognitions go much deeper, much further back"—back to the point of a priori forms. Referring to both Saint Anselm and Saint Augustine, the character Anselm batters Stanley with instruction: "I'm proving the existence of God, God damn you. Saint Augustine says a man who is going to make a box has it first in his art. The box he makes isn't life, but the one that exists in his art is life. 'For the artificer's soul lives, in which all these things are, before they are produced'" (570).

We see forms because in God these forms exist beforehand. Wyatt frantically insists on Hubert's reality because he is aware of the analogy—he senses, that is, that if the original of his copy does not exist, then it is also very possible that the original of artistic forms—godhead—does not exist either. Finally, then, the question of Hubert's existence does, for Wyatt, come down to a matter of the existence or nonexistence of God. As Wyatt, responding to the verification of another original, Bosch's *Seven Deadly Sins,* says, "Thank God there was the gold to forge!" (735).

13. Quoted in Friedlaender, *Van Eyck to Bruegel,* 33.

14. Ibid., 35.

15. Sir Martin Conway, *The Van Eycks and Their Followers* (New York: Dutton, 1921), 183.

16. Panofsky, *Early Netherland Paintings,* I:142.

17. Quoted in Koenig, "'Splinters from the Yew Tree,'" 80.

18. Quoted in ibid., 81.

5

Dryad in a Dead Oak Tree
The Incognito in *The Recognitions*

JOHN SEELYE

> Fairy folks / Are in old oaks.
> —English folk rhyme

The demands of *The Recognitions* are both great and singular, and those readers who have admired the book undoubtedly share tastes that distinguish them from the reviewers and general readers who didn't.[1] They all, presumably, admire satire and appreciate the odd, the grotesque, the bizarre, and the recondite. For *The Recognitions*, as William Gaddis is at pains to suggest, is straight out of Hieronymous Bosch's fantastic landscapes; it is queer in all senses of the word; it is a twentieth-century fairy tale. If recent events are any reliable indication, the homosexual novel is on the rise; in the future, any assessment of this movement will have to deal with *The Recognitions*, which may prove, at that later time, the Queen Mab of them all. Not that it is, like the *Thief's Journal* or *Our Lady of the Flowers*, a "*Dichtung* and *Wahrheit* of homosexuality," nor is it, like *The Naked Lunch*, a paranoid nightmare, a dreary, de Sade-like catalogue of sodomic enormities. Nor is it even a psychological investigation of homosexual mores and attitudes. And yet it is, nonetheless, an excursion into fairyland.

The idea of recognition is the main dramatic theme of Gaddis' book. The title is drawn from the Clementine *Recognitions*, which, it is explained

This essay was written during the early 1960s for the abandoned special issue of *Prairie Schooner* that was discussed in the Introduction. It is published here for the first time, with few changes other than excisions from the original text—Eds.

by one of his characters, is the original of the Faust story. But the Clementine cycle is also a romance, a search of son for father: "recognition" there refers both to the acknowledgment of truth and the acknowledgment of kinship. "True father and true son" is obviously a fitting motif for any explication of Christian doctrine. Japhet and his eternal search has become one of the great themes of Western literature, largely through the agency of the picaresque tradition. It is the most important narrative theme in *The Recognitions,* for about it are grouped the many true and false acknowledgments of the book. The two main stories, that of Wyatt Gwyon and Otto Pivner, turn upon this theme, and they have as a third and lesser counterpart the relationship between Agnes Deigh and her mother in Rome.

There is another kind of "recognition" implied in the title, however, which — as in the narrative sense — requires acknowledgment, a realization or perception of an existing quality. In this instance, the quality is not hidden from the characters in the book, but from its readers. This aspect of *The Recognitions* is carried out in the modern manner: by a reticulated system of allusions. It is this quality of Gaddis' work that has led to a mistaken comparison with Joyce, but before *Ulysses* there was Melville's *The Confidence-Man,* and it is to that peculiar novel that Gaddis' bears close comparison, both in theme and technique. There are several references, of course, direct and oblique to Melville and Hawthorne in Gaddis' novel, but more important is the Mephistophelian element, the system of masquerades and betrayals that resembles very closely the method of *The Confidence-Man.* The metaphysical burden of *The Recognitions,* also, as in Melville's satire, is carried by the theme of the questioning search. And, finally, no one familiar with the strange relationship between Melville and Hawthorne can fail to react to that electric phrase, "shock of recognition."

Indeed, Gaddis' work holds so much in common with the later novels of Melville and Hawthorne that there is a possibility that *The Recognitions* may be an attempt to extend the stylistic experiments of the American Renaissance: in it one can find technical and thematic reminders of *Moby-Dick, Pierre, The Scarlet Letter,* and *The Marble Faun,* as well as *The Confidence-Man.* Moreover, it depends, as I have suggested, upon that hidden ironic vein, that secret level of validity that distinguishes so much of nineteenth-century American writing. It is not, however, an anachronism. *The Recognitions* could only have been written in the present era, this century of toilet training and traumatic self-consciousness.

The archetypal search for the father — that distinctly Melvillean theme — has an additional implication in this age of Freud. Thus, Otto, on his circuitous way to a bar where he is to meet his long-lost dad, the inept Mr. Pivner (whom he does not meet; instead he makes mistaken contact with Mr. Sinisterra, a counterfeiter, who later establishes an "inevitable comradeship" with Wyatt [rebaptized "Stephen" by Sinisterra] whose mother he has long ago killed), turns over in his mind the dilemma before him: "It was a problem until now more easily left unsolved; and be damned to Oedipus and all the rest of them. For now, the father might be anyone the son chose. The instant their eyes met in forced recognition, it would be over."[1] There follows two hundred pages later a comic interlude in which Otto selects a "father" from the bar patrons; in his muddled mind there has long been a false recognition: "At about the time he learned that he had a father, or should have one, Albert, King of the Belgians, was killed mountain-climbing. It was not difficult to relate the two: he told that his father had been killed mountain-climbing, and so took upon himself the peculiar mantle of a prince." Thus, the man whom Otto selects as his "father" is a clichéd version of what the cliché-ridden Otto imagines a prince to be: "The man signaled the bartender, raising a hand which caught Otto with the gold flash of a signet ring, and affirmation, a summons which drew taut the muscles in his legs, ready to stand and deliver, [. . .] pledge fealty, inherit the signet and the kingdom its seal perpetuated" (507).

But the man with the ring lacks the green scarf that is the prearranged sign; the green scarf is instead worn by Sinisterra, the counterfeiter-murderer, who has come to the same bar to leave some "queer" with a contact. This improbable Plautine device leads to another comic episode, in which Otto receives $5,000 from the man he thinks his father and who thinks him "queer" because he has been, throughout the interview, "rubbing his ankle up and down against what he believed to be the center leg of the table" (517). Previously, Otto has tried to pick up a blond at the bar, but having lost his wallet (as well as, variously, a briefcase, manuscript, and the scarf worn by Sinisterra), he has had to stall for time. Having received the money, he can pay his bar bill and go to his room, which is next to the blond's. Still acting on the assumption of an earlier, probably mistaken arrangement, Otto enters the woman's room to find her in bed with the man wearing the gold signet ring—the latest, but one, in a series of false fathers:

> —Now just who the devil was that?
> —Don't worry, honey, it's only a fairy I met down in the bar.
> —A fairy?
> —You know, queer. He said he was a writer, and they're always queer nowadays. (521)

The plotting of this incident recalls Restoration comedy, and like so many of those farces, it turns on the ambiguousness of sexual identity. Otto is often assessed as homosexual, and this burlesque theme (there is no indication that he is anything but normal) emerges from the Oedipal fact of his quest. Even his searching glances in the bar suggest the cruising gaze of a militant homosexual, and the matter of the green scarf suggests the traditional (perhaps apocryphal) blazon of identity. (A character in Genêt's *Deathwatch* is called "Green Eyes," a characteristic ascribed by Joyce in "An Encounter" to foreign sailors and perverts.)

The green signal and the Oedipal theme merge once more when Otto and Mr. Pivner finally have a brief, mistaken meeting side by side in a lavatory. Mr. Pivner, embarrassed by the obscene grafitti on the wall in front of him, lowers his eyes,

> glimpsing in that brief embarrassed sweep, the face beside him, a haggard face drawn over a sharp profile which stared intently ahead. And his eyes were drawn slowly back up this figure his own height, near the same stature, slowly up, then snagged, drawn up short, and back, caught on a corner of green. And he was staring at that, down at the bit of wool protruding from the coat's pocket, waist-level, when the whole face turned on him, turned bloodshot eyes in a desolation of contempt. (566–67)

Mr. Pivner, like his son, is occasionally mistaken for a homosexual, and that his innocent glance should be wrongly interpreted by Otto, that their casual meeting at the Oedipal crossroads should result in such a horrid encounter is one of those absurd ironies that characterize *The Recognitions:* the green that was supposed to be the welcome flag of true recognition proves to be the warning signal of mistaken perversion.

The color green is ubiquitous and thematically ambivalent in *The Recognitions.* When associated with Otto, it carries connotations of wealth. Green is also associated with Wyatt, whose eyes burn green in moments of excitement or anger. Stanley (the bathysiderodromophobic composer, who has Oedipal problems too) possesses eyes that, when confronting Otto, burn green; and Ellery, a television writer, wears a green necktie. The impotent Negro critic who appears throughout the satiric episodes wears a green wool shirt, and late in the book Stanley meets a publicity man who wants to get Esme into a movie contest and who wears a green silk necktie and drives a "lime-green" convertible. Green, the traditional color of growth and promise, seems to symbolize, on the one hand, the mistaken values of "filthy lucre" (as epitomized in the person of Recktall Brown), and, on the other, the artist's inner flame of imagination.

The Oedipal theme is complicated by the interwoven sexual relations of Gaddis' male characters. For instance, the scarf that Sinisterra wears when he meets Otto was brought home by his son, Chaby, a junk-peddler, to whom it was given by Wyatt's mistress-model, Esme, an addict, in whose room it was left by Otto, who thinks he loves her. Since all three men are sexually involved with Esme, the scarf (like the earrings of Madame de . . .) is a token of this mutual involvement. Certainly the Joycean motif of homosexuality implied by a shared woman is early intimated in *The Recognitions* through a conversation between Esther (another of Wyatt's women with whom Otto later sleeps) and Wyatt:

> —Do you think he's homosexual too? she asked calmly.
> —Otto? How in heaven's name . . . what do you mean, too?
> —Nothing, she said, looking down. (106)

The recognition of this metaphor supports Gaddis' logic in having much of his comic relief supplied by a fantastic congerie of gay types who mince ridiculously around and about the activities of the main characters. These types, with their mock marriages and petty tragedies, their chorus of sweetly smutty remarks, are, curiously enough, the only happy people in the book. It is almost as if Gaddis were creating a mock pastoral out of the underworld of perverted romance that is the domain of the "queers," the fairyland that the homosexual conclave maintains independent of the larger, "normal" microcosm. Certainly the pastoral image is that which the homosexuals have chosen for themselves, with their election of the type-word, "Corydon," as well as the whole system of catchphrases and cant by which the reticulations of the grapevine are maintained.[2]

Without question, the pastoral theme is suitable to a satiric landscape, a kind of oasis in the wasteland. What is "queer" suggests a lost ideal, perhaps—"fairies," after all, are the relics of a lost religion. Thus, a Dionysian revel of some four hundred homosexuals is regarded by Gaddis as a wry reminder of a golden age: "There was, in fact, a religious aura about this festival, religious that is in the sense of devotion, adoration, celebration of deity, before religion became confused with systems of ethics and morality, to become a sore affliction upon the very things it had once exalted" (311). This band of lisping swains and false maidens is a Comus-like rabble whose center is the sinister art critic, Basil Valentine. Rudy, a fairy queen "dressed now in silver lamé," carries about a copy of *De Virginibus Velandis* lent "her" by "Val." That "Val" is Valentine can be verified by Rudy's perfume, which is obviously of the art critic's manufacture: "'A very dear friend makes it himself. *Fuisse deam,* that's what he calls it. An aroma remained, you could tell a goddess had just appeared,' Rudy said, waltzing toward the dance floor" (313). This Ovidian tag is first uttered by Valentine during an interview with the art dealer sub rosa, Recktall Brown, and Wyatt. Wyatt, it is early made clear, uses oil of lavender as a medium in his forgery of old masters, and this scent becomes a leitmotif associated with the martyred artist. The countertheme is provided by Frank Sinisterra's use of lavender in his counterfeiting processes.

But, as his knowledgeable reference ("Oil of lavender, eh?") indicates, Basil Valentine is also a member of the lavender gang, and the link established between Valentine, Rudy, Wyatt, and Sinisterra implies that lavender, like green, is no simple token of recognition. The art critic's name, for instance, can be read in part as an anagram for the Latin root of the word. In America, moreover, what is often called "lavender" is actually sweet basil (*Ocimum Basilicum*: "royal fodder"). "Lavender," in the quaint "language of flowers," once meant "acknowledgment" (hence, recognition), and in the cant of fairyland, "It takes lavender to smell lavender" now means, similarly, "It takes one to know one."

This sort of knowledge is bile, perhaps, but it brings out the true colors of Gaddis' book. For Basil Valentine is undoubtedly the major representative of the demonic element in *The Recognitions,* the chief tempter of the saintly Wyatt. A Jesuitical conniver, whose dread of mortality is twice betrayed by his aversion to a fallen curl of human hair, and by his perhaps unconscious pun—"No reproduction is nice" (233)—and who is called "The Cold Man" by Esme, Valentine has the power of prophecy: "I suppose you . . . well, let's say you eat your father, canonize your mother, and . . . what happens to people in novels? I don't read them. You drown, I suppose" (262). He also claims to have the "one secret" the pagan gods have to teach, those gods that, when superseded, "become demons" and fairies. This secret is mentioned three times, twice by Valentine. The first time, he is talking to Wyatt and brings up the "secret" during what appears to be a homosexual approach: "Here you are, and I shall teach you, I shall teach you the only secret worth knowing, the secret the gods teach, secret that Wotan taught to his son . . . " (387). The next time this "secret" of Woton is mentioned by Valentine, the reference is more precise and is made under much different circumstances.

The secret is "the power of doing without happiness," and the revelation occurs in a "cat-house" here, in the city zoo, but with sufficient ambiguity to undercut Valentine's humorless approach: "The broken cries from the next cage had stopped, given over to heaving and groans" (551). This episode, which occurs at the center of the book between Otto's interview with Sinisterra and the most destructive cocktail party of an incremental series, has an emphasis that is both scatological and grotesquely sexual. It reaches a climax before a cage of copulating pumas, where Wyatt (now without a name) exchanges glances with a woman who has averted her face:

So she continued to stare at him, where he stood held in Valentine's grip there, for moments, finding sanctuary where she could recover all so abruptly assaulted, in eyes which shared nothing, recognized nothing, accused her of nothing: but those moments passed and, recovering, she groped for escape. But that lack of response held her, that lack of recognition no more sanctuary than the opened eyes of a dead man, that negation no asylum for shame but the trap from which it cried out for the right to its living identity. (552)

The three figures, at this moment, are held in emblematic stasis, a figurative grouping that recalls the allegorical pageants of Hawthorne and Melville: Valentine grips the evasive Wyatt who holds, with his empty eyes, the hapless woman, who, in turn, clings desperately to her child (the same search-and-denial later characterizes the meeting between Otto and his father). The brief episode is concluded when the woman, preferring shame to the emptiness offered by Wyatt, turns back to the cage and the knowing satyrical faces of the men surrounding it. Only Valentine, perhaps mistaking emptiness for innocence, continues to seek the soul of a damned man.

The third mention of Valentine's proffered "secret" is made by Wyatt after he has stabbed the false critic almost to death (the Valentine in Goethe's *Faust* is stabbed when he attacks Faust). Confronted by Fuller, the dead Brown's former slave, Wyatt confesses to have "taught him the lesson . . . the only lesson the gods can teach." The "power of doing without happiness" is death, and with the death of Valentine Wyatt is "as free as the day I was born. Here! Here! . . . don't go near there, don't touch him."

> —But maybe Mister Valentine in danger of recoverin, sar.
> —But . . . no, don't touch him. You never know what they may . . . have
> in their hair. (692)

What Valentine will have in his hair, plainly, are horns, those modified antennae that are the Devil's mark. Mephistophelian, cosmopolitan, erudite, and death to the soul, Valentine is unable to countenance the ultimate creative act; impotent, corsetted, a compulsive washer of hands, this archetypal critic substitutes commentary for creation, and is a figure familiar to homosexual circles. The Devil, as it were, is a queer.

Queerness connotes that which is strange, odd, possibly suspicious, and the idea of queerness in Gaddis' book draws its nourishment from hell: "For evil spirits invent for themselves certain counterfeit representations of high degree, that by this means they may deceive the followers of Christ . . .'" (719). Stanley, the composer with a prophetic delusion of decomposition and who may be placed between the obsessed Wyatt and the obsessive Otto, speaks more than he knows when he declares, "The devil is the father of false art" (464). The world of *The Recognitions* is a world of false art, and, as in Stanley's vision, it is a crumbling, cracking, House-of Usher world about to fall into oblivion. "Everything's sort of contraceptive, everything wherever you look is against conceiving, until finally you can't conceive any more" (459). The contraceptiveness of the modern world, the essential sterility of the wasteland, is the situation central to Gaddis' book; that is why his hero is a forger, his chief villain an effeminate art critic who sponsors the hero's activities. *The Recognitions* is *Caleb Williams* written sideways.

For the strange problem posed here, which lies beneath the metaphorical clothing of false art and the ambiguous imitation by the hero of Christ (and Saint Stephen), beneath the suggestion of holy masquerade ("He even said once, that the saints were counterfeits of Christ, and that Christ was a counterfeit of God" [483]), beneath the panoply of counterfeit presentments, the hints of obscene blasphemy, is the microcosm suggested by the one word, "queer."

Women in *The Recognitions,* such as Esther and Esme, serve rather minor roles as junctions or thematic connections; save for the episodes concerned with Agnes Deigh, who seems to represent a bountiful sterility, the action is dominated by men. It is the world of Vic Tanny's every other day each week. And the maleness of *the Recognitions* is one of the terms of the metaphor discussed above. Pandemonium is also a kind of Vic Tanny's, and Gaddis' book is a *Paradise Lost* out of *The Dunciad,* a vision of the demonic microcosm, a mock epic for moderns, divided into a trinity in which a multiplicity of matched, unfructive indirections celebrate the eternal dichotomy of father and son ("all of it cluttered with separation, everything in its own vain shell, everything separate, withdrawn from everything else. Being looked at by God! Is there separation in God?" [690]). It is essentially an evil world, and evil cannot bear fruit but feeds upon its own self, like corruption, incessantly:

> But evil on itself shall back recoil,
> And mix no more with goodness, when at last
> Gather'd like scum, and settl'd to itself,
> It shall be in eternal restless change
> Self-fed and self-consum'd; if this fail,
> The pillar'd firmament is rott'nness,
> And earth's base built on stubble. . . .
> (*Comus:* 593–99)

Comedy expunges evil; satire celebrates it and draws upon contemporary types to ornament the eternal Pandemonium. Thus, the Madison Avenue world of *The Recognitions* is that absurd reference necessary for the satirist, the tinsel on the Xmas tree. But satire, as in Pope's attack on Grub Street hacks, must rise above the individual, contemporary instance. It must take fire from its materials, ignite them to a kind of apotheosis. It must do this by kindling the hot center of a culture's entrails, and this, I would suggest, Gaddis has done. Beneath the decorative matter of publicity men and advertising agents is an intense matrix of ecclesiastical references, Christian, heretical, pagan. Allusions to the Clementine *Recognitions* are but the most important of many references to early Christian doctrinal writings, and this level of discourse is made tangent with the narrative through the progress of Wyatt-Stephen toward his thirty-third birthday, and through the subject matter of his art. It is the immense weight of this esoteric material that sponsors the necessary combustion.

The stuff of Gaddis' book is often self-consciously mythic. Indeed, his use of anthropological material, the wisdom of comparative mythologies, is often so pervasive and obvious as to outweigh the narrative element. Like the style of this book, Gaddis' many references at times seem mannered and superficial. But these surface allusions are not mere *appliqué*. They are outcroppings of a deeper, more subtle matter, the elements of which are simple and fundamental, and, which, taken together, evoke the crumbling rock upon which the structure of our Western civilization is built. Moreover, the elements of this structure are part and parcel with the metaphor discussed above: the demonism underlies the Trinity by means of the ambiguous father and son (and unholy ghost of motherhood) allusions that permeate the fabric of the book.

The satanic counterpart of the Eucharist, the central ritual of Christianity, is cannibalism, and in the person of Wyatt these two themes are met: the person of Wyatt, like the substance of the Host, is fed upon by those who surround him. Chief among these parasites is the sexually cannibalistic Esther, who is always "analyzing, dissecting, finding answers," who wants to "meet the latest poet, shake hands with the latest novelist, get hold of the latest painter, devour . . . " (95). Wyatt's relationship with this hungry woman is put forth in Eucharistic terms:

> Moments like this (and they came more often) she had the sense that he did not exist; or, to re-examine him, sitting there looking in another direction, in terms of substance and accident, substance the imperceptible underlying reality, accident the properties inherent in the substance which are perceived by the senses: the substance is transformed by consecration, but the acci-

dents remain what they were. The consecration has apparently taken place not, as she thought, through her, but somewhere beyond her; and here she sits attending the accidents. (94)

The allusion seems clear, especially since the myth of Osiris appears severally in *The Recognitions,* and in at least one place is related to the Eucharist ceremony: "The god killed, eaten, and resurrected, is the oldest fixture in religion" (536). But in Gaddis' mythology, the killed and devoured god is the long-sought father, not the son; Wyatt is devoured spiritually until his body is a shell, but Reverend Gwyon's ashes, mistaken for a gift of oatmeal, are accidentally baked into a loaf of bread and devoured by his son. The properties of this substance are peculiar in more ways than one:

> — Have you looked at the bread? I don't mean tasted it, but just look at it. It's practically turning red.
> — My husband would know what it is, said the woman with the ring, examining a piece of the bread. She broke it, and the fine gray texture crumbled. [. . .]
> — Micrococcus prodigiosus, he pronounced [. . .] Looks like blood, doesn't it. (883–84)

This transubstantiation continues ambiguously until the woman extends "that hand" and withdraws "it more slowly, separating her fingers and glancing down surreptitiously to see what the sticky gray matter lodged between them might be" (880). The stuff of Reverend Gwyon is nothing more than mortal, the accident a matter of chemistry; in Gaddis' world, moreover, the ancient enigma of "Homoousian or Homoiusian," "Homo or Homoi," merges with a more earthly rite, that one for which Sodom was destroyed: "Near him, someone obligingly derived *faggot* from the Greek *phagein.* 'Phag-, phago-, -phagous, -phagy, -phagia' . . . the voice whined. 'It means to eat," (593–94). Gaddis' phony etymologies, like the people who originated them, are debased, perverted, turned to the foul profanations of his pagan fairies: "Oh! so pretty for Christmas Eve, all red and shiny like a candy cane" (571). The ritual of the Eucharist, as in a Black Mass, becomes an obscenity: "I've come across something about the bread being baked on her loins, the wafer for profaning the Eucharist, but what in heaven's name do you want to know this sort of thing for? A novel?" (372). The voice here is that of Basil Valentine, the dryad who inhabits the metaphorical oak of *The Recognitions,* the emblem of that afflatus that motivates and inspires the mechanism of disguise, affectation, counterfeiting, and forgery. Since it evokes, as well, the nature of Godhead and sacrifice, the metaphor is truly sacramental, but the sacrament is unclean, baked from the blackest bread. As in all dark satire, "eating" suggests cannibalism, the ultimate theme of Timonism, and the body of the Host becomes strange flesh, hot from hell.

To recognize this shocking metaphor is to realize that *The Recognitions* is a black book indeed, is to understand the alchemical beast lurking beneath the ecclesiastical colors of the jacket. Like Pandemonium, Gaddis' novel is a "perfectly ordered chaos," whose structure is perversely defined in terms of the most holy order: a book for burning, it burns with a flame of infinite intricacy, deep within which can be discerned, dimly at first, and then more clearly, a savage smile betraying "the white teeth of violation."

Notes

1. William Gaddis, *The Recognitions* (1955; reprint with corrections, Cleveland and New York: World Publishing Co., Meridian Fiction, 1962), 303. Subsequent references to the work will be cited parenthetically in the text.

2. Again, this is a theme that evokes hostility and that must not be pushed too far. I would like to point out, however, that "Corydon" (cf. Gide's book of the same name) provides the obvious anagram "Don Cory," the pseudonym adopted by the author of several studies of homosexuality published in the 1950s and 1960s. "Damon" is another pastoral analogue, as is "Damon and Pythias" (*The Recognitions,* 498, 505); and one of the central characters in a popular cartoon strip that features two adventurous males and a series of women resembling female impersonators is a truck driver called "Nomad," a mirror version of Damon.

6

Peer Gynt and *The Recognitions*

STEVEN MOORE

> The main thing is to remain sincere and true in relation to
> one's self. It is not a matter of willing this or that, but of
> willing what one absolutely must do because of one's self,
> and because one cannot do otherwise. Everything else leads
> only to falsehood.
>
> — Henrik Ibsen

In his elaborate first novel, William Gaddis incorporated a huge body
of referential material garnered from world literature, mythology, and
mysticism as a backdrop against which Wyatt Gwyon's quest for salvation
is played. Parallels and analogies are thereby suggested that not only clarify aspects of Wyatt's struggles and raise them to mythic proportions, but
in turn often shed illumination on the original sources themselves, aiding
the reader to make the "recognitions" demanded by the novel's title. Gaddis' use of Ibsen's equally elaborate drama, *Peer Gynt,* is an instructive example of this process and, more important, may provide a key to certain
problematic areas in the difficult novel.

Both novel and play share a concern for redemption and the attainment
of selfhood, or, in C. G. Jung's phrase, the "integration of the personality."[1] However, the exact nature of redemption, and whether the protagonist actually attains selfhood, are questions that have been asked of both
works. The validity of Solveig's role as the means of Peer's salvation has
been debated since the play's publication in 1867. One of the earliest reviewers found the "happy" ending banal and "a little absurd,"[2] and Ibsen
scholars have yet to reach a concensus on the artistic and theological integrity of Peer's fifth-act redemption. "Nobody," Michael Meyer hopes,
"any longer takes the last act of *Peer Gynt* at its face value, as the return

of an old man to his youthful love; such an ending would have been, for Ibsen, most untypically banal and sentimental, two adjectives which recur frequently in contemporary criticisms of it."[3] How, then, are we to take this last act? or more pertinently, how did Gaddis take this last act? A variety of readings have been suggested, the most persuasive of which emphasize Peer's passivity: his redemption, such that it is, is conferred upon him, not actively won. "If Peer is to be saved at all," translator William Archer wrote to Arthur Quiller-Couch, "it is clearly to be by no active effort of his own."[4] He goes on to argue that "whether seriously or ironically, it was a supernatural salvation that Ibsen had in his mind."[5] This form of redemption was as unsatisfactory to Archer (who labeled it "rank supernaturalism") as it must be to most modern readers. "Work out your own salvation with fear and trembling" advises Saint Paul (Phil. 2:12), and it has become difficult to admire any form of salvation in which the redeemed does not take an active part.

This, at any rate, is the conclusion Wyatt Gwyon draws after exploring the various avenues of redemption still open to modern man, and he almost fails to achieve integration for the same reason that Peer fails: a stunted attachment to the mother.

If this sounds like psychological reductionism of the worst kind, it takes only a careful reading of both texts to vindicate such an interpretation. Wyatt has the misfortune to lose his mother by the age of four. Her ghost appears to him at the moment of her death and thereafter her absence (and her inadequate replacement in the person of Aunt May) leaves an emptiness in him that he spends most of the novel trying to fill. At an early age he begins a portrait of his mother (taken, significantly, from a photograph of her *before* her marriage), and his inability or reluctance to complete the portrait (some fifteen years pass before he does) becomes a symbol of his inability to establish a satisfying relationship with another woman. "Finish it," his wife Esther astutely says of the portrait. "Then there might be room for me."[6]

Wyatt takes the portrait with him when he leaves Esther to forge paintings for Recktall Brown. It is not until he listens to Esme read the opening of the Grimm Brothers' "The Frog King" that he finds in Esme's features the lines of completion needed for the portrait of his mother: "She sat, her head half turned; and her face emptied of the curiosity and life of an instant before. If anything of life was left, it was a vague look of yearning, but that without expectation" (273)—a deliberate echo of "the unchanging, ungratified yearning in the face of Camilla on the living-room mantel" (33). She is thus contrasted with Esther, who had always complained of his failure to live up to her great expectations of him, and Esme appears to qualify for the anima figure (again Jung's phrase) that Wyatt has been seeking. But when Wyatt realizes his portrait of his mother has become a portrait of Esme, a subconscious apprehension of the incestual nature of the attraction (coupled, consciously, with the guilt in knowing that the portrait is a study for his next forgery) causes him to shy away from Esme's advances, and he sends her on her way.[7]

Had Wyatt given in to Esme at this point, finding in her the mother he lost in Camilla, he would have been in much the same situation as Peer Gynt at the end of Ibsen's play. Among Ibsen's many commentators, those with a psychological background seem to have noticed that Peer can give himself to Solveig only after she has become—in appearance as well as psychologically—his mother. For example, Georg Groddeck, who included a psychoanalytic reading of *Peer Gynt* in his *Exploring the Unconscious* (1933), remarks that from the opening scene the relationship between Peer and Aase is not the usual one between a grown-up son and his middle-aged mother, but rather that of a little boy and his young mother—a psychological rut Peer stays in throughout the play:

> It is only after a long and roundabout journey that Peer Gynt can bring himself to the point of allowing another woman to have the honor of mothering him. This new mother, one need hardly say, is Solveig; she is the reincarnation of Aase. Peer Gynt feels that from the start. This and this alone it is that prevents him from remaining with her, for she is sacred to him, as a mother must be to her son. Never can she be for him a mere woman.[8]

It is only after Aase's death and when Solveig herself is middle-aged that Peer is able to give himself to her. Groddeck goes so far as to suggest that the successful staging of the play would be where a physical resemblance between Aase and Solveig is emphasized. His arguments, too extensive to be rehearsed here in full, are convincing enough to necessitate a reevaluation of Peer's redemption at the end of act 5. When Peer cries, "My mother; my wife; oh, thou innocent woman!—/ In thy love—oh, there hide me, hide me!"[9] it is clear that Peer has not progressed psychologically beyond the first scene and has reaffirmed his ideal love as that for his mother. We hear the cry not of a self-realized man but of a little boy who misses his mommy. And there the play, and perhaps Peer's life, ends.

Wilhelm Reich, whose "Libidinal Conflicts and Delusions in Ibsen's *Peer Gynt*" preceded Groddeck's essay but remained unpublished until recently,[10] lays greater emphasis on Peer's incestuous fixation and Oedipal conflicts.[11] Wyatt's fixation, of course, is on the memory of his mother rather than the woman herself, and it is maintained by the unfinished portrait and her gold earrings, but the psychological principle is the same: his inordinate attachment to his mother obstructs a mature relationship with any other woman. Reich reaches the same conclusion as Groddeck regarding Peer's fifth-act redemption: "We now understand that Peer's redemption can take place only when Solveig has become as old as his mother was at the onset of his psychosis."[12]

Holding out for a girl just like the girl that married dear old dad would be more disastrous for Wyatt than it was for Peer; where Peer is an old man in act 5 and probably dies if not at the end of the play (as some critics have suggested) then shortly thereafter, Wyatt is in his early thirties. Wyatt's process of integration would halt upon falling into Esme's arms, as Peer's does in Solveig's lap. Esme *is* the ideal anima figure for him in that she, alone of all the characters in *The Recognitions,* is capable of selfless love. But with the unresolved relationship to his mother simply shifted onto Esme's shoulders, such a union—even ignoring Esme's schizophrenia and heroin addiction—would be far from ideal. This move on Wyatt's part would be romantic in Denis de Rougemont's sense that intense romantic attraction, if not akin to the death instinct, leads not to personal growth but to decay.[13] Providentially, Wyatt loses track of Esme and instead returns to Spain, where his mother is buried, to confront and resolve the original source of his psychosis.

Bearing all this in mind, we are now in a position to understand Wyatt's own half-dozen or so references to Ibsen's play. After delivering his last forgery to Brown a week or so after the encounter with Esme and drunkenly revealing his various dilemmas, Wyatt visits Basil Valentine to deposit the evidence of his forgeries. Valentine tries to subdue him and asks what he has been up to, and Wyatt answers that he has not been "up" to anything, but rather:

> —Down to, consorting with mermaids in the bottom of a tank where the troll king lives (here a cough interrupted; and Basil Valentine held his breath)—God love him. I had willingly fastened the tail to my back, and drank what he gave me, you know, but there, when he tried to scratch out my eyes. "I'll scratch you a bit till you see awry; but all that you see will seem fine and brave."
> —So you've been to see Brown, have you? [. . .]—What's the matter, what's the matter? he said suddenly, —groaning like that, what is it?
> —I'll explain . . . as soon as I . . . yes . . . get settled . . .
> —My dear fellow . . .
> —It's a liberty I'm taking today, pretending I weigh three hundred pounds. Damn it, will you allow it? "I min Tro, i mit Håb og i min Kjaerlighed" . . . eh? No, it didn't work out that way, I tell you. There's Solveig locked up

with a dangerous man, human and industriously mad, he may save me yet like Luther saved the Papacy. (375)

The two quotations will be recognized by those familiar with Ibsen's play. The first is from Peer's encounter with the troll king in act 2, scene 6; and the second is Solveig's famous line, "In my faith, in my hope, and in my love," from the end of the play. But the context requires some elucidation. Mermaids entered into the discussion Wyatt held with Fuller previous to Brown's arrival (346–48), and the "bottom of a tank" (i.e., lake) is the residence of the Grimm Brothers' frog king. Solveig and the dangerous man refer to his former wife, Esther, and her current lover, Ellery, both of whom Wyatt saw briefly en route from Brown's to Valentine's. Esme, then, seems to be equated in Wyatt's mind (especially after her advances) with the troll king's daughter, the Green-clad One, who leads Peer to her father's mountain court. At this point, Wyatt is contemplating a return to his father to resume his studies for the ministry, and consequently Esme is seen not in the role of redemptress but the temptress of *Peer Gynt*. (Esther, a failed Solveig, has long been abandoned as his redeemer.) Valentine, however, interprets the allusion to Solveig as a reference to Esme and 175 pages later, though only a few days hence, mocks what he infers are Wyatt's romantic delusions:

> Basil Valentine turned and laughed in his face. — Really, really my dear fellow. No, he said, clutching the single gray glove before him. —The "somber glow" at the end of the second act, is it? the duet with Senta, is that it? . . . "the somber glow, no, it is salvation that I crave," eh! "Might such an angel come, my soul to save," your Flying Dutchman sings, eh? Good heavens! And up they go to heaven in a wave, or whatever it was? Really! And all that foolishness you were carrying on with the last time I saw you, that "I min 'Iro . . ." and the rest of it, that Where has he been all this time? and your Solveig answers In my faith? In my hope? In my, . . . good heavens! You are romantic, aren't you! If you do think you mean all this? And then what, They lived happily forever after?
> — But listen, listen, she . . .
> — No, no, it's too easy. After all, you know. [. . .] He did not speak until threatened by the voice beside him, then went on derisively, — And Saint Rose of Lima! Why, this sudden attempt to set the whole world right, by recalling your own falsifications in it? And then? Happiness ever after? Then you will be redeemed, and redeem her, and . . . good heavens knows what! And then, what next? First it's Shabbetai Zebi, now it's the Flying Dutchman? Listen to me, he went on, his voice dropping, — this lost innocence you're so frantic to recover, it goes a good deal farther back, you know. And this idea that you can set everything to rights at once is . . . is childish. (551)

Valentine, it would seem, understands the source of Wyatt's confusion better than Wyatt does himself. In this crucial section (part 2, chap. 6) Valentine is alerted to several references by Wyatt to his mother and makes the connection between Esme, Camilla, and their combined appearance in the portrait Valentine calls a "Stabat Mater." When Solveig is added to the gallery of romantic redemptresses Wyatt has been naming (Senta from Wagner's *Flying Dutchman,* the king's daughter from "The Frog King," Arianrhod from the Welsh *Mabinogion,* Isis from Lucius' *Golden Ass,* Saint Rose of Lima), Valentine can only dismiss Wyatt's concerns as "childish" —an apt word in light of the psychological implications under consideration. He realizes, as Wyatt will later, that redemption cannot come from without—from a Solveig capable of conferring salvation—but must be worked out "with fear and trembling" from within.

An immature relationship with one's mother is not only childish but ultimately destructive, as the fates of many of the other characters in *The Recognitions* attest: Anselm castrates himself after an encounter with his domineering mother;[14] Charles is left to die after his smug Christian Science mother abandons him; and Stanley, concerned with his mother throughout the novel, finally dies as a result of the organ work dedicated to her. (None of these, it will be noticed, has a satisfying relationship with a woman in the course of the novel.) "You know, the trouble with you," Max taunts Anselm and Stanley, "you're all mothers' sons" (534), as is Peer Gynt, and as is Wyatt until he adjusts to the loss of both his mother, Camilla, and his mother-surrogate, Esme, and rediscovers the meaning of love with the Spanish girl, Pastora.

Wyatt could never pursue this course as long as he was involved with the Valentine-Brown syndicate. Brown recommends crass materialism as the only reasonable goal in life, and the only advice Valentine can offer, "the only secret worth having," is "the power of doing without happiness" (552).[15] Such advice, however, is as limiting as the troll king's dictum, "Troll, to thyself be—enough!" (*Peer Gynt,* act 2, sc. 6) or the Boyg's advice, "Go roundabout" (act 2, sc. 7). That Gaddis associated the troll king with the Boyg—both of whom advocate passive resignation over active integration —is indicated by a gloss Gaddis provided his Italian translator to a reference to the Boyg earlier in that same important chapter:

p. 545 1.27   the "Boyg" was the troll king in Ibsen's "Peer Gynt" who wanted Peer to marry his ugly troll daughter and, in order to cure Peer of his 'pestilent nature'[16] and make him see as trolls do, says he will scratch his eyes so that Peer will "see awry; but all that you see will seem fair and brave."

The reference is to Brown, as elaborated on page 375 lines 15–19, Brown as the Boyg-troll king having perverted Wyatt's vision so that the false looks beautiful.[17]

Together, the Boyg and the troll king form a combination represented in *The Recognitions* by Valentine and Brown, both of whom try to pervert Wyatt's vision. Although Peer stops short of allowing the troll king to scratch his eyes until he sees awry, his subsequent career is an embodiment of the troll king's advice: "To thyself be—enough!" Wyatt, to his credit, more quickly realizes that the way of the world is not his way. The world of *The Recognitions* is the world of trolls, where the false looks beautiful, where counterfeit is taken for genuine, and where people are to themselves not true but simply enough. In his introduction to the edition of *Peer Gynt* Gaddis used, William Archer quotes Ludwig Passarge's interpretation of the Boyg as "a symbol of the mass of mankind, *perpetuum immobile,* opposing its sheer force of inertia to every forward movement." He goes on to explain: "This would make it nearly equivalent to 'the compact majority' of *An Enemy of the People;* or, looking at it from a slightly different angle, we might see in the scene an illustration in action of that despairing cry of Schiller's Talbot: 'Mit der Dummheit kämpfen Götter selbst vergebens.'"[18] Brown is consequently not only the troll king who urges conformity but also the Boyg in his capacity as chief representative of the inert masses against whom Wyatt, and any creative person, must struggle. Valentine, on the other hand, despises the masses and thus errs at the other extreme, an extreme that Gaddis associates with Gnosticism. In his notes, Gaddis wrote:

> . . . Basil Valentine, who is the gnostic presumption . . . is finally stricken down with insomnia, for his very refusal to realize and grant the worth of matter, that is, of other people. The essence of his gnosticism is largely an implacable hatred for matter. It is that element of aescetecism (*sic*) common in so many religious expressions turned, not upon the self, but upon humanity.[19]

Brown interacts with people only to bilk them; Valentine does not interact with them at all. Both are to themselves enough. Now the masses in *The Recognitions* are, for the most part, no better than trolls (as Ibsen felt the majority of his fellow Norwegians were), but following the cynical paths advocated by Brown and Valentine will not help Wyatt in the least. If Camilla has hold of Wyatt's private conscience, then Brown and Valentine have hold of his public conscience; all three must be exorcized before he can progress.

Act 5 of *Peer Gynt* and part 3, chapter 5 of *The Recognitions* (the last chapter in which Wyatt appears) find the protagonists in similar circumstances. Most significantly, both have undergone a symbolic death at sea; realistically, of course, Peer escapes from the shipwreck and Wyatt dies only in the eyes of Esme, who is convinced the moribund sailor recovered midvoyage is Wyatt himself. But psychologically both exemplify the "rebirth fantasy" common to literature and myth.[20] Both Peer and Wyatt must, at this point, come to terms with the past in order to redirect the future. As Peer makes his way to Solveig, the voices of his unconscious—anthropomorphized as the Strange Passenger, the Button-moulder,[21] the Lean One, and assorted thread-balls, withered leaves, sighings in the air, dewdrops, and broken straws—weigh his past deeds in the balance and find him wanting. His symbolic death notwithstanding, Peer is unable to make the final sacrifice necessary to be born again: "To be oneself is: to slay oneself," the Button-moulder explains (act 5, sc. 9), to kill the childish ego and allow the mature self to emerge.[22] But this answer, as the Button-moulder anticipated, is lost on Peer, and he ends on Solveig's lap in the same childish state as when the play began.[23]

Wyatt, on the other hand, seems to have taken to heart the Lean One's prescription in the following scene:

> Remember, in two ways a man can be
> Himself—there's a right and wrong side to the jacket.
> You know they have lately discovered in Paris
> A way to take portraits by help of the sun.
> One can either produce a straightforward picture,
> Or else what is known as a negative one.
> In the latter the lights and the shades are reversed,
> And they're apt to seem ugly to commonplace eyes;
> But for all that the likeness is latent in them,
> And all you require is to bring it out.
> If, then, a soul shall have pictured itself
> In the course of its life by the negative method,
> The plate is not therefore entirely cashiered,—
> But without more ado they consign it to me.
> For ulterior treatment I take it in hand,
> And by suitable methods effect its development.
> I steam it, I dip it, I burn it, I scour it,
> With sulphur and other ingredients like that,
> Till the image appears which the plate was designed for,—
> That, namely, which people call positive.
> But for one who, like you, has smudged himself out,
> Neither sulphur nor potash avails in the least.

> *Peer.*
> I see; one must come to you black as a raven
> To turn out a white ptarmigan? Pray what's the name
> Inscribed 'neath the negative counterfeit
> That you're now to transfer to the positive side?
>
> (act 5, sc. 10)

The name inscribed 'neath the negative counterfeit of Gaddis' protagonist had been Wyatt; as Stephen, the name originally intended for him by Camilla (27), he will no longer try "to make negative things do the work of positive ones" (590), as Esther had earlier accused him of doing. Blocked throughout the novel by his guilt and fixations, he finally realizes "it's only the living it through that redeems it" (898) and takes as his motto Saint Augustine's dictum "Love, and do what you want to" (899). On that note we leave the protagonist, not defeated by childish fixations, as we left Peer, but victorious over the remorseful past and well on the way to individuation.

Ascertaining the proper relationship to self and society, to the world within as well as the world without, constitutes one of the major themes of *The Recognitions,* and Gaddis found in *Peer Gynt* an analogue that could be incorporated with advantage. *The Recognitions* may be a repudiation of the myth of romantic redemption glorified in such works as *Peer Gynt, The Flying Dutchman,* and *Faust,*[24] but it shares with them the age-old concern with the proper development of the inner and outer man. The allusions to (and quotations from) *Peer Gynt* and the large number of other works appearing in the novel are not then, as some early reviewers charged, showy examples of erudition on the young author's part, but an attempt by Gaddis to achieve the kind of multiple perspective Wyatt finds so intriguing in his beloved Flemish painters; they succeed in giving *The Recognitions* the depth and symbolic resonance that distinguishes truly great literature.

Notes

1. *The Integration of the Personality* (1939) is the title of Jung's first book-length study of alchemy (and a book that Gaddis used for most of his alchemical references), but the phrase is common to many of Jung's writings (cf., Ensaf Thune's application of the phrase in "The Paradox of the Boyg: A Study of Peer Gynt's Humanization," *Modern Drama* 19 [March 1976]: 91).

2. F. Bætzmann in *Aftenbladet,* quoted in Michael Meyer's *Ibsen: A Biography* (Garden City, N. Y.: Doubleday & Company, 1971), 268.

3. Meyer, *Ibsen,* 272.

4. Quoted in Rosalind Pitman's "William Archer and *Peer Gynt,*" *Notes and Queries* 218 (n.s. 20 [July 1973]): 256.

5. Ibid., 256. Timothy Schiff comes to the same conclusion in "Providence and Dispensation in Henrik Ibsen's *Peer Gynt,*" *Scandinavian Studies* 51 (Autumn 1979): 375–91.

6. William Gaddis, *The Recognitions* (1955; reprint with corrections, Cleveland and New York: World Publishing Co., Meridian Fiction, 1962), 88. Subsequent references to this work will be cited parenthetically in the text.

7. When Valentine asks Wyatt the next morning who the subject of this painting is, Wyatt admits it is his mother and immediately his face draws "up in lines of confusion as though he had just remembered" (338). This confusion, perhaps more than anything else, causes Wyatt to retreat to his father in part 2, chapter 3.

8. Reprinted (V. M. E. Collins' translation) in *Ibsen: A Collection of Critical Essays,* ed. Rolf Fjelde (Englewood Cliffs, N. J.: Prentice-Hall, 1965), 64.

9. The translation is the same one used by Gaddis, viz., that of William and Charles Archer (New York: Charles Scribner's Sons, 1907).

10. The paper was presented to the Vienna Psychoanalytic Society in 1920 and is translated by Philip Schmitz in *Early Writings* (New York: Farrar, Straus and Giroux, 1975), 3–64. As with Groddeck's essay, the many insights in this long essay resist summary; suffice it to say, Reich's analysis is very thorough and convincing. At that time, Reich was still an orthodox Freudian and had not yet developed the singular theories for which he is generally known and often dismissed.

11. A full exposition of Wyatt's Oedipal conflict would require an essay in itself. The symbolic keys to the conflict can be found in the bird imagery (Wyatt as robin, Reverend Gwyon as wren); Wyatt's imitation Memling (in which the tortured Valerian is modeled after his father); and the role of the father-king in anthropological and religious ceremonies cited in the novel involving the death of the son.

12. Reich, "Libidinal Conflicts," 48. It is no coincidence, then, that when Wyatt meets Esme she has an abandoned daughter of four somewhere (196)—Wyatt's age when Camilla abandoned him. Even if Esme's child is imaginary (276–77), the symbolic importance remains.

13. De Rougemont's *Love in the Western World,* trans. Montgomery Belgion (New York: Harcourt, Brace, 1940), was another of Gaddis' source books.

14. Anselm's habit of going about on all fours—"ritu quadrupedis," as he calls it, after the manner of Saint Teresa (197, 300)—makes psychological sense when we learn that "His mother is the sweetest little Boston woman, [. . .] *awfully* interested in dogs" (309).

15. This "secret" is from Bernard Shaw's *The Perfect Wagnerite* (4th ed. 1923). In his synopsis of Wagner's *Valkyrie,* Shaw writes, "With the son [Siegmund] he himself [Wotan] leads the life of a wolf, and teaches him the only power a god can teach, the power of doing without happiness" ([New York: Dover, 1967], 35).

16. Actually, "pestilent" is a mistranslation on the Archers' part. According to Henri Logeman, *hersens* is a colloquialism, and the line should read, "this 'ere human nature" (*A Commentary, Critical and Explanatory on the Norwegian Text of Henrik Ibsen's "Peer Gynt",* Its Language, Literary Associations and Folklore* [1917; reprint, Westport, Conn.: Greenwood Press, 1970], 116–17).

17. Quoted in Peter W. Koenig's "'Splinters from the Yew Tree': A Critical Study of William Gaddis' *The Recognitions"* (Ph.D. diss., New York University, 1971), 92. I assume Gaddis is purposely condensing the Boyg and troll king into one symbolic figure; however, the

note for the Italian translator was written some ten years after the publication of the novel, and perhaps Gaddis simply forgot the distinction.

18. Pp. xxviii–xxix. The quotation from Schiller—"With stupidity the gods themselves struggle in vain" (*Jungfrau von Orleans,* act 3, sc. 6)—is used in Gaddis' second novel, *J R* (New York: Alfred A. Knopf, 1975), 189.

19. Quoted in Koenig, "'Splinters from the Yew Tree,'" 93.

20. See Reich, "Libidinal Conflicts," 43–44. Some critics have argued that Peer actually drowns during the shipwreck and that the balance of act 5 is a hallucination at the moment of death, but this reading has not found widespread acceptance.

21. The Button-moulder's occupation (see act 5, scenes 7, 9, 10) probably accounts for the unusual image, "streets were filling with people . . . like buttons from a host of common ladles" (329), an image repeated by Wyatt on the top of page 376.

22. Groddeck, *Exploring the Unconscious,"* 76–77; see also Logeman's long gloss on this line, in *A Commentary,* 333–35. Wyatt knows what the Button-moulder is talking about and thus answers Valentine's taunt that his plans are suicidal: "Suicide? this? Do you think there's only one self, then? that this isn't homicide? closer to homicide?" (546).

23. In a 1972 BBC television production of the drama, the director astutely lap-dissolved at this point back to a tableau of Aase cradling Peer just as Solveig does at the end.

24. The influence of *Faust* on *Peer Gynt* has often been noticed (see, for example, A. LeRoy Andrew's early "Ibsen's *Peer Gynt* and Goethe's *Faust," Journal of English and Germanic Philology* 13 [1914]: 238–46), but space does not permit an examination of the confluence of both works on *The Recognitions.*

7

"il miglior fabbro"
Gaddis' Debt to T. S. Eliot

Miriam Fuchs

If *The Recognitions* seems complicated and often obscure, one aspect
of it remains clear, and that is the profound impact of T. S. Eliot. Perhaps only a discerning reader will realize the formal impact of the poetry—
the shifting points of view, the juxtaposition of past and present, and the
spatialization or organization of events according to location rather than
chronology. Even a casual reader, however, will sense the thematic impact
of Eliot's poetry—arid landscapes, mourning women, questers, imposters,
fertility figures, chapels, bells, burials, and resurrections. Although the majority of shared motifs comes from *The Waste Land* and *The Four Quartets,* echoes can be heard from many of Eliot's poems.

Something as specific as "Twit twit twit" from *The Waste Land* (l. 203)[1]
becomes the title of a book that Max or one of his friends brings to a
Greenwich Village bar. Prufrock's fear that his female companion would
rebuke him with "'That is not what I meant at all. / That is not it, at
all'" is muttered by Otto Pivner when Esme seems less than enamored with
him. Otto insists: "Oh, look, that isn't what I meant. [. . .] That isn't what
I meant at all."[2] Guests leave a party saying, "Yes, well ghood night, eh?
Ghood night . . . goo night, goo night, goo night . . ." (680), just as friends
leave the London pub in *The Waste Land:* "Goonight Bill. Goonight Lou.
Goonight May. Goonight. / Ta ta. Goonight. Goonight" (ll. 170–71).
Someone asks Stanley, "Is it 'Ils vont prende le train de sept heures' or 'de
huit heures'" (182), and the answer may be found in Eliot's "Lune de Miel":
"Ils vont prendre le train de huit heures." Stanley quotes, "It's 'birth and
copulation and death'" (193) from "Fragments of an Agon" in *Sweeney
Agonistes,* while a literary critic disdains "claims of time past and time
future, both contained in this limicolous present" (626), varying the opening of *The Four Quartets:* "Time present and time past / Are both per-

haps present in time future, / And time future contained in time past."
The "Murmur of maternal lamentation" heard in *The Waste Land* (l. 368)
metamorphoses into Mount Lamentation, which Wyatt sees from his window while he grows up in his father's New England parsonage. The most
frequent echo derives from J. Alfred Prufrock, who reassures himself that
"there will be time" to face all that he fears. When Otto asks Esme if she
loves him, she answers, "If there were time" (484), and as Mr. Pivner waits
day after day for Otto to call, "And still, even in sleep, he knew there would
be time" (293). After his wife's death, Gwyon imagines her protestations
right up to Purgatory: "If there had only been time. [. . .] If only there
were time. [. . .] if you'll only tell me what I should do . . ." (15). Gwyon
knows there is a lesson in Camilla's death, but believes "There would be
time" (ibid.) to discover it, and thirty years later he is still muttering the
same refrain (419). Stanley also worries about being summoned to Purgatory without enough preparation. Unlike Mrs. Porter and her daughter
in *The Waste Land,* he rarely washes, since the "overwhelming question"
is: "Would he have time to wash himself to perfect newness, dress in un-
worn, uncreased garments?" (321).

These examples should not give the impression that Gaddis borrows
liberally and randomly from Eliot; the paraphrases and quotations are part
of the form and substance of *The Recognitions*. It is as though characters
and conflicts of *The Waste Land* are placed in a midtwentieth-century sound
chamber so that their monologues, dialogues, inflections, and gossip are
remarkably familiar. The chamber reverberates with other sounds as well,
but Eliot's are an essential component. Voices rise out, fleeting but unmistakable, as testimony of underlying beauty, calm, and harmony, of (as Basil
Valentine tells Wyatt) the only secret worth knowing. The secret of *The
Recognitions* is the secret behind the cacophony of *The Waste Land* and
the knowledge revealed through the harmonies of *The Four Quartets*. There
are many perspectives through which Gaddis' dense, difficult, and brilliant
novel may be understood, and Eliot's poetry is one of the most important.

Gaddis believes with Eliot that "inexplicable splendour" lies under the
grime of our "unreal" cities, and, like Eliot, he darts from one location
to another to reveal the extent of that grime. Also like Eliot, Gaddis creates a spatial construct in which voices at various locations seem to vi-
brate simultaneously in pretentious hypocrisy. The "splendour" is hard to
detect.

For example, in part 1, chapter 1, the third-person point of view cuts
across Paris like a camera, creating a montage from a single evening in
August. As it scans the Right Bank, the Terrace of the Dôme, the Pont
d'Auteuil, the Bourse, Montmartre, and the Montrouge Cemetery, part of

one conversation is juxtaposed to another. The same procedure is used in New York, where Wyatt, his acquaintances, and countless anonymous citizens board buses and subways to locations in Greenwich Village and Central Park, or walk up and down the avenues. J. Alfred Prufrock hopes he will have enough time "To prepare a face to meet the faces that you meet," and the third-person voice of *The Recognitions* expands on his words: "It broke up and spread itself, in couples and threes and figures of stumbling loneliness, into the streets, into doorways, they all went into the dark repeating themselves and preparing to meet one another, to reassemble, rehearse their interchangeable disasters . . . " (315). The lives of these people are, by necessity, an ongoing charade because they have renounced or lost track of their beginnings. Without this knowledge, they have no future and no opportunities for authentic growth.

Eliot's work emphasizes the need to recognize the past as a point of origin—personal, ancestral, religious, historical, and cultural. To serve as negative examples, he shows one wastelander after another enacting rituals that none of them understands, thereby debasing the fundamental meaning. In "East Coker" of *The Four Quartets,* Eliot insists that "In my beginning is my end," and without acknowledging an origin there is only fragmentation. Many characters in *The Recognitions* who are severed from their origins remain hopelessly isolated from their community and from those who care about them. Wyatt conceals part of his past from his wife Esther, and, as in *The Waste Land,* their sexual encounters become automatic and loveless, a series of isolated gestures. With masculine aggressiveness, Esther mirrors the male pursuers of *The Waste Land* who settle for impersonal responses, since lovemaking is an impersonal ritual. Their staccato dialogue could very well belong to the clerk typist and the carbuncular young man: "Wyatt? What. How are you? Fine. I mean how do you feel? Empty" (100).

Wyatt's trade as a forger of old Flemish masters elevates the execution of line above the origins of conception. Since his goal is perfection, success is ensured by reproducing what has already been produced and refined. Only years later does Wyatt realize that his respect for the perfect forgery has forestalled his own growth, something that "East Coker" warns against: "The knowledge imposes a pattern, and falsifies, / For the pattern is new in every moment / And every moment is a new and shocking / Valuation of all we have been." His knowledge is false because in using another artist's masterpiece, Wyatt accepts a pattern but rejects possibilities of newness. The pattern contains nothing that is his own and is therefore too limited a beginning to be authentic. Gaddis puns on someone else who also sacrificed an essential part of himself for a supposedly higher goal, "Origen, that most extraordinary Father of the Church, whose third-century enthusiasm led him to castrate himself so that he might repeat the *hoc est corpus meum, Dominus,* without the distracting interference of the rearing shadow of the flesh" (103). Those who distort or abjure their personal origins, in effect, castrate their own maturation. Wyatt similarly ignores Esme's authenticity by seeing only those parts of her he can use to forge Madonnas. In contrast, Esme understands her origins and her basic nature—her free sexuality, even her addiction to drugs. Despite the disorder of her personal life, she possesses a transcendent and "inexplicable splendour" that draws other people, except Wyatt, to her.

Gaddis continues to unearth endless varieties of contemporary grime —fraud, forgery, plagiarism, counterfeiting, fear, neglect, deceit, and corruption. He also recreates the tensions between burial and resurrection, between winter and spring. Part 1 of *The Waste Land* is entitled "The Burial of the Dead," and part 1, chapter 1, of *The Recognitions* is about just that. Gwyon and his wife Camilla cross the Atlantic by ship, and she is stricken with appendicitis. The surgeon on board is forced to operate, but Frank Sinisterra, impersonating a doctor, is fleeing the American authorities who want to arrest him for counterfeiting. Like Madame Sosostris, Sinisterra's talent is limited; he cannot redeem Camilla's future, nor can "the wisest woman in Europe" (1. 45) see as much of the future as she should. After Camilla dies on the operating table, Gwyon does not allow her to be buried at sea (like Phlebas the Phoenician), and she is interred on the rise behind a Spanish village that possesses wasteland qualities. In the poem there is "Rock and no water and the sandy road / The road winding above among the mountains / Which are mountains of rock without water (11. 332–34). San Zwingli is similarly "built of rocks against rock, streets pouring down between houses like beds of unused rivers" (16). The prophet of *The Waste Land* insists that life can be resurrected, and Camilla, true to the symbolism of her name, becomes the flowering corpse, the dying and reviving goddess of *The Recognitions.* Those who gradually sense Camilla as part of their own origins, and those who perceive her eternal spirit as integral to their own temporal selves are moving out of the disintegration of *The Waste Land* toward the integration of *The Four Quartets.*

Wyatt is luckier than his mother. He is almost, but not quite killed by his doctors, and it seems to be Camilla's spirit that redeems him. Gaddis echoes both "Gerontion" and *The Waste Land* to emphasize the corruption of the physicians who are baffled by Wyatt's illness:

Winter thawed into sodden spring, cruel April and depraved May reared and
fell behind, and the doctors realized that this subject was nearing exhaustion, might, in fact, betray them by escaping to the dissection table. [. . .]
With serious regret, the doctors drew their sport to a close, by agreeing on
a name for it: *arathema grave*. After this crowning accomplishment, they
completed the ritual by shaking hands, exchanging words of professional
magic, mutual congratulation and reciprocal respect, and sent the boy home
to die. (42–43)

As in *The Waste Land,* April is cruel for not bringing relief to Wyatt, who
has been dying all winter. Although spring arrives, it reaches depravity before effecting renewal. "Depraved May" is taken directly from "Gerontion":

> In the juvescence of the year
> Came Christ the tiger
>
> In depraved May, dogwood and chestnut, flowering judas,
> To be eaten, to be divided, to be drunk
> Among whispers; by Mr. Silvero
> With caressing hands, at Limoges
> Who walked all night in the next room;

Wyatt parodies Eliot's Christ, appearing in spring but falling into the hands
of imposters who divide and mutilate their victim. The doctors' sham
rituals around Wyatt's emaciated body echo the actions of Mr. Silvero,
Hakagawa, and Madame de Tornquist, who all fail to resurrect the body
of Christ. In the "juvescence" of his twelfth year, Wyatt is sent home to
die. It is no wonder, then, that an anonymous voice later reminisces about
an earlier time of youthful innocence: "In Istanbul in the summer, [. . .]
it was Istanbul, wasn't it? We used to take long rides in the cistern, in the
summer . . ." (74). Even though the rides occurred in the summer, the
gentleness and nostalgia bring to mind Marie's recollection of sledding in
The Waste Land: "And when we were children, staying at the archduke's, /
My cousin's, he took me out on a sled, / And I was frightened. He said,
Marie, / Marie, hold on tight. And down we went" (ll. 13–16).

Wyatt's father quietly puts his ailing son in touch with eternal spirits.
Gwyon understands the ineffable relationship between Camilla's spirit and
the Barbary ape he brought home from Spain. The whole family silently
understands this connection, especially after the animal uproots Aunt May's
beloved hawthorn tree, an action that quickly leads to the death of Wyatt's
fanatic Calvinist aunt. No one mourns. Gwyon brings the ape to Wyatt's
bedside and murders it in ritual sacrifice. Wyatt screams in pain, imagin-

ing that nails are being driven through his feet. Sacrifice of the animal, in which Camilla seems reincarnated, leads to Wyatt's recovery.

In contrast to characters such as Wyatt, who eventually struggle to "unweave, unwind, unravel / And piece together the past and the future" ("The Dry Salvages"), are the hordes of humanity who ignore the past and debase their origins. Otto Pivner connects "Nothing with nothing" like the masses in *The Waste Land* (1. 302) despite his attempts to connect everything to himself. His origins belong to other people because he steals aesthetic vocabulary from Wyatt, romantic phrases from Esme, mannerisms from observing his reflection in mirrors. He counterfeits his past (Did he, in fact, graduate from Yale?), and so he has no future. He immediately transforms his experiences into the play he is writing so that he hardly has any present. The moment he thinks something significant has occurred to him, Otto imagines his protagonist, Gordon, one step further in the play. Symbolically, Otto is writing himself out of existence. When Dr. Fell calls him by the name of Gordon, Otto answers.

Agnes Deigh's husband relinquished his last name when he married. Giving up his original identity contributes to the sterility of their marriage. Agnes and her husband live apart, do not make love, meet occasionally for breakfast. Agnes' sexuality suffers further when she cannot convince guests at a party that she is really a woman, not a man in drag. Dozens of other characters similarly show the disastrous results of denying origins and debasing traditional rituals. Obfuscated by ignorance or greed, the quest for renewal becomes a travesty. Tony Tanner summarizes the congestion of wastelander activity in *The Recognitions:* "Life becomes a sort of ongoing carnival of clutter, filling up with stuff at the same time as it seems to be coming apart and falling to bits."[3]

The antipode to the confusion, barrenness, and rootlessness is the "inexplicable splendour," apprehensible to only a few. Concealed but immutable, it is the fulfillment that derives from knowing one's beginnings. It is the recognition of the eternal and the sacred in the midst of the temporal and the profane. Those in *The Waste Land* who understand the challenge of such splendor are most often the first-person personae. These include the subjective voices of the German aristocrat, the speaker who addresses Stetson, the Thames poet, the Old Testament poet, Ferdinand from *The Tempest,* Tiresias, the Fisher King, Buddha, and Saint Augustine. Their lines rise above the discontinuous twits and jugs of the poem to blend into a single, coherent, but fluid consciousness.

Robert Langbaum explains these personae, who usually speak very briefly, as comprising a single protagonist but not in the usual sense. The "I" is the total of each voice from each epoch; it "acquires delineation or identity not through individuation but through making connection with ancient archetypes."[4] Each voice—the saint, the poet, the king, whoever —is a tribute to the order of the past and a lament over the chaos of the present. For instance, as the woman in the burnished bedroom reproaches her companion for knowing nothing, seeing nothing, and remembering nothing, the voice of Ariel from *The Tempest* breaks through: "I remember / Those are pearls that were his eyes" (ll. 125–26). This line nostalgically recalls a beauty to which the woman is oblivious. Other lines of first-person personae similarly recall harmony and lyricism: "By the waters of Leman I sat down and wept . . ." (l. 183); "Sweet Thames, run softly, for I speak not loud or long" (l. 184); "O Lord Thou pluckest me out" (l. 309); "We who were living are now dying" (l. 329); "Shall I at least set my lands in order?" (l. 426). These and other lines lament that the past has been severed from the present, and "East Coker" urges the same need to recover the past: "There is only the fight to recover what has been lost / And found and lost again and again." A similar fight takes place in *The Recognitions*. Evidence of authenticity may be found beneath a forgery, expressed by a murderer, conveyed by a drug addict, or obscured by insipid and incessant talk; but it exists, enduring and everlasting.

An ever-present consciousness, represented by the "I," finds its way into *The Recognitions*. The meaning of the first-person voice is contrasted to the meaning behind the third-person voice. For instance, when Esme realizes that Wyatt will never love her, will use her only as a starting point for his forged Madonnas, she tries to discard what he "stole" by referring to herself in third person. Otto asks if she has been modeling, and Esme replies: "Sometimes she did" (482) and "She does not see him anymore" (483). "You'll be all right alone? Now she will" (484). One afternoon Agnes Deigh writes to a dentist, asking for the meaning behind his middle initial, which just happens to be "I." Stanley's translation of a Michelangelo poem laments the theft of the "I":

> O God, O God, O God,
> Who has taken me from myself
>   from me myself
> Who was closest (closer) to me
> And could do more than I
>   most about me
>   What can I do? (322)

Basil Valentine, the art dealer who sells Wyatt's forgeries, expresses the fragility of the authentic "I": "There's as much difference between us and ourselves as between ourselves and others?" (553). When Wyatt, in despair, declares that "*No one knows who I am*" (439), he is right, and only painfully and gradually does he learn the expansive implications of the "I." Recognition of his inviolable self will lead him to a profound unity, a unity understood by each "I" of *The Waste Land*.

The fleeting first-person voices of *The Waste Land* emerge unpredictably, and together they establish a subtle but unmistakable presence. Camilla's spirit also manifests itself in unlikely places and through unlikely characters, and it unifies the living and the dead, Catholicism and Protestantism, Spain and America. Wyatt perceives it at the moment of Camilla's death even though he cannot know she has died. Her spirit emanates through the Barbary ape Gwyon brings home from San Zwingli as though metempsychosis has taken place. In addition, Camilla's body is mistaken for the little girl next to whom she is buried. Instead of exhuming the remains of the Roman Catholic rape victim, the Spanish authorities send Camilla's Protestant bones to Rome, where they are canonized and worshiped by thousands of Catholic pilgrims.

Although he does not know it, Wyatt is inextricably linked to Esme through Camilla. Esme becomes the next incarnation of her eternal spirit. As Wyatt's warehouse goes up in flames, Esme discovers a set of earrings. She runs into another room and pierces holes through her ears: "When she came out, wearing the Byzantine earrings, there was blood on them and on her shoulders, running down in singular unpaired lines over her bared breasts" (469–70). Esme cannot realize that she performs an action Camilla performed forty years earlier. A guest had brought the same set of earrings as a gift for the young bride. Without even waiting for him to depart, Camilla had dashed into another room, pushed the needles through her lobes, and "burst in again with wild luster in her eyes, wearing the gold earrings, blood all over them" (14). Doing what she feels she must, Esme naturally partakes in cyclical time and ritual, achieving a deep communion with Camilla.

The instant Camilla's spirit manifests itself, Esme seems transformed, suddenly enriched with the knowledge of the ages. She composes a letter to Wyatt to protest his treatment of her. Her earlier efforts to write amounted to nothing but ludicrous imitations of *carpe diem* poetry. Now her prose is muddled, but sophisticated and abstruse. She writes about the nature of painting, reality, and death, transcending her limitations of self-expression just as her beauty has always transcended her own awareness.

This transformation is important because it represents a successful unity that other characters in the novel strive for. The difficulty of achieving it is stated in "Burnt Norton":

> Words strain,
> Crack and sometimes break, under the burden,
> Under the tension, slip, slide, perish,
> Decay with imprecision, will not stay in place,
> Will not stay still.

Gaddis chooses specific words from this passage to convey Esme's struggle to write before she finds Camilla's earrings:

> The words which the tradition of her art offered her were by now in chaos, coerced through the contexts of a million inanities, [. . .] and when they reached her hands they were brittle, straining and cracking, sometimes they broke under the burden which her tense will imposed, and she found herself clutching their fragments, attempting again with this shabby equipment her raid on the inarticulate. (299)

Both authors place writing in a tactile context where words are rigid, easily cracked, having been corrupted by "Shrieking voices / Scolding, mocking, or merely chattering, / Always assail[ing] those who try to purify them ("Burnt Norton").

Camilla's presence infuses not just Esme, but also Wyatt, though he must first journey back to Spain. His experience seems right out of "The Dry Salvages":

> But to apprehend
> The point of intersection of the timeless
> With time, is an occupation for the saint—
> No occupation either, but something given
> And taken, in a lifetime's death in love,
> Ardour and selflessness and self-surrender.

Wyatt is the quester, embedded in linear time, finally meeting the buried corpse, now part of sacred time, on consecrated ground, where heaven and earth intersect. Camilla, of course, is soon to become a saint through error, and Wyatt learns from her that love and necessity become, at some point, synonymous. Self-surrender does not mean obliterating one's self and origins for a work of art; it does mean, however, that one surrenders the notion of perfection (and thereby surrenders forgery) in order to accept the imperfections of a life that must be lived through.

Unassailable knowledge emerges not just through the omnipresent "I," but also through a second device—spatialization. Resembling the straight cut in film editing as opposed to the dissolve, spatialization rests on the assumption that physical location is as effective as chronology in unifying material. An author is therefore free to jump from one city to the next as Eliot does in *The Waste Land*. *The Four Quartets* is similarly built upon a spatial foundation, for history is perceived according to geography, not linearity. "Burnt Norton" refers to a house in Gloucestershire and "East Coker" to Somersetshire, England; "The Dry Salvages" to rocks near the Massachusetts coastline; and "Little Gidding" to an Anglican village in seventeenth-century England. Although time shifts back and forth and scenes constantly change, the geography provides a clearly discernible structure that cuts across the boundaries of time.

Sharon Spencer describes this technique as a device by which "every location in space, every *lieu,* is infused with its own time, or simultaneity of times."[5] Since each chronological period is subsumed by the location, a spatialized work lacks sharp divisions between past, present, and future. Gaddis often achieves this blurring of time. Neither the third-person narrative nor the characters are particularly precise about time, and voices drone on for too many pages at a time, from too many separate conversations, for chronology to remain clear. But location is crucial. For instance, the motif of barren terrain heightens the reflexive quality of *The Recognitions* and provides unity. Whenever a tourist approaches San Zwingli, nearly identical words describe it. It is first mentioned as close to a "rock-strewn plain" (7). Next comes an expanded version:

> San Zwingli appeared suddenly, at a curve in the railway, a town built of rocks against rock, streets pouring down between houses like beds of unused rivers, with the houses littered like boulders carelessly against each other along a mountain stream. Swallows dove and swept with appalling certainty at the tower of the church. (16)

More than an abundance of rocks suggests that Gaddis was thinking of "What the Thunder Said." The mountains need water, a chapel is present, and Eliot's hermit thrush is now swallows, reminiscent of the line, "*Quando fiam uti chelidon*— O swallow swallow" (l. 429). This same passage is repeated almost word for word in part 3, chapter 3, when Sinisterra approaches the village just as Gwyon did: "San Zwingli appeared suddenly, at a curve in the railway" (776). There are only slight differences. Gwyon had climbed "to the pines behind the tower," and Sinisterra climbs "the hill toward the town." Gwyon had "paused to breathe the freshness of manure," and Sinisterra pauses to sniff the surrounding pines before noticing "the delicious freshness of cow manure." Both voyagers rediscover "senses long forgotten under the abuse of cities."

When Wyatt goes to the monastery where Gwyon recuperated after Camilla's death, he finds the old man who tolls the bells of a secluded chapel
(which appear in both *The Waste Land* and *The Four Quartets*). The old
man turns out to be the murderer of the little girl next to whom Camilla
was buried. Rather than being sent to prison, he was allowed to live close
to the location of his sin, where he daily recalls the action by tolling the
bells. The old man possesses the only secret worth knowing and attempts
to teach it to the younger penitent. But one morning Wyatt finds the entrance to the monastery locked. Suddenly he realizes that the murderer's
penance has taught him something about the enduring nature of sin, but
that he himself must complete the lesson. *The Four Quartets* could be used
to describe Wyatt's progress. "The Dry Salvages" suggests that such "moments of agony . . . are likewise permanent" and that "We appreciate this
better / In the agony of others, nearly experienced / Involving ourselves,
than in our own." The old man's agony has involved Wyatt, but now he
must see himself as the sole source of his sins and the sole origin of his
future. Each moment lived and each selfish act reverberate endlessly; what
might have been in his life and what actually took place "Point to one end,
which is always present" ("Burnt Norton").

Wyatt cannot reverse time in order to redeem the past. Gaddis and Eliot
both believe that the most fulfilling and authentic way to perceive life is
spatially and eternally, absorbing chronology into larger dimensions and
harmonies. Wyatt decides that living in the present means he will "marry
someone else's mistake, to atone for one of your own somewhere else, dull
and dead the day it begins" (898). One person's beginning must intersect
with another person's middle, which may intersect with a third person's
end, and so on. This is the means by which contraries are resolved: "And
right action is freedom / From past and future also" and "Time the de-
stroyer becomes time the preserver" ("The Dry Salvages"). Wyatt makes
his decision:

> —And how do you atone? By locking yourself up in remorse for what you
> might have done? Or by living it through. [. . .] Or by going back and living
> it through. [. . .] If it was sin from the start, and possible all the time, to
> know it's possible and avoid it? Or by living it through. (896)

He can't return to Esther or Esme, and he can no longer live in a rarefied
atmosphere of perfection, which is merely a sham. Living, giving, and allowing himself to receive from others is the only secret worth searching
for and worth knowing.

Wyatt's lesson takes place approximately nine hundred pages through the novel. It is a dramatic climax to the coherent narrative thread of his life. Knowing that the plot will motivate a reader to push forward through hundreds of pages of spatialized conversations, Gaddis withholds the climax as long as possible. *The Recognitions,* though, is about both missed and successful discoveries. The reader who concentrates on a linear pattern will probably miss the central message of the novel that first appears hundreds of pages earlier. The reader who thinks spatially, looking for recurrent patterns, settings, and dialogues, can discover the theme when it first occurs. Gaddis shares with Eliot the insistence that sacred knowledge is everywhere, and so he inserts it in earlier chapters, as Eliot inserts it in the "I" personae of *The Waste Land.* The knowledge is described in *The Four Quartets,* but it is placed in each section so that it will harmonize with the next.

Characters who express timeless knowledge are themselves unaware of what they know—another missed recognition. For example, Agnes Deigh writes to the dentist, Dr. Weisgall. She apologizes for having informed the police that she saw him through a window beating a young woman. Told by police that this was his own daughter, she writes: "'Dear Doctor Weisgall. Perhaps it is not until late in life that we realize that we do not, ever, pay for our own mistakes. We pay for the mistakes of others, and they . . .'" (556). Her words nearly match Wyatt's final recognition: "To run back looking for every one of them [mistakes]? every one of them, no, it's too easy. [. . .] the sin is only boring and dead the moment it happens, it's only the living it through that redeems it" (898). The meaning is the same: although knowledge may come late, each person is not punished directly for his mistakes and cannot atone directly for them; he is punished for someone else's and atones for someone else's, just as that person does for him. Agnes' letter seems unimportant only because the reader is probably concentrating on Wyatt, not on the content of a letter written by a character who has nothing to do with the linear tale.

Mrs. Deigh is not the only person to express the central idea of the novel. Frank Sinisterra also learns that he has not been punished directly for killing Camilla on his operating table. When he meets Wyatt in Spain and learns that Wyatt is Camilla's son, he knows it is time to atone. Time past and time future are contained in time present, and Sinisterra's words echo Agnes Deigh's letter: "No, you can't You can't . . . not to them, but you . . . if you've like sinned against one person then you make it up to another, that's all you can do, you never know when you . . . until the time comes when you can make it up to another. Like I once . . . this woman, I . . ." (814).

Perhaps even more ironic than these lost lessons is the fact that Wyatt himself expresses the problem of seeing behind a familiar form. Describing a revelation from Picasso's *Fishing at Antibes,* he explains:

> —When I saw it all of a sudden everything was freed into one recognition, really freed into reality that we never see, you never see it. You don't see it in paintings because most of the time you can't see beyond a painting. Most paintings, the instant you see them they become familiar, and then it's too late. (92)

Wyatt forgets his own words about looking past the predictable in order to reach what is meaningful, and his warning applies also to the reader of *The Recognitions.* The conventions of a particular form may cause a reader to apprehend less than what is there. Like the fixed and mechanical lives of wastelanders that forestall individual development, an automatic and conventional response to *The Recognitions* will delay an understanding of Gaddis' themes.

Another way to discover the central idea of this novel is to go beyond its dizzying surface to the work of T. S. Eliot. Wyatt's development can be viewed in the context of *The Four Quartets,* while the civilization that crumbles around him can be viewed in the context of *The Waste Land.* This comparison in no way diminishes the individual accomplishment of William Gaddis. In fact, it was Eliot who said that skilled writers will always benefit by being looked at in relation to the great writers of the past, while the derivative writers will be exposed: "It is a judgment, a comparison, in which two things are measured by each other."[6] Understanding Eliot as the echo in the garden, the voice behind the waterfall, the pattern behind the prose is essential. First, it provides a literary background for this difficult novel, and second, it reveals *The Recognitions* as among the most sophisticated and rewarding literary works of the twentieth century.

Notes

1. All quotations from Eliot's poetry have been taken from *Collected Poems: 1909–1962* (New York: Harcourt, Brace & World, 1963).

2. William Gaddis, *The Recognitions* (New York: Harcourt, Brace & World, 1955), 447. Subsequent references to this work will be cited parenthetically in the text.

3. Tony Tanner, review of *The Recognitions, New York Times Book Review,* 14 July, 1974, 27.

4. Robert Langbaum, "New Modes of Characterization in *The Waste Land*," in *Eliot in His Time: Essays on the Occasion of the Fiftieth Anniversary of "The Waste Land,"* ed. A. Walton Litz (Princeton: Princeton University Press, 1973), 100.

5. Sharon Spencer, *Space, Time and Structure in the Modern Novel* (New York: New York University Press, 1971), xx.

6. T. S. Eliot, "Tradition and the Individual Talent," in *Selected Prose of T. S. Eliot,* ed. Frank Kermode (New York: Harcourt Brace Jovanovich, 1975), 39.

8

Love and Strife in William Gaddis' *J R*

STEPHEN H. MATANLE

The Problem of Chaos

William Gaddis' *J R* is a novel without conventional narrative divisions. And yet this apparently seamless novel is about things coming apart at the seams. In this sense, *J R* continues the investigation of a problem that Gaddis identified in his notes for *The Recognitions* as "the separating of things today without love."[1] Characters in *J R* find themselves separated from each other, and from themselves, in a variety of ways. The human body is fragmented, reduced to separate parts, and physical contact among characters is often hazardous. This situation is compounded by a kind of ocular chaos, a fragmentation of the visual field, for which eyeglasses are a metonymy. Most important, human communication, reduced to disembodied speech, frequently generates misunderstanding and disorder.

Jack Gibbs, a science teacher and failed writer, is the novel's preeminent authority on disorder. In fact, his first speech in the novel is an impromptu lecture on precisely this subject. Interrupting a studio lesson, Gibbs makes a futile effort to enlighten his students by challenging their assumptions about order:

— Before we go any further here, has it ever occurred to any of you that all this is simply one grand misunderstanding? Since you're not here to learn anything, but to be taught so you can pass these tests, knowledge has to be organized so it can be taught, and it has to be reduced to information so it can be organized do you follow that? In other words this leads you to assume that organization is an inherent property of the knowledge itself, and that disorder and chaos are simply irrelevant forces that threaten it from out-

side. In fact it's exactly the opposite. Order is simply a thin, perilous condition we try to impose on the basic reality of chaos . . .[2]

Although Gibbs is talking specifically about the reduction of knowledge
to information, the significance of his remarks transcends this immediate
context, for in the world that he inhabits, chaos is inherent in virtually
every aspect of human life.

Gibbs is concerned throughout *J R* with the difficulty of imposing order on "the basic reality of chaos . . . " This notion clearly informs the
book he has been trying to write, as well as his attitude toward it. He describes it to Amy Joubert as "a book about order and disorder more of
a, sort of a social history of mechanization and the arts" (244). Order is
both the subject and the strategy of the book. A history of organization,
it represents Gibbs' effort to organize imaginatively the past. However, the
book exists only as a fragment. Begun over ten years ago, it remains unfinished. When Gibbs finally tries to resume work on the book, he can
barely "get going on it" (583). Victimized by various distractions and by
a lack of energy, he spends most of his time reading aloud from the first
part of the book, losing his place, making a few minor changes, and searching for his notes. However, when he accidentally finds the notes in one
of the cardboard boxes crammed into the Ninety-sixth–Street apartment,
he is appalled by the evidence of his own ambition: "'God hundreds of
them' . . . finally coming to rest on H-O with the torn carton drawn close
'started with eighteen seventy-six have to get them all back in, Christ how
did I, look at that what did I think I was doing!'" (586). By "getting a
fresh start" (565) on the book, Gibbs had hoped to restore some order
to his life and to demonstrate to Amy his strength of purpose. Yet his work
is repeatedly interrupted by telephone calls, a nice irony, since the notes
for his book "started with eighteen seventy-six" (586), the year the telephone was invented. His energy dissipated and his concentration fragmented, Gibbs finally abandons the book. In a sense, his "social history"
is a victim of what it diagnoses, as it succumbs to the very conditions it
describes.

Gibbs' preoccupation with order and chaos also informs his frequently
allusive speech. For example, when he accosts Edward Bast and Amy Joubert in a New York cafeteria, he weaves allusions to T. S. Eliot's "Hyste-
ria" into his speech: "Get those breasts to stop shaking we may be able
to collect some fragments of the afternoon I'll concentrate on that " (120).
Like the speaker in Eliot's prose poem, Gibbs embarks on a project to com-
bat distraction. Trying to convince Edward Bast that Amy is "out on her
feet," Gibbs claims that "in spite of its appetizing symmetry woman's body's

an absolute God damned chaos" (ibid.). In *J R,* however, it is not merely the female body that is a chaos, but the human body. Furthermore, this notion is reinforced by Gibbs' several allusions to Empedocles.

The Rule of Strife

In an early scene in *J R* a character named Gall, who has been hired by a foundation to write a book on its "in-school television support program" (39), visits the school on Long Island where much of the novel's action takes place. Stopping to copy down the motto inscribed above the main entrance, he explains to Mr. Ford, the program specialist: "it might make a good epigraph for this book when I find out what it means" (20). A little later in the novel, during a conversation in the school principal's office, Gall asks Jack Gibbs about the motto: "That line over the main entrance here? in Greek? I thought, is it Plato? or . . ." (45). Gibbs suggests that he "try Empedocles," and while Gall tries to spell it, Gibbs continues: "I think it's a fragment from the second generation of his cosmogony, maybe even the first . . ." (ibid.). In any case, it represents a stage in the life of the world "when limbs and parts of bodies were wandering around everywhere separately . . ." (ibid.). A few pages later Major Hyde, a member of the school board, complains: "I'm trying to have a serious discussion with these Foundation people on closed-circuit broadcast and you butt in with arms and legs flying around somebody's eyes looking for their forehead what was all that supposed to be!" (48). Gibbs replies: "He was asking about one of the pre-Socratics, Major, the rule of love and the rule of strife in the cosmic cycle of Emp . . ." (ibid.). Like some of Gibbs' other allusions, such as the one to Eliot, this allusion to Empedocles is partly a characterization of his immediate environment and partly a reflection of his ideas about order and chaos.

Gibbs' advice to Gall, that he "try Empedocles," is curious in a couple of respects, not the least of which is that the inscription over the main entrance does not come from Empedocles. Furthermore, Gibbs knows this. As Whiteback, the school principal, explains: "It was his idea to make it look like a quotation from Herkahm, yes from the classics that is to say simply by adding curlicues to the letters in that motto his friend Schepperman gave us which sounded ahm, sounded all right at the time of course until we found out it was communist" (456). In fact, the motto is a familiar quotation from Marx's *Critique of the Gotha Program:* "From each according to his ability, to each according to his needs." Thus, without

the curlicues, the motto reads: "FROM EACH ACCORD . . ." (20). However, once this mystery is solved, it still remains unclear why Gibbs attrib-
utes the quotation to Empedocles. The answer, I think, is that Gibbs is
being ironical. Far from embodying Marx's ideal, the school's teachers and
administrators are almost uniformly incompetent, and the children's needs
are routinely ignored. This discrepancy is further emphasized by the implicit contrast between Marx's vision of harmony and Empedocles' "rule
of strife." More important, Gibbs' allusion is, at least in part, a response
to what is going on around him. In the wake of Edward Bast's unortho-
dox presentation on Mozart, the principal's office is in chaos. Hurrying
to switch off the television set, Major Hyde trips over somebody's foot.
A control knob comes off in Congressman Pecci's hand. Bodies are cropped
arbitrarily by the television camera. Meanwhile, Bast relates the "fairy
tale life" (40) of Mozart, interspersed with scatological excerpts from
Mozart's letter of 28 February 1778 to his cousin Maria Anna Thekla.
This scene of disorder, then, inspires Gibbs' allusion to Empedocles.

Empedocles' world is ruled by two forces, Love and Strife. The function of Love is to unite, to make one out of many, and incidentally to cause
rest. The function of Strife is to separate, to disperse things without apparent design, and incidentally to cause movement. These two forces rule
in periodic alternation. Love combines and binds the elements into the
Sphere, a single, homogeneous whole. However, at a certain time, "fixed
. . . by a broad oath,"[3] the power of Strife begins to increase until it finally destroys the perfect balance of the Sphere and "scatters the elements
randomly, so that they enter into haphazard combinations with one another."[4] According to Denis O'Brien, "Strife's share is essentially a process,
a battle, a time of change and conflict, a time of increase and decline, where
there is no place for victory and so for peace and permanence."[5] Now if
this is the nature of Strife's influence, it seems reasonable to assume that
the world of *J R* may be represented as being ruled by Strife. Much of the
novel's action happens in a "town where all allusion to permanence had
disappeared or was being slain" (18). Moreover, one of the novel's major
concerns is the separation of a common language into different modes of
discourse. As O'Brien suggests, "our own world falls in the period of movement when the power of Strife is on the increase."[6] Furthermore, "as time
goes on, the power of Strife in the world becomes even greater, the different parts of our bodies will no longer be able to hold together."[7] This
is precisely the situation dramatized by *J R*. The body is incoherent, fragmented into a variety of parts, deprived of stability and balance.

The possibility that *J R* represents a world that is ruled by Love is easily
dismissed. The separating power of Strife clearly holds sway over most of

the human relationships in the novel. Love is either absent or deformed by selfishness. Edward Bast suffers from a hopelessly romantic obsession with his cousin Stella, underscored by his trying to set to music Tennyson's "Locksley Hall." Stella in turn uses Edward's desire in order to retain control of a family business. When Miriam Eigen asks her son how much he loves her, he replies: "Some money . . . ?" (267). And Jack Gibbs, the only character in the novel who says "I love you" (501), waits for Amy Joubert to return from Switzerland and then, according to Thomas Eigen, avoids her: "When she finally called he wouldn't speak to her, heard her voice he pretended he was an old black retainer" (725). Most of the marriages in the novel end in divorce, and families are consequently divided and dispersed. There is not even any guarantee that members of one's family are blood relations. "Dad" diCephalis turns out to be "An elderly drifter" (685) who eats dog food and plays the saxophone. His true identity is unknown, as both Dan and Ann diCephalis have assumed that he is the other's father. In these and other instances, human relationships fail to exhibit the cohesion that characterizes the rule of Love.

In his poem *On Nature,* Empedocles emphasizes the effects of Love and Strife on the development of mortal creatures. Furthermore, he sometimes conceives of the Sphere, produced by the increasing power of Love, in anatomical terms. For example, in fragment 29 Empedocles defines the Sphere negatively. It consists in the absence of protrusions: "For there do not start two branches from his back; [he has] no feet, no swift knees, no organs of reproduction; but he was a Sphere, and in all directions equal to himself." By contrast, fragment 57 describes a world no longer whole but divided into a variety of parts: "many foreheads without necks sprang forth, and arms wandered unattached, bereft of shoulders, and eyes strayed about alone, needing brows." This is the fragment which Gibbs refers to in his conversation with Gall. In that same conversation, Gibbs summarizes fragments 59–61, a description of the stage in which "parts are joining up by chance, form creatures with countless hands, faces looking in different directions . . ." (45). These same images reappear later in the novel as Gibbs is jostled in Penn Station: "elbows found ribs and shoulders backs 'place is like the dawn of the world here, this way' . . . countless hands and unattached eyes, faces looking in different directions" (161). The narrative description here corroborates Gibbs' analogy between the subway passengers and Empedocles' "creatures" by employing images taken directly from Empedocles. Yet the reduction of the body to its parts is not confined to the passengers on the subway.

Throughout *J R* characters are consistently presented in terms of their hands, feet, elbows, knees, eyes, backs, shoulders. And these separate parts accidentally come into contact with others. In the second scene of *J R*, one of the novel's many bodily collisions occurs:

> Bast's elbow caught Mrs Joubert a reeling blow in the breast, she dropped the sack of coins and he stood for an instant poised with raised hand in pursuit of that injury before the flush that spread from her face to his sent him stooping to recover the sack by the top, spilling the coins from its burst bottom into the unmown strip of grass, and left him kneeling down where the wind moved her skirt. (19)

A moment later, as Bast tries to recover the spilled coins, Amy Joubert steps on his hand. Jack Gibbs, wherever he goes, creates a disturbance when he tries to arrange his limbs. For example, sitting beside Amy on the train, he finally manages to get "one knee wedged over the other looking deliberately slumped, a foot dangling in the aisle" (244). On a similar occasion, Amy complains: "Your knee can you move your knee, Jack can't you just sit . . ." (476). J R, a sixth-grader and the title character of the novel, is as restless as Gibbs. Sitting next to Edward Bast on the train, J R tries to arrange himself:

> He wedged a sneaker more tightly into the seat ahead bringing the heap higher with his knees, sinking slowly until a nostril came in reach of his thumb, finally —I just wondered, I mean can you make much doing that? writing this here music I mean? he paused, his elbow grinding against the arm hung limp beside him. (127)

The human body in *J R* is an awkward assemblage of limbs. Moreover, characters tend to move clumsily and abruptly. This tendency is emphasized only when their movements accidentally resemble dance steps. For example, Whiteback, as he moves toward his car, is described as having "retired in the box step of the rhumba" (19), and Jack Gibbs, in a New York cafeteria, makes "an abrupt turn that the right bar of music just then might have claimed for a moment from a tango" (115). One might expect the body to behave more gracefully in erotic contexts, but this is not the case. In fact, during the sexual act, limbs often seem to have been "caught in some random climax of catastrophe" (137). This is, in Empedocles' terms, simply one more instance of the dominance of Strife over Love.

In the only idyllic scene in the novel, Jack Gibbs and Amy Joubert spend a weekend together, during which they frequently make love. However, it is sometimes difficult to know precisely what they are doing. Even the simplest descriptions of their bodies seem fragmented: "The weight of her leg warm over his gone rigid for his twist away leaving only his back to her

where she kissed his shoulder in the darkness and clung as though for
warmth until, as of its own weight, it eased away" (483). In this passage,
the merely contiguous relations among separate parts of the body suggest
a certain tension between Love and Strife. Indeed, Gibbs has just experienced the frustration of impotence induced by alcohol and eagerness. Yet
even when the descriptions concern sexual acts, the lovers' bodies are never
represented as whole, but rather as constellations of fingers, shoulders,
knees, elbows, and orifices:

> . . . where his lips moved she suddenly fell wide, hand drawing closer strip-
> ping vein and color as his knee rose over her and jarred the telephone, still
> holding closed as though against a sudden plunge, or sudden loss, when
> the telephone rang, her arms came free, came up, her shoulders' struggle
> against his knee come down and legs drawn tight in a twist away as the tele-
> phone box went to the floor and she got the receiver wrong end round. (493)

This passage is not unlike those describing the faction of limbs on the train.
The fragmentation of the body makes it difficult to visualize the action.
Moreover, this is characteristic of the entire novel. The reader cannot always easily "see" what is going on. Instead, he must rely on what he "hears."
Yet discourse too is ruled by Strife, whose influence may be observed in
the plurality of voices, the separation of words from the things they name,
and the disembodiment of speech.

The Plurality of Discourse

J R consists almost entirely of dialogue, of "voices meeting and parting" (155). Perhaps the most prominent characteristic of verbal discourse
in *J R* is its heterogeneity. The novel is traversed by all kinds of discourse:
social, economic, legal, political, scientific, literary. As these modes of discourse intersect, compete, and absorb one another, it becomes increasingly clear that no one of them is privileged. Each authorizes itself.

The extent to which these various modes of discourse succeed in asserting their authority depends largely on their instrumental value. Early in
the novel, Jack Gibbs asks the school principal about the source of his
nearly incomprehensible jargon: "Speak of tangibilitating unplanlessness,
where'd you pick up that language, Whiteback?" Whiteback defends his
jargon by relying on an implicitly instrumentalist view of language: "You,
you have to speak it when you talk to them" (50). In a world of duplicity,

you use double-talk. There is no true word, no inevitable correspondence between sign and referent. Thus, when Edward Bast accuses J R of using a word without knowing what it means, J R replies, "so why should I have to know exactly what it means?" (296). After all, he is paying a lawyer to know what words mean.

Yet lawyers, in *J R* at least, are not always the most reliable arbiters of disputes about the meaning of a word. In a conversation with Anne and Julia Bast, a lawyer named Coen offends and confuses the two elderly sisters by using words like "bastard," "lunatic," and "emancipated" in their special legal sense. Mr. Beaton, of the law firm Beaton, Broos and Black, must explain to Amy Joubert that he is using the word *charity* "in its tax law connotation" (212). Words such as *charity* are especially susceptible to being degraded in *J R,* presumably because they do not refer to anything tangible. One of the clearest examples of what an instrumentalist view of language can do to words is J R's definition of "goodwill." Near the end of the novel, Bast complains about J R's attempt to "find out how much all that goodwill is worth" (654), and J R replies, "No wait hey I mean holy shit I don't mean where everybody's crazy about us and all, see goodwill that means the excess of the purchase price over the value of these net tangible assets." Bast, of course, violently protests: "That's not what it means!" (655). However, Bast is wrong insofar as he fails to recognize the extent to which meaning is contextual.

Several of the novel's characters, including Bast, resist the dissociation of signs from their referents. Amy Joubert, for example, clings sentimentally to a reference theory of language. When she sees the words "ethical product" used to describe a prescription drug, she is appalled. On another occasion, Mr. Davidoff, a public-relations man, addresses her social studies class in front of the Treasury steps. After listening to him talk about "standing here in the cradle of American history" (82), Amy wonders "who ever stood in a cradle" (118). Amy Joubert shares with Esme, a character in Gaddis' first novel, *The Recognitions,* a sense that words have been hopelessly debased, that language is "in chaos, coerced through the contexts of a million inanities."[8] But whereas Esme tries to recover that moment when words were indistinguishable from the things they named, Amy merely laments its passing. In *The Order of Things,* Michel Foucault describes this rupture by invoking the story of Babel:

> In its original form, when it was given to men by God himself, language was an absolutely certain and transparent sign for things, because it resembled them. . . . This transparency was destroyed at Babel as a punishment for men. Languages became separated and incompatible with one another

only insofar as they had previously lost this original resemblance to the things
that had been the prime reason for the existence of language. And the languages known to us are now spoken only against the background of this
lost similitude, and in the space that it left vacant.[9]

The story of Babel, then, dramatizes the fall of the word from its original
harmony with the world. Language is henceforth dispersed, and the space
"left vacant" by "this lost similitude" is filled with a proliferation of words,
a multitude of voices, a plurality of discourse.

One of the most distinctive voices in *J R* belongs to Whiteback. In a
conversation with Vern, the district superintendent, his speech is characteristically hesitant and diffuse: "Yes well of course we ahm, community-
relationswise that is to say Vern you don't get popular support without
the ahm, how did that Flesch woman put it yes without the support of
the community of course she had a gift for expressing ideas and my job
is ahm . . ." (220). Whiteback in fact has two jobs. He is both the school
principal and president of the bank. As such he exemplifies the confusion
and disorder generated by competing modes of discourse. When Gibbs asks
whether he has considered giving up either the bank or the school, Whiteback replies: "Yes well of course the ahm, when I know which one of them
is going to survive" (340–41). Near the end of the novel, the question is
effectively settled when the school is purchased by the J R Corp and operated by a Mr. Stye, "which he's like this branch manager" (649). By that
time, however, Whiteback has been given a job with the FCC.

The irony of Whiteback's new career is impossible to miss, since his
own powers of communication are so feeble. Intimidated by the very language he insists on using, Whiteback often finds himself hopelessly en-
tangled in tautologies and circular arguments. On one such occasion, he
tries to explain that he has had to turn down Dan diCephalis' application
to refinance the mortgage on his house because of an irregularity in its
construction. It is perhaps worth quoting a substantial portion of this
speech, as it typifies Whiteback's use of language:

> —Yes no nobody's blaming you Dan, we know you didn't build it yourself
> it was, of course it was the builder who ahm, who built it of course but
> the, since the term of a mortgage is related to, dictated by the number of
> years the house is reasonably expected to stand depending on its, directly
> related to the way it's built, constructed you might say, the wall studs having
> a direct bearing on the part of the structure so that of course the farther
> apart they are in a given space the fewer there are of them because the fewer
> there are of them the farther apart they have to be placed. (226–27)

In cases such as this, one might say that Whiteback's language is speaking him, dragging him along behind it. Yet in spite of its redundancy and circumlocution, this instance of Whiteback's speech seems quite lucid compared to his telephone conversations. In the course of the novel, he has a telephone line to his bank installed in the principal's office. As a result, bank business and school business furiously compete for his attention, the two telephones sometimes "ranting at each other" (180), as they are elsewhere in the novel left lying "on desks, hung from cords, berating one another" (52).

For some of the characters in *J R,* the telephone is no longer a convenience. During his romantic weekend with Amy, Jack Gibbs complains that he is "always afraid the damned telephone's going to go off the minute we . . ." (499). Indeed, the telephone does "go off" in the passage quoted earlier. For Gibbs, the telephone is like a bomb or a loaded gun, capable of reducing him to "dead weight" (504) with its ring. Similarly, the Bast sisters are constantly irritated by wrong numbers and offers of free dance lessons. Since the telephone seems only to disrupt their privacy, they feel that selling their telephone stock would be "like selling some poor soul shares in a plague . . ." (229). Instead of improving communication, the telephone increases frustration and misunderstanding.

The telephone effectively eliminates any possibility of checking language, since it reduces the available channels of communication to one, the human voice. Now while this feature of the telephone promotes confusion, it also offers certain advantages to J R, whose financial manipulations affect nearly every other character in the novel. When the Hyde kid suggests that J R, because of his age, is going to get into trouble borrowing money from a Nevada bank to buy thousands of surplus navy picnic forks, J R dismisses the warning:

> —I mean these funny hours my mother's always working how do I know when she's going to walk in, like I mean this here bond and stock stuff you don't see anybody you don't know anybody only in the mail and the telephone because that's how they do it nobody has to see anybody, you can be this here funny lookingest person that lives in a toilet someplace how do they know, I mean all those guys at the Stock Exchange where they're selling all this stock to each other? They don't give a shit whose it is they're just selling it back and forth for some voice that told them on the phone why should they give a shit if you're a hundred and fifty all they . . . (172)

J R uses the telephone to conduct business because it transmits only his voice, which he is able to disguise by stuffing his filthy handkerchief into the mouthpiece. J R's success, then, depends on his being absent to others, on his using the telephone to disguise the fact that he is a scruffy urchin in a torn sweater and sneakers, "frayed, knotted, and unshorn in other details" (57).

Since voices in *J R* are frequently "boxed," it is not always possible to appeal to gestures or facial expressions to check the meaning and intention of speech. This is to some extent a problem both for the characters and for the reader. For example, *J R* begins in the middle of a conversation, whose participants are not immediately identified or described. The reader is cast adrift on a stream of dialogue, cut loose from the conventional moorings of attribution and exposition. As most of the dialogue in *J R* is unaccompanied by descriptions of mental processes, feelings, motives, or facial expressions, we have no way to verify precisely the intended meaning of what we "hear." Refusing to allow his language to articulate subjective experience, Gaddis eschews interior monologue or other techniques for exploring consciousness from the inside. Our only sense of the characters' thoughts, intentions, and desires must be derived from what they say to one another. Similarly, the characters themselves draw inferences from each other's audible speech and observable behavior.

Yet visible perception in *J R* tends to be unreliable. On those occasions when a character responds to visual cues, he is likely to misinterpret them, as Edward Bast does when he "sees" Amy Joubert holding a cigarette which is really a cracker: "she'd turned the profile of her raised chin and, one finger delicately cocked, her hand risen with a white cracker to her parted lips where Bast abruptly thrust a lighted match" (117). Depending on visual signals for information about the world, one risks not only embarrassment but also injury. Thus, Mr. Skinner, a textbook salesman, is involved in one of the novel's several automobile accidents when the school janitor directs him into traffic. As Whiteback explains, "he says Leroy signaled him right out that blind corner in front of a truck, one of those big asphalt trucks . . ." (46). Perhaps the most revealing instance of the unreliability of visual perception occurs when Amy Joubert tries to make J R see the moon. J R has just suggested that "everything you see someplace there's this millionaire for it?" (473), and Amy is horrified at the idea:

    —And over there look, look. The moon coming up, don't you see it? Doesn't it make . . .
    —What over there? He ducked away as though for a better view, —No but that's, Mrs. Joubert? that's just, wait . . . (474)

Amy fails to convince J R that there are objects in the world whose worth is intangible, but Edward Bast, near the end of the novel, renews her effort:

> —But she's can't you see what she, why did you duck away! can't you see what she was trying to tell you she . . .
> —What tell her it's this top of this here Carvel icecream cone stand? tell her does she want to bet her ass if there's a millionaire for that? (661)

Both J R and Amy are apparently looking at the same object, yet each sees something different. Furthermore, there is no way to know which of them is right. Since the narrator confirms neither perception, we are faced with an unresolved conflict between Amy's romanticism and J R's instrumentalism.

While Amy and J R practice incompatible ways of seeing the world, other characters have difficulty seeing it at all. One such character is Whiteback, whose glasses metonymically reduce him to a cipher. Near the beginning of the novel, for instance, Whiteback is momentarily blinded by the sun, which "caught him flat across the lenses, erasing any life behind them in a flash of inner vacancy" (18). On another occasion, "catching light from nowhere, his lenses went blank" (175). However, Whiteback is once again merely an extreme example of a general phenomenon, a kind of ocular chaos in *J R*. Few of the novel's characters look directly at one another. Instead, their gazes are deflected, and lines of vision fail to intersect. Such is the case in this description of Amy, her uncle, and her father:

> Mrs Joubert sitting knees clenched reading through tortoise shell glasses, looking up just then elsewhere to ask —must I read all this now? elsewhere the weather side of Cates hunched, back to door, reading papers with a look pinched through gold rims that rose abruptly and glanced off hers to cross the desk lusterless with —just the cobalt? where Moncrieff's glance over heavy black half frames and the huddled permanent of a secretary had already passed them both and returned. (94)

These glances do not connect the characters. Instead, they reinforce the separation already suggested by the metonymic reduction of the characters to different styles of eyeglasses.

The world of *J R,* then, is characterized by disorder and instability. In Empedocles' terms, it is ruled by Strife, whose function is to separate. Thus, we discover that the human body in *J R* is fragmented, separated into parts, deprived of unity and equilibrium. Language is separated into different forms of discourse, and signs are separated from their referents. Finally, voices are "boxed," disembodied. In fact, *J R* ends with just such a voice: "So I mean listen I got this neat idea hey, you listening? Hey? You listening . . . ?" (726). It is, of course, J R talking on the telephone, and there is an ominous note of excitement in his voice.

Notes

1. William Gaddis, notes for *The Recognitions,* 1945–51, as quoted in Peter W. Koenig, "Recognizing Gaddis' *Recognitions,*" *Contemporary Literature* 16, no. 1 (1975): 67.

2. William Gaddis, *J R* (New York: Alfred A. Knopf, 1975), 20. Subsequent references to this work will be cited parenthetically in the text.

3. Empedocles, fragment 30, trans. Kathleen Freeman, in *Ancilla to the Pre-Socratic Philosophers* (Oxford: Basil Blackwell, 1956), 56. All further references to Empedocles' fragments will be cited parenthetically in the text.

4. Helle Lambridis, *Empedocles: A Philosophical Investigation* (University, Alabama: University of Alabama Press, 1976), 59.

5. Denis O'Brien, *Empedocles' Cosmic Cycle: A Reconstruction From the Fragments and Secondary Sources* (Cambridge: Cambridge University Press, 1969), 101.

6. Ibid., 2.

7. Ibid.

8. William Gaddis, *The Recognitions* (New York: Harcourt, Brace & World, 1955), 299.

9. Michel Foucault, *The Order of Things,* a translation of *Les mots et les choses,* (New York: Vintage, 1973), 36.

9

Disclosing Time
William Gaddis' *J R*

Susan Strehle

In his second novel, *J R*, winner of the National Book Award for 1976, William Gaddis contrasts two different perceptions of time. Most characters in the novel reify time, seeing it as the spatial product of their clocks. Closing off the processual flow of past, present, and future, these characters tell time in disjoined fragments. They inhabit a narrow, atomized present, largely stripped of past memories and future anticipations. Patterned allusions reveal a cultural past reduced to rubble, and scattered references suggest the disintegration of most characters' personal past. Because they try to seal off and forget the past, they also close off the future. Most repeat themselves with neither growth nor change; the sterile circles of their recurrent words and acts roll out of a kind of future, determined beyond change, that is no future. In opposition to his characters, the narrator of *J R* maintains an open relation to time, which he presents as unbroken process. Refusing the narrow measurements by which his characters quantify time, the narrator emphasizes instead its continuous unfolding in open-ended cycles rather than closed circles. In the unified dimension of narrative time, past anticipates future and future proceeds out of past. Set off, then, against the chaotic fragmentation and futile repetition that form the matter of the novel is the unbroken unity of its manner.

The notion of two different and conflicting sorts of time—public and private, objective and subjective, mechanical and psychological—has acquired a prominence in twentieth-century writing from modern philosophy. Henri Bergson's formulation of the dichotomy has shaped recent thinking about time. In *Time and Free Will* (1889), Bergson contrasts spa-

Reprinted from *The Journal of Narrative Technique* 12, no. 1 (Winter 1982):1–14, by permission of the author and publisher.

tialized, successive time of the sort science posits with *durée,* the experienced time of human psychology. While man perceives time both ways, he sees it more vitally as *durée,* which emphasizes interpenetration rather than separation: consciousness assumes the form of duration "when our ego lets itself live."[1] Taking Bergson's ideas further, Martin Heidegger grants absolute priority to experienced time in *Being and Time* (1927), where he argues that the study of being must be grounded in an exploration of time. Providing background that explains Heidegger's position, Georges Poulet traces shifting concepts of time and meaning in his introduction to *Studies in Human Time* (1950). Briefly, the source of meaning for man's existence has changed from a God outside time to a history of public time to the individual's private, experienced time. Thus, human meaning logically attaches, for Bergson and Heidegger, to durational or lived time. In different ways than Bergson, Heidegger also assumes that man may perceive time authentically (as time) and inauthentically (as space). In his late lecture "Time and Being" (1969), Heidegger explains "true time" as an open, continuous unity in which "futural approaching, and the reciprocal relation of both brings about the opening up of openness."[2] When man uses chronometers to measure time as a distance between now-points, he spatializes, divides, and closes off the unified opening of "true time." Hence, for Heidegger, one chooses between "true" and false modes of being when one chooses between experienced time and spatialized, successive time.

As the burgeoning criticism on time in modern fiction attests, the conflict between these two kinds of time informs the structure, techniques, and even the subject matter of recent novels. Critics have identified a common pattern in early twentieth-century novelists' presentations of public and private time: public time occupies the novelist-as-historian, who uses it to provide a framework within which his characters experience private time. In one perceptive study, Theodore Ziolkowski explains, "Objective time is stressed, then, in order to give shape to the narrative. . . . While the author keeps a firm grip on the chronology of public time, the hero is rapidly led into a state in which he experiences a kind of timeless suspension."[3] Similarly, David Higdon asserts, "Public—objective—clock time may indeed have little to do with characters, but it has everything to do with structure."[4] The tension between the two generates meaning, for the public-time form infuses the private-time content with value. In works like *Ulysses, Mrs. Dalloway, The Sound and the Fury, The Trial,* and *The Magic Mountain,* then, characters inhabiting lived time encounter the demands of an external world through the public time that also shapes their stories.

But one other typical feature of the modern novel, the antiheroic protagonist, opens up the possibility of quite the opposite treatment of time. If a novelist wished to suggest, as Bergson and Heidegger have given him license to do, that men may live in false and inauthentic relations to time, he might place his characters in public time. Discussing Spengler's Faustian man, Hans Meyerhoff describes a character who resorts to ceaseless striving to counteract time's inevitable drift toward death. His striving, writes Meyerhoff, "is a way of forgetting time. . . . It enables the individual to live within the dimension of a permanent 'now,' without past or future," embracing the moment while rejecting duration.[5] To emphasize such a character's confinement in public time, the narrator would place himself in private time, thus retaining the juxtaposition by which both views of time take on meaning. In *J R,* Gaddis has used this innovative strategy, inverting the temporal opposition common to early modernist novels in order to present a far bleaker view of character. The figures of *J R* epitomize false relations to time, from which emerge their diseased relations to each other and to themselves. But the narrator, demonstrating an alternative *durée* or true time, tells his characters' story in a manner disclosing the solution to their temporal problems.

To indicate his characters' reification of time, Gaddis fills the novel with clocks that fragment temporal flow. The clocks at the Long Island school sever pieces of time: "The wall clock beyond them dropped its longer hand with a click for the full minute and hung, poised to lop off a fragment of the next."[6] Repeated references to these school clocks underline their splitting motion: they "severed a minute's remnant" (228), "clipped away identical minutes" (174), and "disposed of the hour with a click" (332). The arbitrary divisions made by these clocks close off past and future from the present: "The face all simple purpose across the corridor suffered a tic, reduced the future and extended the past by twenty seconds" (463). Similarly, a clock in the office of a large corporation breaks up the essentially continuous flow of time:

> For time unbroken by looks to the clock the only sound was the chafing of an emery board, and the clock itself, as though seizing the advantage, seemed to accomplish its round with surreptitious leaps forward, knocking whole wedges at once from what remained of the hour. (256)

The narrator refuses to quantify time; he does not say how much time is unbroken but regards time as an undivided "round." For the secretaries beneath this clock, however, time appears in severed wedges because they spatialize it, watching the pie-shaped units that lead to closing time.

While the public clocks break hours efficiently, most of the privately

owned clocks of the novel are themselves broken, reflecting their owners'
maimed notions of time.[7] Thomas Eigen, who sacrifices the large in his
preoccupation with the minute, keeps a broken "clock with one hand pointing the minute" (406). Dan diCephalis, constantly inarticulate, owns "a
clock with a broken chime" that makes futile attempts to declare the hour
throughout the novel (57, 164, 316). Expressing his romantic nostalgia over
his past, Edward Bast's clock runs backwards. While he works out a complicated conversion chart to identify the present hour, his sense of time
remains distorted by his idealized recollections of his childhood. Piles of
boxes obscure the bottom half of another clock, most often glanced at
by Jack Gibbs in the East Ninety-sixth–Street apartment, so that "after
three o'clock nobody knows what time it is till like nine" (552). Appropriate to Gibb's sense of futility, the visible half of the clock bears the legend
"NO DEPOSIT NO RETURN," and the disappearance of the hands in
each reference to it reinforces the suggestion of lost time: smoke drifts
through the room "to climb NO DEPOSIT NO RETURN and fail against
the arc of the clock where the long hand pursued the small, passed it, de-
scended and was gone" (572). This half-clock summarizes the discontinuity and fragmentation in all of the characters' perceptions of time: cut off
from a past that has left no deposit, they envision a future that can bring
no return.

For the central characters of *J R,* the personal past fragments as all relationships that have provided unity and stability disintegrate. Among those
whose marriages break up are Amy Joubert, Jack Gibbs, and Thomas
Eigen. Love relationships dissolve, too, between Rhoda and Schramm, Jack
and Stella, and Terry and Kenny. Parents and children separate. Ann di-
Cephalis abandons her children, Lucien Joubert steals his son away from
Amy, Jack Gibbs and Thomas Eigen lose their children to divorces, and
J R himself appears to live "in a home without, I don't know. Without
grownups I suppose" (246). Most characters find themselves isolated from
all sustaining relationships, like Edward Bast, who loses in various ways
his father, his uncle, his aunts, his cousin Stella, and all of his friends.
Similarly, the inanimate symbols of past unions fall apart. Of the many
collections of fragments in the novel, the most recurrent is a box of ruined
toys that belong to Thomas Eigen's son David; besides a broken crèche
with an armless Virgin who has lost her baby Jesus, the box contains "a
sheep with one leg gone, a red mitten, a broken music box, marionette
in a tangle of strings, car with no wheels, Piglet torn from his base" (406).
These fragments first appear just after Eigen's wife leaves him, taking the
boy, and Eigen moves the broken pieces around through the rest of the
novel (591, 618, 726). When the Bast family disintegrates, the corporation

they have founded comes apart, despite the efforts of Norman Angel "to hold things together here" (144). With all its broken unions, torn paper, split seams and even spilt milk (164), *J R* resembles the postlapsarian world of Humpty Dumpty.

Because they perceive the past as irreparably shattered, Gaddis' characters display an uncommon will to forget. Since honest recollection discloses their failures and, worse, their responsibility for those failures, most characters either distort or obliterate memory. Minor characters like the diCephalises, Davidoff, and Hyde appear to have no past, springing full grown and devoid of memories into the present. The major characters reveal strikingly little about their own past lives; the scant information about them usually comes from other characters. Gibbs, for example, rarely mentions his disastrous marriage, which we learn about from Norman Angel, and the Bast sisters provide our only accurate glimpse of Edward's lonely childhood. What the characters tell others about their past is at best selective, designed to arouse pity and deflect blame; Amy Joubert describes her relation to her ex-husband as "playing against him and helping him win" (488). At worst, they resort to outright lies; claiming to have lived Schramm's past, Gibbs tells his daughter his leg was hurt "fighting the Germans in his tank" (159). Most often, however, they close off and hide the past. So Amy and Gibbs, during an intense affair, never reveal enough about their previous lives to realize that they share concerns over divorces, lost children, and her retarded brother Freddie. In trying to cut off the past from the present, they not only falsify their accounts of themselves but also doom their relationships to each other.

Like the personal past, the cultural past appears reduced to "a heap of broken images" among Gaddis' characters. The vast majority have no cultural heritage at all; the few who do find no meaning in the pieces they accumulate. In the allusive fragments throughout *J R,* art has either been stolen, as a student plagiarizes Emerson's "Brahma" (179), or reduced to the casual bon mot. More than any other character, Jack Gibbs collects and uses disconnected bits of culture. He carries a list of incomplete sentences from Pascal, Taine, Nietzsche, Forster, and others (486) and refers to it on occasion (121, 394). In conversation he steals and twists lines from Eliot's "Prufrock" (282, 284, 390), and from his apparent favorite, Yeats' "To a Friend Whose Work Has Come to Nothing" (131–32, 398, 605). He alludes briefly to Southey (396), Conrad (408, 631), Blake (493), and Hart Crane (621). He fractures lines from Eric Segal: "Love means being able to say you're sorry" (494), and Elizabeth Akers Allen: "Backward turn backward oh time in thy flight, make Tom Mister Grynszpan" (278). In discussing entropy with Eigen, he invites him to "read Wiener on communication" (403); later he appropriates an idea from Norbert Wiener's book, *The Human Use of Human Beings*. Wiener details the "technical difficulties" that prevent the telegraphing of a human being: "To hold an organism stable while part of it is being slowly destroyed . . . involves a lowering of its degree of activity, which in most cases would destroy life in the tissue."[8] Gibbs echoes, "Question of technical difficulties though, run into problems of preserving life in the tissue when you lower the organism's degree of activity to keep it stable" (498).

The references to Wiener establish that Gibbs' name is another ironic allusion to a lost bit of history; Wiener's book begins by describing the importance to modern physics of the virtually unknown Josiah Willard Gibbs (1839–1903). A quiet, unmarried gentleman-scholar who taught at Yale from 1871 until his death, J. W. Gibbs developed a geometrical model of the second law of thermodynamics and broke ground for the twentieth-century physics of contingency and statistical probability.[9] While his contemporary, James Clerk Maxwell, immediately recognized the significance of Gibbs' contributions, Maxwell's early death and Gibbs' own retiring nature left his theories in obscurity until 1920. But according to Wiener, "It is, I am convinced, Gibbs rather than Einstein or Heisenberg or Planck to whom we must attribute the first great revolution of twentieth century physics."[10] In Gaddis' reductive irony, Jack Gibbs teaches physics at an elementary school, exchanges his namesake's quiet earnestness for a manic cynicism, contributes no original theory but instead steals many of his lines, and cannot finish any piece of work. Between J. W. and Jack Gibbs lies the distance between significant wholes and disparate fragments.[11]

The characters' sense of a decimated past appears most clearly in recurrent allusions to cycles that emerge ironically incomplete in the novel. One group of allusions invokes Richard Wagner's *Der Ring des Nibelungen,* a four-part operatic cycle of fall and redemption. The opera begins, of course, with the dwarf Alberich's theft of the Rhinegold, and ends when the ring made from the gold is restored to the Rhinemaidens.[12] In Gaddis' ironic treatment, teachers schedule a performance of the entire *Ring* by elementary and junior high school students. Most characters are familiar with the whole cycle (though Congressman Pecci confuses the first part with Rhinegold beer), but they leave it incomplete. The project goes no further than a rehearsal of scene 1 of "The Rhinegold," during which the Rhinemaidens—crass, uninnocent, and avaricious—insist on having real coins to protect. J R, aptly cast as Alberich, "seemed indeed to know his part, and had got off with the Rhinegold" (36). Thereafter, its producers abandon the opera without staging the restoration of the gold or the redemptive conclusion to the dwarf's fall. This incomplete production of the *Ring* reveals the characters' willingness to cut off the cultural past; that the amputation occurs after the fall but well before the redemption reflects the hopelessness to which their vision of time condemns them.

In another pattern of allusions, Jack Gibbs makes several references to Empedocles, each of which concerns fragmented limbs and monstrous combinations of body parts (45, 161, 406). Gibbs tells Eigen that human life consists of grotesque unions: "Only audience sit through it's Empedocles, shambling creatures with countless hands eyes wandering around looking for a God damned forehead parts joining up all wrong make a hell of a musical" (407). Gibbs refers to only one phase of the cosmic cycle Empedocles proposes. Believing the world is ruled alternatively by love and strife, Empedocles sees cosmic history as a regular cyclical movement between wholeness and disintegration. During the increase of strife, men and women will be torn into pieces: "For a time perhaps they will cling together in monstrous combinations. Then separate limbs will wander disconsolately about the world on the eve of the dissolution of all things" until the increasing power of love reverses the process.[13] Gibbs abandons the cycle before the redemptive countermovement to reunite whole creatures; he fractures the cosmic cycle at the point where life itself is most fragmented.

Other references establish ironic links between Edward Bast and Philoctetes. In the Philoctetes legend, which survives most notably in Sophocles' play, cyclical movement appears in the hero's exile and return, wounding and healing, suffering and redemption.[14] Edward Bast's experiences parallel the first part of this cycle. When his somewhat senile aunts try to remember the year of Edward's birth, they correlate it with his father's composition of an opera version of *Philoctetes* (12). Edward's hand is wounded during his first appearance in the novel (19), as in one version of the myth Philoctetes was wounded in the hand.[15] Edward's abandonment by his comrades, exile from his family, and suffering in isolation resemble the Philoctetes legend; his artistic power promises to echo the archer's. But the parallels turn ironic, and the cycle incomplete, because Bast can accomplish no release from suffering. In place of the compassionate young Neoptolemus, whose loyalty cures and frees Philoctetes, the ruthless J R arrives instead to "help out" Edward. From the island of Manhattan where Edward is marooned, there appears to be no return home; in fact, the last time he goes home, he finds no house on the lot. While the wound from the opening scene heals, Bast gets sicker and more exhausted during the novel until he winds up hospitalized for several weeks near the end. Like the other allusions, the Philoctetes references introduce a cyclical pattern, to break it at the point of suffering and loss.

These allusive patterns operate on two levels, suggesting the two visions of time in *J R*. As fragments, the allusions elaborate the characters' notion of time as public, divisible object; as moments in undivided cycles, they illustrate the narrator's sense of private temporal continuity. The broken cycles recall a statement by Stanley, a character in Gaddis' highly allusive first novel, *The Recognitions:* "That's where the curse is, fragments that don't belong to anything. Separately they don't mean anything, but it's almost impossible to pull them together into a whole."[16] Perceiving the past in just this way, as fragments belonging to nothing, the characters of *J R* abandon cyclical continuity when they forget the original sources of their allusions. But the narrator's distance from his characters also appears in these allusions: Not only *do* the fragments belong, but they belong to originals that treat time as unbroken process, as cyclical "round." As a consequence of the characters' reification of time, they see shards where the narrator evokes unified process.

As they lose both the personal and cultural past by closing off fragments of time, Gaddis' characters also sacrifice the future. So cut off from the past that they can neither learn from it nor change its patterns, they doom themselves to a future that endlessly reiterates the past. In their eternal returns to their own previous words and actions, they enact a profane form of what Mircea Eliade identifies as a "will to devaluate time" by a return to origins, "in illo tempore."[17] Eliade demonstrates that the repetition of archetypal gestures abolishes concrete, historical time and participates in mythical time. But having sealed off mythic archetypes with the rest of the past, Gaddis' characters reiterate only their own empty words and aimless gestures. These repetitions do not liberate from time but rather condemn them to it. Without conveying them to the timelessness of origins, the cycles in which they return to themselves decapitate the future.

On the smallest scale, they repeat endlessly their own empty jargon. While the speakers' names are rarely supplied, their hackneyed phrases, like ironic Wagnerian leitmotifs, identify them. Mr. Hyde reiterates "what America is all about" (25, 27, 38, 179); while Ann diCephalis repeats "more inspiration in one finger . . ."(53, 54, 165). Principal Whiteback has a large collection of vapid phrases, including "in terms of the ongoing situation," "motivating a meaningful experience," and "tangibilitating the full utilization potential," each of which appears dozens of times; John Cates has only one, "hear me," expressed as a command at the end of most of his sentences. The PR man Davidoff forever hires "topflight name" assistants with "two edged swords" to cut "the tip of the iceberg" while he stays "on deck" when "the firebell rings." Miss Flesch's "all that bla bla bla" and

J R's "holy shit" epitomize the meaninglessness of these repeated formulas: seldom have signifiers been so empty.

Perhaps because so many of them have so little new to say, Gaddis' characters also repeat and quote each other. Davidoff hears stockbroker Crawley making a telephone statement to the press (83); later, when his boss asks him to prepare a press release on an entirely unrelated issue, he dictates Crawley's statement (95). Similarly, Hyde talks to Davidoff and later repeats him, word for word, without acknowledgement (217, 222). To justify his rapacious corporate policies, J R quotes Amy Joubert, Cates, and Moncrief at various points. Dan diCephalis has heard his wife's formulas so often that every time she mentions inspiration, he mutters "finger" (53, 54, 165). So too, after innumerable conversations with J R, both Bast and Davidoff lapse at one point into "holy shit" (446, 540). Living in an enclosed, stale world where few characters generate new ideas or words, most find themselves borrowing, stealing, or simply repeating other people's language.

On a larger scale, whole conversations recur throughout the novel. Because most characters cannot solve problems, they talk about them repeatedly: Whiteback juggles the "retreads" or retarded children from room to room, as he explains in almost every scene set in his office (176, 224, 330, 453). Some characters ride hobbyhorses in every appearance: Hyde turns most conversations in the principal's office to his civil defense shelter and its waste-disposal system, while Zona drones about her problems with her maid. Other characters find nothing new to talk about, as Rhoda and Bast discuss the day's mail each evening in the apartment, while Gibbs and Eigen repeatedly exchange the same litany of despair over Schramm's death, their divorces, and their inability to write. Future conversations inevitably follow the same lines as past ones: the old man upstairs with a crippled wife appears to beg for Schramm's apartment five times after Schramm's death, beginning every time, "Hello Mister . . . ?" or "My vife, Mister . . . ?" (285, 372, 379, 563, 588). These patterns of repetition in the barrage of words comprising J R suggest a future, determined beyond change, that is no future.

Like the words they speak, the motions made by Gaddis' characters are circular and repetitive. They travel in treadmill rotations between New York City and Long Island. At one point Gibbs gets off a train on Long Island, meets Amy Joubert in the station, and gets right back on the next train to return to the city with her (475). J R first appears in the novel watching a little girl snap a change purse open and closed, while "his foot returned to forcing back, and forth, and back, the idle vent on a floor grating" (31–

32). Whenever Ann diCephalis arrives home, she repeats the same circular routine: "Foyer, hall, bathroom, foyer, snap, snap, snap, she started the round of turning on lights" (310); whenever her husband arrives, he repeats it in reverse: "diCephalis started a round of turning off lights. Foyer, hall, bathroom, foyer, closet, side door, snap, snap, snap, snap" (55). At the apartment, Rhoda gets into and out of the bathtub while the upstairs neighbors repeatedly bob a piece of gum up and down on the windowsill. Below, the five Puerto Ricans called the cinco Jones move the motorless car that is their clubhouse back and forth across the street (401, 548, 585, 632). Almost all of the characters expend their energy in self-canceling and futile motions, best summed up by the acts of spilling, gathering, and respilling that occur in nearly every scene.[18]

Larger patterns of circular behavior structure the novel, as most characters complete a revolution on the wheel of fortune to end as they began. At home, they run through cycles of marriage, divorce, and remarriage; at work, bust, boom, and bust follow each other in regular alternation. Because they can neither assimilate the past nor transform their relation to it, those characters who have not broken the circle in death have, by the end, reverted to earlier states. Amy Joubert loses and recovers her son, finds and abandons a teaching job, gains and loses an idyllic affair with Gibbs. She divorces one bad husband only to marry a worse, Dick Cutler, of whom she has said, "That would be like, like marrying your issue of six percent preferreds . . ." (214). Amy's retarded brother Freddie escapes from his family's control to enjoy a brief vacation with Gibbs, but as the novel ends, Eigen arranges Freddie's return home. J R begins penniless, makes several million dollars, loses it all and ends, having learned nothing from his experience, ready to begin the whole process again: "So I mean listen I got this neat idea" (726). Most characters compulsively reenact their previous patterns of failure.

These circular and futureless modes of behavior emerge, as I have suggested, from inauthentic relations to time: by denying duration, the characters bury the past and close off any meaningful future. In his two central characters, Gibbs and Bast, Gaddis indicates both the prevalence of circular behavior and its inevitability. Gibbs falls into the common pattern of empty repetition while Bast demonstrates, by exception, the characters' freedom to break the circle. To emphasize the differences between their solutions, Gaddis links the two men with several common problems. Both had lonely childhoods and were neglected by their parents; while Bast's mother died soon after his birth and his father ignored him (65), Gibbs' parents sent him off to a boarding school when he was five because he was "in the way" (247). Both have been infatuated with Stella, the most destructive woman in the book; Gibbs had an affair with her before his marriage, and Bast has idolized her since childhood. Stella preys on the fear of failure both men share. Bast tells her, "You let people try to do something they can't you know all the time they can't you let them try anyhow" (72), and Gibbs explains the results: "Finally realize she's not asking a God damned thing never expected a God damned thing you end up not asking a God damned thing of yourself" (524). Both Bast and Gibbs struggle to write in the squalid, chaotic apartment that metaphorically stands for the larger world of the book; while Bast writes music and Gibbs a study of mechanization of the arts, both similarly try to "hold all these notes together" (287).

Gibbs, however, gives up, just as he has always given up in the past. Unable to create himself, he begins and ends the novel living vicariously through artists who can: Schramm at the start, Schepperman at the end. His clearest chance at a "fresh start," a phrase he uses throughout the novel, arrives in the week he spends with Amy Joubert. Amy provides Gibbs with new clothes, a new belief in his own worth, and a new reason to finish his book. Living in an apartment with no clocks, they follow the natural cycles of various appetites, and Gibbs gains a sense of *durée*. Then she is forced to leave, and they return to public time: "Jack ask them what time it is . . . ?" "What day it is, he muttered" (506). Gibbs' old problems recur with the return to clocks and calendars; he sits in the Ninety-sixth–Street apartment endlessly revising old sentences, unable to make sense of the fragments of old notes or to write anything new. He blames his failure on the frequent interruptions, just as he has blamed his wife, his parents, Stella, and others for earlier failures. Unwilling to confront it honestly, he leaves his past in the same state he leaves his book: scattered fragments about which he tells himself comforting lies. Because he can expose neither his failures nor his excuses to Amy, he must also sacrifice his hopes for a future with her. When she calls, he pretends to be a servant, telling her that Gibbs has cleared "out to a place yonder call Burmesquik set him up a little factory there" (725). Referring to one of Mozart's scatological letters to his cousin, quoted earlier by Bast, about a "village called Burmesquik where the crooked areseholes are manufactured" (42),[19] Gibbs defines the sort of future left to him. As the novel ends, Gibbs sits in Schramm's apartment reading to Schepperman, appropriately making no progress at all: "been on page thirty-five for two hours" (724).

In contrast, Edward Bast breaks out of the circle; he recovers his past, rejects the myths he has made of it, and thus leaves off repeating it. Stella clears his way toward a more realistic understanding of his parents when she tells him his father refused to marry his mother for fear she would disrupt his work, and his mother committed suicide. Suggesting that his father made the same mistakes as he has, this information deflates the idol Bast has constructed. Bast also understands, finally, that Stella destroyed his studio in her search for papers that would give her control of the estate; seeing her clearly for the first time, he rejects her. But his most significant liberation occurs when Bast discovers that he does not have to compose to prove anything to his father or to himself. Released from clock time into lived time in the hospital, he replaces his earlier belief that he has value only if he composes with a new awareness that his music has worth because he composed it:

> —I always thought I had to write music all of a sudden I thought what if I don't, maybe I don't have to I'd never thought of that maybe I don't! [. . .] I've been thinking of things you've said as though just, just doing what's there to be done as though it's worth doing. (687)

To this point, Bast has written music out of unquestioning obedience to his father's past demands; at the end, however, he chooses to compose out of a desire to fulfill his own present promise, to use his talent in the service of something worth doing. By accepting his present in the context of a past seen whole, Bast escapes the failure around him and sets off to "do what you have to" (725). He gains an authentic future by ceasing to strive in public time, by beginning to inhabit the open continuity of private time.

In his growth at the end, Bast breaks through to the vision of time that the narrator has suggested all along: an experienced time unified, linked, and continuous. The novel uses a conventional linear chronology in an unconventional way: the narrator neither divides nor spatializes successive time as his characters do but treats it as flowing process. With chronology, he suggests that the past shapes the future and illuminates continuous temporal links between separate incidents; so J R hires the cheapest assistants he can buy, ignores their incompetence, and witnesses the collapse of his corporation. This approach to time underscores its open unfolding. But the narrator disrupts the spatial succession commonly associated with chronological time, so that locations, speakers, and topics of conversation often change radically from one page to the next. The narrative follows a character from one location to another, leaps through television lines between the principal's office and the classrooms, and jumps telephone wires between various places. In one instance, Cates and Beaton have been talking in the offices of Typhon International; Beaton places a call to Crawley, makes and loses the connection, and the narrative continues with a conversation between Crawley and Bast at the other end of the line (437). By conjoining chaotic spatial leaps and continuous temporal flow, the narrator insists on time's fundamental difference from space: that is, unlike his characters, he refuses to reify time.

To emphasize the unified process of time, Gaddis rejects conventional forms of narrative divisions. Without chapters, sections, or even open spaces in the text, the two months spanned in the book flow unbroken. Moreover, the uneventful times normally omitted between narrative sections appear in *J R*. The narrator skips no days, though he treats them at different lengths; the first occupies seventy-five pages, while the others pass in a paragraph. At the diCephalis home, one Sunday appears as follows:

> Morning made a tentative approach as though uncertain what it might discover. [. . .] [D]oors banged, the toilet held a round of flushing, smoke rising from the toaster lay a blue pall down the hall and the morning still lingering outside appeared to have decided to stay there, dwindling to the gray of afternoon. [. . .] and finally the gray yielded to dark. (316)

This brief day, in which nothing of importance occurs, appears in the novel to connect Saturday to Monday. Even the hours of the day blend, with the "tentative approach" of morning "dwindling" to afternoon, which "yielded" to dark. Refusing to break up the text, the time within it, or the individual days of that period, the narrator of *J R* unfolds a continuous passage of time.

The narrator also sweeps aside the artificial divisions with which the characters reify and measure time. For all of the concern with clocks and calendars expressed in it, the novel is not fixed by either. We never learn in what year the events take place; we may guess at the months, but none are named. Only one partial date appears; J R visits the Ninety-sixth–Street apartment on presumably, 21 November (531). Because days of the week bring recurrent events, even the sporadic mention of the day fails to place the narrative in specific time. Every Thursday Gibbs has visitation rights with his daughter and usually misses the visit, and every Friday many of the characters who live on Long Island travel in to New York. Moreover, despite all the clock-watching that goes on in the novel, we are never told what time it is. The narrator defines the relative position of the hands but withholds absolute readings: "The long hand crept from NO DEPOSIT, passed the short, the second hand swept past them both to NO RETURN, reappeared and was gone" (573). While characters look to their clocks to fix a precise fragment of present time, the narrator watches instead the unending round of the hands.

In place of clock and calendar time, the narrator substitutes the natural cycles of seasonal and solar time. *J R* begins in early autumn, with a glimpse of leaves "becomingly streaked blood-red for fall" (17); it ends as winter sets in, with repeated references to dead leaves blowing in the wind. Solar cycles locate the progressive days of the season, as the narrator observes the regular alternation of light and dark. One day passes behind a closed door with "sunlight crossing the room, leaving it behind in shadow, in darkness" (496); one night arrives with the wind "blowing off the day and finally letting the darkness settle, and damp, for day to return like a rumor of day and lurk in the sky unable to break" (231). These natural cycles reveal time's open-endedness. Although the novel begins and ends amid the dying of life in the fall, the very emphasis on seasonal time points to the unending process in which fall, winter, spring, and summer revolve. The cyclical alternation of day and night in the novel reinforces its presentation of time as eternally open process.

With his treatment of narrative time, Gaddis suggests solutions to his characters' temporal problems. Perceiving time as fragmented object, the characters sever a limited present from a lost past and deny their ability to change; seeing time as unified process, the narrator uncovers their freedom. While the characters illustrate a determined relation to time with the closed circles of their reiterated behavior, the narrator creates an open continuity with the natural cycles that pattern the progressive movement of time. The characters narrow their present by the precise divisions with which they measure it; the narrator expands the present by linking it with open-ended flow. In one of the most remarkable achievements of *J R,* Gaddis resolves his characters' inauthentic and futureless relations to public time with an open, continuous, private disclosing time.

Its use of a private narrative time accounts in part for the difficulty that threatens to make *J R* one of the great underread novels of our times. The novel's other challenging features — its paring away of description and narrative transition to focus almost exclusively on spoken words; its depiction of a characteristically banal level of language; its inclusion of what Bartheleme's dwarfs call "sludge" or "stuffing," words and scenes that fill in between others; its failure to place conversations and characters for the reader — relate to its treatment of time: they emerge from the narrator's refusal to coerce, to editorialize, to elevate, to channel his material into public structures or to command his meaning into logical forms. In thus redefining the narrator's role, Gaddis at once departs from the standards of early moderns like Joyce and Faulkner and opens up a new measure for postmodern art. The moderns aimed, finally, to defeat time: to negate the private-time experience and the public-time frame by absorbing both in a timeless realm of aesthetic suspension. That Bloomsday is 16 June, that Molly's infidelity occurs at 4:32, that Quentin commits suicide on 2 June 1910, that Gregor Samsa wakes at 6:30—on the one hand, these locate the personal epiphany in the public domain of clocks and calendars, but on the other, they suggest that any moment in either kind of time is properly subsumed in an eternal, timeless unity. Gaddis, by contrast, celebrates time. For him, the moment is subsumed in or united with only ongoing time, which cannot be escaped or transcended. In time, Gaddis discloses an authentic site for consciousness and original possibilities for the novel.

Notes

1. Henri Bergson, *Time and Free Will,* trans. F. L. Pogson (New York: Macmillan, 1910), 100. For the influence of Bergson and Proust on literature, see Margaret Church, *Time and Reality: Studies in Contemporary Fiction* (Chapel Hill: University of North Carolina Press, 1963).

2. Martin Heidegger, *On Time and Being,* trans. Joan Stambaugh (New York: Harper Colophon, 1972), 15.

3. Theodore Ziolkowski, *Dimensions of the Modern Novel* (Princeton: Princeton University Press, 1969), 202–3.

4. David Leon Higdon, *Time and English Fiction* (London: Macmillan, 1977), 3.

5. Hans Meyeroff, *Time in Literature* (Berkeley: University of California Press, 1955), 70.

6. William Gaddis, *J R* (New York: Alfred A. Knopf, 1975), 31. Subsequent references to this work will be cited parenthetically in the text.

7. Ziolkowski notes that in modern novels, clocks are summoned "as a negative symbol by the subjective consciousness of an individual who wishes to assert his own private time against the claims of public time. Clocks in modern literature seem to exist only to be ignored, dropped, shattered, deformed, or improved upon" (*Dimensions,* 188). In Gaddis' novel, by contrast, characters break their clocks but never ignore them. Lacking any private time to assert, these characters cannot improve upon but only mirror the deformed state of their chronometers.

8. Norbert Wiener, *The Human Use of Human Beings,* rev. ed. (1950; reprint, Garden City, N. Y.: Doubleday, 1954), 103–4.

9. Useful accounts of Gibbs' life and accomplishments can be found in Raymond J. Seeger, *J. Williard Gibbs* (Oxford: Pergamon, 1974), and J. G. Crowther, *Famous American Men of Science* (New York: Norton, 1937), 227–97.

10. Wiener, *Human Use,* 10.

11. Many of Gaddis' names are ironic allusions and puns: Mr. Hyde has no kindly Jekyll side, Skinner removes women's clothes, accident-prone Schramm bears several scars, and so on. Edward Bast apparently owes nothing to Forster's Leonard Bast but turns out to be illegitimate.

12. For a discussion of cyclical elements in the *Ring,* see Robert Donington, *Wagner's "Ring" and its Symbols* (New York: St. Martin's Press, 1963), 263–64.

13. D. O'Brien, *Empedocles' Cosmic Cycle* (Cambridge: Cambridge University Press, 1969), 2.

14. Edmund Wilson discusses these cyclical movements in *The Wound and the Bow* (Cambridge, Mass.: Riverside, 1941), 272–95.

15. In Theodectes' play, Philoctetes is wounded in the hand; see R. C. Jebb, *Sophocles: The Plays and Fragments* (Cambridge: Cambridge University Press, 1898), xxxi.

16. William Gaddis, *The Recognitions* (1955; reprint, New York: Avon Books, 1974), 658.

17. Mircea Eliade, *The Myth of the Eternal Return,* trans. Willard R. Trask (Princeton: Princeton University Press, 1954), 85.

18. The repeated pattern of spilling, as it illuminates Gaddis' interest in entropy, is treated in my article "'For a Very Small Audience': The Fiction of William Gaddis," *Critique* 19, no. 3 (1978): 61–73.

19. The translation is not Bast's but that of A. Hyatt King and Monica Carolan, *Letters of Mozart and His Family,* 2d ed. (New York: St. Martin's Press, 1966), 1:499–501.

10

Art as Redemption of Trash
Bast and Friends in Gaddis' *J R*

Johan Thielemans

When *J R*, the massive second novel by William Gaddis, was published in 1975, its central anecdote about a sixth-grade boy as financial wizard attracted most attention. Understandably so, as the plot was witty, seemingly farfetched, and not without relevance to the daily dealings at the heart of an American, capitalist society. In short, Gaddis revealed that the financial maneuvers on the stock market are well within the reach of a boy of twelve. The deeper irony of the novel seemed to escape most critics when they failed to note that J R's mentality recurred with the adult bankers and company directors of Wall Street. Gaddis implies that the capitalist system of buying and selling, disregarding any moral or human consequence, can function only when its participants possess the blind enthusiasm of a bright child. The character of J R is neatly counterbalanced by that of the businessman Cates, who sums up the argument in these terms: "It buys something or it don't buy it what the devil you think a market economy's all about."[1] Gaddis argues, however, that our human activity cannot be reduced to its value of exchange. In this respect, the novel is a head-on attack on several basic American myths.

The critique of the system is carefully articulated in a complex dialectical structure in which two terms are constantly seen to be in opposition: money and art. The reality of *J R*, that of crass materialism and blind financial speculation, contrasts sharply with the ideals and the pursuits of a group of artists, who have an enormous need for love, for being accepted. This causes a painful dilemma. The artist creates in order to be recognized by kindred souls. The society knows only how to express its appreciation

Published here, with changes, from a longer version of a lecture given at the Second American Literature Symposium in Warsaw, Poland, during June 1980, by permission of the author.

by way of money, so this appreciation is devalued. Consequently, true appreciation becomes impossible and the artist has to live with the feeling of being rejected. In the novel's exploration of several questions relating to the meaning of art, the value of the artist's life, and the influence of money upon creative activity, the reader recognizes to what extent *J R* is a further development of themes already present in the earlier *Recognitions* (1955).

The basic dichotomy at the heart of the novel can be described in at least three ways. First, we could reduce the book to a study of the elements that shape the values of life in contemporary America. In other words, we could see the book as a study of the nefarious influence of money, and the fact that *Money* is the first word in the text might encourage the reader to do so. Money is a force that prevents people from being kind, sensitive, and fully integrated. Those who possess it are revealed to be permanently maimed psychologically, and those who have to do without it are painfully aware of the fact that in the given social context only money is able to create a space of freedom in which an individual may fully develop his personality. This explains the horror and attraction it exerts. The drift of Gaddis' argument is clear: money is a curse. Ideally, we should be able to do away with it. In this respect, his rejection and his hatred have echoes that reach back both to left-wing and right-wing traditions, as such a radical position can be found both in such Marxist authors as William Morris and in fascist sympathizers such as Ezra Pound.

A second approach would suggest a formulation of the problem in terms of the struggle between mind and matter. Spiritual values are seen to be present in art, but for these values there is no organic place in present-day society. This implies a struggle that may cost lives, and the victims are always on the side of the creative minds. Material interests cheapen artistic intentions, and, although artists cannot do without some form of money in order not only to survive but also to create, they always have to pay a heavy price any time they come into contact with it. No wonder that they all dream of a world where money would not be the central mover and touchstone of all human activities! It appears that only a rigorously moral abnegation makes it possible to escape from money's alluring but deadly embrace.

Though in a different context such ideas might have a politically mobilizing effect, they lose any such quality by being inserted into a third argument that clearly has postmodern echoes. The fight between art and money, between the artist and the values of capitalism, is transposed into a vaster, grander scheme: that of the opposition between order and chaos. Money creates an ever greater degree of the latter. Gaddis chooses as model the conflict between information and noise from communication theory.[2] Order promises a form of humane life, but, as everything is governed by entropy—of which money is the main instrument—order fails to materialize. It is within this ineluctable context of inescapable deterioration that artists wage a losing battle, which, nevertheless, is sometimes crowned by victories. These occur when a work of art is seen to escape from the fatal cycle. Works of art are messages from a different dimension of reality. Their status seems to be that of perfection, a quality that manifests itself only in the work of art and that has quasi-Neoplatonic overtones. Whenever a work of art manifests an inner vision, all the misery, disorder, and trash on the level of everyday life are transcended. They receive a justification and at the same time become tolerable, as it is now revealed that they are but a screen behind which the sublime hides. To get beyond the screen is a crowning achievement. At the end of the book, the alchemical nature of the process is described when the author Thomas Eigen looks without comprehension at the score young Edward Bast has feverishly written:

—And some papers, I put down some papers when I . . .
—Well Christ what do they look like.
—They don't look like anything Mister Eigen, just a lot of papers with crayon . . .
—Wait look under the, those?
—Yes, yes here they are look. They don't really look like anything do they.
—Yes fine, now . . .
—A lot of, like a lot of chickentracks don't they, look. I mean it's all still just what I hear there isn't it.
—Fine yes! now . . .
—I mean until a performer hears what I hear and can make other people hear what he hears it's just trash isn't it Mister Eigen, it's just trash like everything in this place everything you and Mister Gibbs and Mister Schramm all of you saw here it's just trash! (725)

One pressing question is whether both the making of art and the sensibility for artistic communication guarantee in any way a life that is more fulfilling, satisfying, or, in short, happier. If the artist's role is seen to be so important in the scheme of things, there must be a temptation to idealize him and to present him under an idolatrous light reminiscent of certain nineteenth-century conceptions. Although nowhere in the book is this explicitly stated, it is nevertheless clear that the many plots involving artists are explorations of this theme. Their lives are tormented as they are imprisoned in the tension between total failure and equally total success. It is this basic uncertainty about the final result of artistic activity that condemns the ambitious artist to the status of a failure till eventually he is able to prove that his personal obsessions were worthy of attention after all. But before he has reached this point, his life is miserable indeed, and the artist feels crushed under his superego.

In order to see more precisely how Gaddis confronts his readers with his conceptions, we should now turn to the text and describe the different types of artists in *J R*. Each of them is, as it were, part of the answer to the question about the value of art and artist.[3]

Given the rules by which the world is governed, given the judgments in that world according to which something is perceived to be valuable, it will be obvious that for Gaddis the true artist is the supremely useless human being, as his activities occur in a field that is beyond the reach of money. The value of a perfect work of art cannot be expressed by a price, so much so that in a world governed by the market it becomes an absurd concept. But the relation between the world of art and the world of the market is a dynamic one, and at each and every moment the money world tries to find a function for the artist and his work. It tries to turn him from someone useless into someone useful. Once the artist allows himself to be used in this way, his activities can be rewarded by money. If the artist gives in to the temptation, however, he discovers it is always detrimental to his talent. On this point Gaddis espouses a conservative view whereby the primacy of high culture is undisputed and the occasional excellence of aesthetic objects produced within a commercial context is not even taken into consideration.

Before dealing with each of the different artists, I should point out that, as a group, they cover a wide range of activities: there is a composer, a painter, and a number of authors. They have in common an awareness of being failures. They all feel rejected by the world, which may take the form of parents, spouses, children, or lovers. Without exception, they behave clumsily, which makes their lives into a constant battle against objects.

Composers, as readers of *The Recognitions* know, are members of a special category of artists. In *J R* that category is represented by Edward Bast, a young man who belongs to a family of musicians, composers, and businessmen. James Bast, his uncle, presumably,[4] is a fêted conductor who wrote an excellent opera, *Philoctetes*. Edward wants to compose too, but shy and impractical as he is, he is not sure about his own talent. Nevertheless, he has plans for a major opera, but later changes to an oratorio, and finally thinks of a suite for small orchestra, these different projects showing his dwindling ambitions. Edward's ideal is to make a nonexistent world come into existence. When he comments on Wagner, the composer he most admires, he refuses to accept the fact that Wagner asked the audience to suspend its belief. For him, Wagner did something of a totally different nature:

> — No not asking them making them, like that E flat chord that opens the Rhinegold goes on and on it goes on for a hundred and thirty-six bars until the idea that everything's happening under water is more real than sitting in a hot plush seat with tight shoes on and . . . (111)

The claim is an ambitious one and it is only possible for Bast to labor at his ideal in a secluded place where he works and "nothing else happens." Music, he says, is not just another form of work, not merely writing down notes, not part "of all that out there" (69). It is a reality separate from the world. Again he refers to Wagner, who could not compose if his eyes wandered: "He couldn't concentrate if he looked out and let his eyes follow the garden paths because they led to an outside world" (116). The adventures of Bast are all concerned with finding such a secluded place. At the beginning of the book, he has it: a studio adjacent to the house of his aunts. But as the whole area where they live is redeveloped, the house is to be taken down. The studio itself is converted into a clubhouse for teenagers. Bast's search for a place suitable to a recluse is one of the structural elements of the novel.

The second major problem Bast is confronted with is of a financial nature. His family firm faces a severe crisis and it obliges Bast to make a living for himself. As long as he tries to marry business and art, he is not very successful. He tries to get into a school, but his first lesson on closed-circuit television about Mozart is a total failure. He cannot join a musician's union because he cannot prove that he is a concert pianist, the tests being too difficult. Later he meets a number of people who want to enlist his services: He is asked to write ballet music by some dancers but doesn't get paid, as the dancers are fired. He is asked to write some background music, which he calls "some nothing music" (112), for television, but his music is too intrusive for background music. He is asked to provide music for a documentary on zebras. He writes music for a foundation grant procured by J R. He even consents to listen to the radio and to note down the titles of the songs played for checking royalties. The basic irony of this seemingly desperate search for money is that he could get all the money he needs through a simple legal action, claiming part of the estate of Thomas Bast, his legal father, who has just died when the novel begins. One piece of paper—a birth certificate—is all he needs.

In this respect, Bast, who, according to the female characters in the book, is "a boy with a lot of romantic ideas about himself" (148), is clearly an

example of the unadapted artist, out of touch with the realities of the world.
But Gaddis has composed a book too full of ironies and paradoxes to leave
Bast such a simple case. We should not forget that Bast issues from a family in which art and business are equally well represented. His business
experience is put to good use by the boy J R, whom Bast, in his capacity
of teacher, first meets at school. J R is attracted by the forlorn and helpless
young teacher and tries to help him out financially. Bast gradually becomes
J R's business associate, the official representative of the corporation, J R
being too young and too small ever to appear in person at any board
meeting or business conference. Bast is so good at his job that it is even
suspected that he may have more talent for business than for art. We have
seen that Bast is not exactly a good-for-nothing in a hostile world, as a
traditional vision of the artist would have it. He possesses many talents,
both musical and extramusical, that could secure him a respected career.
But Bast ultimately refuses to join the world. We should remember that
his presumed uncle's opera is called *Philoctetes* after the Greek hero who
did not want to leave his uninhabited island but who was lured away from
it by the deceitful Ulysses. In the same way, Edward Bast is constantly
tempted away from his main project, and the whole plot is moved by the
fact that he both refuses to abandon that project and partly gives in to
the pressures of the world. He never makes firm decisions but is always
a pawn in somebody else's game.

When he finally gets his much-wanted seclusion, it is thrust upon him
by circumstances. After a period of lack of sleep and undernourishment,
he is suffering from pneumonia and is taken to the hospital, where he finds
the necessary quiet to work at his major opus. It is at this seemingly blessed
moment that Gaddis makes Bast face the ultimate question of the validity
of his pure, uncontaminated, artistic labor. Bast's roommate, a Mister Duncan from a failed publishing firm, is a compulsive talker. To Bast, he becomes a father substitute and it is through him that Bast is forced to face
the possibility that his artistic ambition is a ludicrous pursuit. His artistic
activity loses its uniqueness and becomes one of the many human undertakings. He says:

> —I was thinking there's so much that's not worth doing suddenly I thought
> maybe I'll never do anything. That's what scared me I always thought I'd
> be, this music I always thought I had to write music all of a sudden I thought
> what if I don't, maybe I don't have to I'd never thought of that maybe I don't!
> I mean maybe that's what's been wrong with everything maybe that's why
> I've made such a, why I've been thinking of things you've said as though
> just, just doing what's there to be done as though it's worth doing or you

never would have done anything you wouldn't be anybody would you, you wouldn't even be who you are now. (687)

In this monologue, Bast reflects for the first time on his actions and sees them in a larger context, beyond the limits of the purely artistic. In fact, the question that is raised concerns the meaning and importance of any human action. The obsession to make a work of art, the compulsion to excel at one self-chosen activity, is suddenly seen as futile. It is the point where everything becomes devoid of sense. It is a point of absolute zero, where the preference of action over inaction loses its relevance. Once this terrifying absolute is introduced, there is no real convincing argument offered to refute it. This insight is not necessarily a tragic or destructive one. For Bast, in fact, it comes as a relief. He even considers for a moment abandoning his compositional work, but the next moment he takes it up again, still pursuing that dream of communicating his inner vision.

As much tortured by his artistic ambitions as Bast is Jack Gibbs, the failed but lucid author. As a young man he works for the General Roll Company, a firm belonging to Thomas Bast, who started a business making player pianos. Gibbs falls in love with Stella, the fascinating, witchlike daughter of the boss, but he is rejected in favor of Norman Angel, who, in exchange for the attractive young lady, will invest his capital in the firm. Thereupon, Gibbs leaves and decides to devote all his time to the writing of a novel "about random patterns and mechanizing" (147). The writing, though, proves such an ordeal that he abandons it and takes to drinking. He marries, has a daughter, gets divorced, and is thoroughly unhappy, as his wife not only tries to make him pay as much as she can but also makes it very difficult for him to see his daughter at regular intervals. In order to make a living, Gibbs teaches physics at J R's school and continually upsets his superiors. He is, from their narrow, bourgeois point of view, a true subversive and a dangerous radical. Eventually, they decide to sack him, which ironically becomes a pointless gesture as Gibbs wins at the races so that he can abandon his job without regrets. He has a new love affair with a young teacher at his school, Amy Joubert, and his idyllic week at her apartment in New York gives him all the strength and courage needed to start working again on his sixteen-year-old project. When he goes back to his old manuscript, he gets terribly depressed. He finds the text totally unsatisfactory and he has the feeling that his ideas have become outdated. At the same time, he feels paralyzed by the fact that he may fail while doing the best he can. As he is steeped in culture, he lives by quoting or misquoting other people. Also, his book, of which we are offered the opening paragraphs, is in many ways a repetition of things thought and said else-

where. For a moment, we touch once more upon the fascinating and daunt-
ing problem of originality, which was at the core of *The Recognitions*.

Jack Gibbs is a tormented human being, feeling that he has not a right-
ful place in the world. His parents did not accept him and sent him off
to a boarding school to get rid of him. He has never grown up and keeps
acting like an unruly child. Making a nuisance of himself is his preferred
form of protest. He divides human beings into two categories: the excellent and the despicable. He proclaims the excellence of artists and thinkers. Many of these belong, remarkably enough, to the German tradition,
as his idols are Wagner, Mozart, Beethoven, Goethe, and Broch. He is fascinated by the urge for destruction that haunted so many creative people,
Van Gogh cutting his ear off being the outstanding example. He has a
spontaneous feeling of solidarity with fellow artists. He tries to prevent
the suicide of Schramm, another failed author; he takes care of Freddie,
Amy Joubert's retarded brother whom he met at boarding school, and who
has the redeeming quality of being moved to tears by hearing music. This
makes Freddie a member of that despised band of sensitive human beings.
Gibbs subscribes to the motto: "The better among us bear one another
in mind (290)"—words stemming from Beethoven's correspondence.

Of course, this implies a radical and dangerous dichotomy, as those who
do not belong to the select group come in for total disdain. Gibbs blames
his former wife but is blind to his own shortcomings: He constantly voices
his concern about his daughter, but he always forgets the day on which
he is supposed to meet her. He is unfair toward the lawyers trying to settle
the Schramm estate. He is unnecessarily rude toward the police officers
coming to investigate Schramm's suicide. His aversion toward the members of the school board, on the other hand, seems fully justified. But it
goes without saying that Gaddis makes Gibbs into an irritating character
both for the other characters of the book and for the reader.

There is one test of humanity in which both Gibbs and Bast fail completely. They both meet J R, the twelve-year-old boy who in many respects
is similar to Gibbs: J R has no father and little contact with his mother.
The similarity is externally stressed by the fact that they both have the
same trouble with their clothes. J R is eager to learn and is always ready
to help other people out. The women teachers at the school recognize his
special qualities and find him very touching. Gibbs and Bast, the artists,
however, despise him. For Gibbs, J R is an intruder. This negative assessment rests on the simple fact that he proves to be immune to music. But
that is highly questionable and much more of a judgment on the narrowness of mind and lack of human feeling on the part of the artists.

Gibbs is engaged in a risky wager. All his misbehavior, he assumes, will be transcended at the moment when he finally delivers the goods: a major contribution to the field of literature. But in this respect Gibbs fails to prove his excellence. He is inhibited by the examples set by his admired predecessors. The possibility that his own writing may not be of the same standard as that of the models paralyzes him and makes it very difficult for him to go on "trying to believe something's worth doing long enough to get it done . . ." (492). And suppose that the best we can do is not good enough, what is left? One of the ways out may be suicide, the ultimate, senseless destruction.

Another failed author, Schramm, is driven to this desperate act. He is the son of a well-to-do industrialist, but his father is opposed to the idea of his son being an artist: he "thought writing was for sissies" (246). During the Second World War, Schramm took part in the battle of the Ardennes. At Saint Fiacre, he held out against the German tanks, as his general had overlooked ordering him to retreat. His action, which was a military mistake, caused a decisive change in the odds and later he was decorated for his act of supposed bravery. But Schramm is greatly tormented by the idea that the general played God to his Faust, making bets on his chances to win. Obsessed by the war, he wants to write a book about his experiences, but he fails to do so. Though he is very good at advising other artists on their problems, and at one point even sees fit to help Bast out of a musical impasse, his own shortcomings overwhelm him and he commits suicide.

The exact motive of Schramm's deed remains obscure: It may be that he couldn't face his artistic failure any longer, the gap Tolstoy mentioned that exists between what one feels and what one can do. Or it could be the lack of productivity that killed him, the fact that he kept being obsessed by words but was unable to commit anything to paper. "Same God damned words," Jack Gibbs says, "waiting for him only thing to do get rid of the God damned container for the thing contained" (283). Perhaps it is a case of jealousy, as his friend Eigen would rather believe. Or it may also be a case of a doomed and unconsummated love for his stepmother, who is younger than he. Finally, there is the more romantic explanation of Schramm imitating his much-admired Hart Crane.

The list of possibilities is revealing, as it consists of the main problems treated in the novel: artistic inadequacy, the tortuous relation between parents and children, the need for acceptance and respect, the lack of understanding between loving partners, and the temptation to prolong the destructive tradition that has manifested itself in so many artists' lives.

In a wider context, Schramm's untimely death is not useless, for it triggers a series of actions. His ambition to turn his war experiences into a meaningful statement is partly realized by Jack Gibbs, who selects for his gravestone in Arlington the following epitaph: "Es ruht im Feindesland," causing a wave of scandal as a newspaper "called the epitaph a desecration to all who fought and lie buried in these hallowed . . ." (724), and partly by Tom Eigen who, after falling in love with Schramm's widow, decides to write a novel about his friend's experiences.

From this we learn that Eigen's story has a happy ending, but his character is too important to be left at that.[5] Eigen wrote a novel, which, after he put in seven years of hard work, only managed to appeal to a minority audience. He started to work on a play, which remained unfinished. In order to support his wife and son, he joined a firm as company writer. In the meantime, he has been plagued by the unfinished work. In the process, his wife loses her respect for him and, being unable to face the idea that he spends so many fruitless hours in his room, decides to leave him. Although for Eigen this is a painful crisis, it allows him to change his life drastically: he quits the commercial job and starts writing with the feeling that he has come out of a long illness. After his friend Schramm's suicide, Eigen meets the latter's wife and begins to write, full of hope, on a new project that he borrowed from Schramm, illustrating one of the ironic propositions in the book that if the subject matter is too close and personal, it is unfit for a work of art, though, of course, *J R* may be read as distorted mirror reflections of incidents and problems from Gaddis' own life.

To complete this gallery, we should briefly mention the painter, Schepperman. He suffers, in contrast to the previous characters, from too much money: a wealthy patroness, Zona Cates, pays him a monthly fee in exchange for all the works he paints. While Schepperman, an abstract impressionist, thinks of his canvases as statements, Zona Cates is interested only in their speculative value and locks them away. Schepperman runs riot after a while and hides in a small room on Ninety-sixth Street, where he finishes a portrait, the most beautiful work he has ever made. Unfortunately, this proved possible only by imprisoning the model in the room. When the model, an old man, breaks out, plaster in the wet paint damages the painting and Schepperman is calmed down by Jack Gibbs reading from Broch's *Sleepwalkers,* another major novel about the decline of values in the modern world.

In Schepperman we have an example of the creative artist who is cheated out of his contribution by speculators. In this, he illustrates the difficult position of the visual artist in present-day America. Nevertheless, he remains capable of producing a perfect work of art. As we have seen, artistic perfection represents the only possible escape from entropic processes. Gaddis' vision, though, is of a deeply ironic pessimism, and that is why he arranges for the perfect canvas to be damaged. He makes several points with this one incident: he shows that it is possible to catch a moment of perfection and to preserve it, a painting being the ultimate triumph over the chaos that is the very substance of life. Unfortunately, the record of that perfection is an object, and as such it must return to the process of deterioration.

The artists in *J R* consider themselves to be of a special kind, as they think themselves more intelligent and sensitive than the common human being. In many respects, their opinion finds support in the surrounding world, which is full of the stupidity, crassness, and greed of the business-man, the banker, the school administrator, and the politician. But whether the awareness of the higher values that express themselves in art guarantee a more harmonious humanity is a position clearly rejected by the author. Fundamental insights into the value of life are discovered by people be-longing to the categories despised by the artists. Wisdom can be learned from a purely commercial publisher such as Mister Duncan or from a vul-gar, uneducated girl such as Rhoda. She wants to succeed; her ambition is to become a famous photographic model. When she finally manages to make this come true, she recognizes in the same lucid way as do the artists how futile her enterprise is. Rhoda concludes that she has stum-bled upon a theme for a novel. Her lucidity is dialectically related to the lucidity of Edward Bast, but hers destroys the pretension of the artist to be unique and to have access to insights outside the reach of the com-mon man.

J R argues that works of art are and remain important despite the im-probable and petty lives of their creators, which clearly articulates Gaddis' conviction that the life of the artist in no way enhances the work of art. Since the novel testifies to so much care, professional pride, and artistic devotion on the part of its maker, its very existence proves that whatever the doubts they have not overcome the author's belief in the ultimate value of his own work.

Notes

1. William Gaddis, *J R* (New York: Alfred A. Knopf, 1975), 696. Subsequent references to this work will be cited parenthetically in the text.

2. Johan Thielemans, "Gaddis and the Novel of Entropy," TREMA [Travaux et Recherches sur le Monde Anglophone] no. 2 (1977): 97–107.

3. It may be necessary to remind the reader of the form of the book: It is written as a long series of dialogues. On the surface, it is of an uncommon complexity, and the reader has to work on the text before it opens itself to him. This means that what is obvious and possibly less interesting in a traditional novel, namely the fabula, becomes in this instance one of the secrets the reader has to unravel. For the reader, plots have to be deducted from oblique information. He can proceed only by reference and cross-reference. Of course, in this respect the book is not unique, and any reader of William Faulkner will be familiar with the pleasure and the occasional frustration that are part and parcel of the reading activity whenever an author invites his reader to become a cognitive detective. What follows is then not only a simple summary of some plots in the book, but the result of tenacious reading and hard thinking.

4. There are many indications suggesting that James in fact fathered Edward.

5. The biography of Eigen is particularly interesting because Gaddis wove so many autobiographical elements into it.

11

Paper Currencies
Reading William Gaddis

STEVEN WEISENBURGER

I have come to debase the coinage.
—Diogenes of Sinope

Borges tells the *ficción* of Pierre Menard, a modernist writer who poured himself into so much of *Don Quijote,* its lore, and its time, that he produced a verbatim duplicate of the Cervantes text.

And yet such a feat of appropriation can be done without Menard's long years of scholarship. One of the minor eccentrics in William Gaddis' *The Recognitions* scrawls counterfeit signatures on the frontispieces of books, *Moby-Dick,* for example, and as he inscribes the text amidst the noise of a party, Mr. Feddle *is* Melville, "sitting in that farmhouse in the Berkshires a century before."[1] Another character, Esme, recreates from her heroin-induced "terror" a perfect duplicate of the Leishman and Spender translation of Rilke's first *Duino Elegy.*

These achievements are in some sense whole and require at least residual powers of empathy. Empathy, however, has been all but depleted in the twenty years between *The Recognitions* and Gaddis' next novel, *J R.* Now one has Jack Gibbs, whose name betokens the entropy afflicting him, and whose habit of mind Gaddis reveals in the symbol of his coat pocket, rarely filled with cash but always with epigraphs taken seemingly at random from an Empedocles, a Marx, a Wagner, or a Hemingway. Many of these quotations have to do with money and decay; some of them are inaccurate. They

Reprinted from *The Review of Contemporary Fiction* 2, no. 2 (Summer 1982): 12–22, by permission of the author and publisher.

are all we see of Jack's unfinished opus on the "social history of mechanization and the arts, the destructive element . . ."[2]

Readers are dealing here in words as transferable properties, currencies
of exchange. In fact one might well take up the fictional testimony of *The
Recognitions* and *J R,* then compose Jack's social history as a chronicle
of monies: the epoch, Menard-to-Feddle-to-Gibbs, as a study in acceler-
ated depreciation, the "destructive element" Jack never wholly comprehends.
For currency is in Gaddis a destroying channel between technology and
art, between the cartel and the artist. Currency spurs usurious practices
instead of simply signifying use-values; and as with so much in Gaddis,
the value of a currency is ever suspect because it may be counterfeited.
Cash, therefore, becomes a warning of something deeply troublesome: the
quoted word as another "money." Writers, like financiers, evaluate and
regulate words through quotation. Words, like paper currency, may be borrowed, copied, stolen, even redeemed. The difference, of course, is that
such literary practices have been raised—through the work of an Eliot,
Joyce, Mann, or Gide—to the status of a Holy Communion.

Gaddis remains broadly ironical about what this may mean. With the
precision of an anatomist, he satirizes the modern obsession with currency,
and especially how that obsession disciplines a scarcely recognized continuity of exchanges—sexual, monetary, artistic, metaphysical. Like Swift's
Houyhnhnms, his fictional characters enact a limited discourse within the
closed system of their culture, a system in which the cash nexus presents
itself as Divine Law. So it is that tracing the pattern of exchanges in *The
Recognitions* and *J R* discloses a satanic regime, and the myriad of counterfeiters, plagiarists, and usurers soon appear not as eccentrics but as ex-
emplars of modernist doctrine. As such they define the real cynicism of
these fictions, books that share with the Greek philosopher Diogenes a
profound desire to debase whole issues of coinage. Gaddis does not, however, share with Diogenes a desire for *sententiae;* his books are encyclo-
pedically big, emblems perhaps of our inability to compose with deft strokes
around principles of beauty and truth. To say this in no way denies the
marvelous consistency of Gaddis' satire, for in many respects he seems the
most disciplined writer of this generation. It is only to make an observation about the mode Gaddis works in.

One might in any case begin with small details and a short excursion
into onomastics. Names, Barthes has written, are the fossils of discourse.
They are the oldest, most durable of coinages. Their traditional purpose
in fiction is to reveal some essential, generic trait of character that the narrative displays in action. But in Gaddis names are tentative; like any coin,
they may be, and often are, exchanged for another. So Wyatt Gwyon be-

comes "Stephen Asche," and Otto Pivner assumes the name of a character in his own play. More interesting, the names often confer identities the characters *do not* possess, and it is the business of narration to reveal this absence. In *The Recognitions,* Otto Pivner's given name signifies exactly what he wants ("riches") but cannot win; so too with Amy ("amity," "love") Joubert of *J R.* Characters sometimes struggle against the fate of their name. Frank Sinisterra's life can be read as the long, absurd failure of his calculated techniques (in counterfeiting) to deny the curse of bad luck signified in his family name, just as Jack Gibbs struggles to hold off the disintegrative chaos signified in his, which recalls the father of entropy theory, Josiah Willard Gibbs. Other names, like Dave Davidoff and Monty Moncrief, or especially Wyatt ("son of Guy") Gwyon ("son of Guy") betoken a pattern of redundancies. They are self-enclosing, wholly patronymical coinages. Still other names are so multifarious as to be an auctorial imposition on characters: for how else may we regard a Recktall Brown or an Agnes Deigh, a Dan diCephalis or an Isidore Duncan?

In Gaddis, names are roles the characters impersonate with varying success, and the gap between the name and the counterfeit becomes one source of irony within the novels. Beyond that, the names are *obvious* counterfeits; obvious because if literary versions of experience are suspect, as they always are in Gaddis, then one purpose of naming is to parody the act of creating fictional currencies. This is true even with titles: the soap opera *Dallas* has recognized in "J R" a melodramatic satanism already waiting to be exploited; and "The Recognitions" is itself, as Gaddis reveals, borrowed from "the first Christian novel" (398). Names, therefore, register at the most fundamental level of writing a distrust of writing. If anything, they are meant to affront literary conventions.

The Irish surname "Gaddis" itself invokes a "son of Gad," a descendant that is to say of the bastard child and seventh son of Jacob, a gimpy-hipped patriarch of Israel, who fixed on "Gad" because it meant "wealth." This is half of that continuity of exchange I mentioned as running through Gaddis' work: the ways in which the generations of men and the generations of money are interwoven. With his protagonists Gaddis invokes the rest. Wyatt Gwyon becomes the seventh in a line of Gwyon forebears to attend divinity school, and like Edward Bast (who may well be a bastard child), Wyatt's greatest dilemma is to produce artworks, to find metaphysical significance, and to do so despite the venal culture they both are born within.

Wyatt Gwyon's inheritance from his forefathers brings a legacy of necessity and guilt. Within the Gwyon line, "each generation was a rehearsal of the one before," and each life is "conceived in guilt and perpetuated in refusal" (18). Each Gwyon seems to counterfeit the previous one, and Gaddis compares them to a line of statues standing against "the vanity of time." Through two centuries only one boy had doubted the family's grand resistance to temporal change, and in despondency he had (like Quentin Compson in *The Sound and the Fury*) "tied a string around his neck with a brick to the other end" and drowned himself in "two feet of water" (ibid.), demonstrating even in his suicide the Gwyons' tenacious sense of necessity. Now Wyatt does not drown himself but he does become mortally sick, and through the illness he recovers a sense of dark, unconscious flow or "recognition," which he always identifies with the half-light of dawn, or with his maternal grandfather's falling into a well, there to glimpse out of its darkness, and in spite of the daylight above, the patterns of stars. (The man is clearly meant to remind us of the saying from Democritus: "Truth lies at the bottom of a deep well.") Contrary to Wyatt's irrational strain from "the Town Carpenter" is his Puritan heritage of election, which carries with it the fear of not being gainful, of not heeding Cotton Mather's warning: "That which is not useful is vicious." The embodiment of this fear, with her "Use-Me Society," is Wyatt's (paternal) Aunt May. One ironical result of this doctrine, despite the family's "disapproval" of everything worldly, is a "fortune" that had "grown near immodest proportions" by the time of Wyatt's childhood (ibid.), though Wyatt sees that wealth as the profit of a con game, a "ruse" whereby the parishioners look upon their weekly offering of coins as a rendering up to God of that which originally was His (26–27). A second result is Wyatt's inability to complete any of his artworks except for those that are copies and are thus profitable, for example, the copy of his father's copy of a circular table depicting the seven deadly sins. Wyatt's sale of this piece is his first link to Recktall Brown, the father of his career as a forger, wherein we see that counterfeiting also runs in dynastic lines. The generations of Gwyon men copy each other; Sinisterra is the last in a line of forgers; and Wyatt is quoted as having said that "the saints were counterfeits of Christ, and that Christ was a counterfeit of God" (514).

Against this nexus of counterfeit monies, men, artworks, and divinity stands Wyatt's inheritance from his mother Camilla. She wants to name Wyatt "Stephen," after the first Christian martyr, though Gaddis certainly wants readers to remember the Greek "stephanos," which (as Joyce had said) means a "crown" or "ring," with its clear antipathy to the regressive linearity of "Wyatt Gwyon." (Interestingly, also Aunt May's watchwords are "NO CROSS, NO CROWN.") Wyatt's legacy from Camilla is also one of chance (she dies as the result of Frank Sinisterra's bad fortune) and of incompletion. As long as he remains under the gun of his father's Puritanism, Wyatt cannot finish the "original" portrait of his mother. His legacy on the maternal side is, therefore, one of failure or, what is the same thing in the American mythos, preterition. It is, furthermore, a legacy of darkness: the darkness, for example, of Camilla's crypt, at the novel's end, or the darkness of the Town Carpenter's well, at the novel's beginning. It is a legacy of flux: Camilla dies at sea, recalling the drowned Gwyon boy; and Camilla's father gazes up from his well at a "sea" of stars. So Wyatt's maternal inheritance stands opposed to Reverend Gwyon's rational, Apollonian Christianity, even in the sun-worship he sees "beneath" Christianity in the cult of Mithras. The division of Wyatt's psyche along these lines continues through his marriage, when Esther feels comfortable with him only in darkness; through his career as an art forger, which Gaddis presents as the fragmentation of artistic perception into copied bits; until his journey to Spain brings Wyatt full circle at the side of his mother's coffin.

Thus, Wyatt's is not, as Bernard Benstock has claimed, a "quest for the father" in the manner of *Ulysses*.[3] If anything, his is an (eastward) motion toward the maternal identity. His motion also counters that in the Clementine *Recognitions,* which Gaddis aptly charts for us with a quotation: "*I am come to destroy the work of the woman, that is, concupiscence, whose works are generation and death*" (338). At the least, Wyatt's is an attempt to strike some fruitful compromise between the demands of his paternal and maternal legacies, a promise Wyatt sees in the equipoise of light and dark at dawn, in the Latin *oriri,* that is to say, wherein he finds a true point of "origin" or "orient." This comes to an artist, Wyatt supposes, "maybe seven times in a life" (102). Gaddis' narrative aside, "Magic number!" implies that such moments of artistic fulfillment weigh against the heritage of counterfeit and decay embodied in the seven generations of Gwyon men, and in the forged table of Bosch's *Seven Deadly Sins.*

A similar dilemma holds in *J R.* Edward Bast's lineage is clouded by the doubtfulness of his conception. Is he the son of Thomas, president of the General Roll Company, whose business it is to reduce music to the separate points, or "holes," of a piano roll? Or is Edward the son of his (nominal) uncle, the composer, James Bast, who cohabited with Edward's mother before she took her life? His legacy from Thomas is one of technology, the rational separation of the musical flux into bits; from James, a devotion to art and an alienation from monetary culture. Both possibilities once were available in the vague figure whom Edward's aunts refer to as "Father," founder of the General Roll Company and musician who used to pay his four children, in coin, at the completion of their piano lessons. The passage of generations separates these aspects. At the same time, the Bast family ruin is shored up by an accumulating fortune, and when Thomas dies intestate, it leaves Edward in a bind. If, as his name suggests, he stands as the "guardian" of the Bast wealth, then Edward must decide whether he means to inherit an artistic or a commercial patent.

Edward Bast's solution to this dilemma is all the more arresting because of its similarity to Wyatt Gwyon's in *The Recognitions*. Through most of *J R*, Bast attempts to support himself by various short-term ventures: teaching, working for J R Vansant, and trying to compose the ninety-six-part orchestration for a film produced to tout a hunting preserve for a group of latter-day Valhallans. He is in fact paid for none of these, and the film project illustrates the fruitlessness of them all. Mister Crawley, his patron, seems to regard his $400 offer for the musical score out of the same "honeymoon with the arts" (409) fervor that went into buying paintings from Jack Gibbs' friend Schepperman. The deal with Bast, however, comes off more like a shotgun wedding. First Crawley fails to grasp the complexities of *performing* the "hen-scratchings" Bast shows him on paper. They mean hiring musicians, for instance; but with the blindness of a Gulliver, the businessman detects only greed behind Bast's requests for more: "Problem is I try to talk to him about art and all he seems to talk about is money" (306). Next he complains to Bast that the marriage to commerce has turned the young man from his "unique gifts" and toward "an almost unhealthy preoccupation with money" (448). Indeed, the relationship does prove unhealthy: like Jack Gibbs and Wyatt Gwyon, Edward does fall mortally ill, though his pneumonia will leave him unable to expend himself in monetized "talk." Like Wyatt's, the respite of his illness thus brings Edward "recognitions" of a flux he can compose. Still more important, the compositions Bast rescues from a hospital trash can at the close of *J R* are the first pieces he completes. They conclude a progress toward diminished complexity: first Edward leaves behind his unfinished grand opera, then a cantata, and a suite, finally to complete some poignant works for cello. Note that his attempts at holding together a multitude of voices, and doing so within the confines of the studio behind his aunts' house, or in any of the rooms J R secures for the purpose, all fail. Nor does Edward ever record Crawley's film score, which, like Thomas Bast's piano rolls, would have become a matter of film-frames and "holes." Instead, Edward's motion, like Wyatt's, is toward the maternal side of his inheritance, toward the model of James, the artist his mother herself had selected against all the demands of conventional morality.

This drama always takes place *inside*. As Wyatt remarks on more than one occasion, "All art requires a closed space." An important figure behind all of *J R* is Josiah Willard Gibbs, the Victorian physicist whose *On the Equilibrium of Heterogeneous Substances* first set forward the hypothesis that compounds mixed within a closed system exchange particles until they reach a state of changeless homogeneity, or "heat death." Jack Gibbs knows that information theorists put forward a similar hypothesis, in the late forties, treating the vulnerability of any closed, complex order of signs to "noise"; "Read Wiener on communication," he says, "more complicated the message more God damned chance for errors" (403). This is especially true of mechanized exchanges. When J R orders a set of business cards for Bast, the first name comes out "Edwerd" (186)—ironically, a recognition of the original Saxon spelling. The "distinguished novelist" in *The Recognitions* mistypes a quotation from Wordsworth—"The world is to muhvh with us, late ans soon, gettijg and spendinf we lay wasre . . ." (946)—though he should have continued to get at its deeper truth: that within a mercantile culture, "little we see in Nature that is ours." Within such a closed order, signs thus begin to jostle against one another in a furious exchange, a "violence all enclosed in a framework," as Wyatt says of flamenco music (123). Metaphors of disease are prominent. Wyatt argues that for the artist to keep faith with these circumstances is "like saying a man's true to his cancer" (262). Jack Gibbs compares his opus on mechanization and art to a terminally ill patient who never gets out of bed (603). These are perfect bodily metaphors for the state of inflated currencies that Gaddis shows us.

Within both novels, signs of monetized exchange flash even in the darkest corners. The neon lights of Mr. Pivner's New York add "a note of metaphysical (Bergsonian) hilarity to the air of well-curbed excitement, in tubes of glass cleverly contorted to spell out cacaphonous syllables of words from a coined language, and names spawned in the estaminets of Antwerp" (302). Here, even that last (coined) phrase was borrowed from Eliot's "Gerontion," a poem that in turn derived *its* first line—"an old man in a dry month"—from A. C. Benson's book *Edward Fitzgerald* (1905). Phrases lifted from Eliot, Rilke, and the Puritan fathers lie scattered throughout part 1 of *The Recognitions;* coinages from Shakespeare are everywhere in Gaddis; here and there are bits of Wordsworth; Edward Bast runs together lines from Wagner's *Ring* and Tennyson's "Locksley Hall" when he performs for his half-sister Stella. In *The Recognitions,* Gaddis' use of the *tiret* instead of quotation marks was doubtless intended to collapse the proprietary boundaries between coinages. In *J R,* his use of the *tiret* and ellipses increases the sense of entropy.

One learns never to take the coins at face value. As simple a quotation as Herschel's comment to Otto, "'Publish and be damned,' the Duke of Wellington said" (191), reveals hidden ironies because: (1) Wellington's curse may be apocryphal; (2) if he *did* write these words as some of his biographers claim, it was not in the context of a writer suffering indignities at the hands of dull critics, which is how Herschel and Otto mean it; (3) Wellington evidently wrote the phrase to a publisher threatening to print a woman client's lurid half-truths unless Wellington paid them both off. As with Joyce's tour through the Wellingdone Museyroom, one is afflicted by a kind of vertigo. The only steady thing is that Otto's assimilation of Herschel's quotation, as with his innumerable borrowings from Wyatt, hinges on his finding a self-accruing point of interest. Exchanges like these are by nature usurious; the currencies must pass through the hands of a middleman who takes his cut, as Frank Sinisterra knows: "Everything's middlemen. Everything's cheap work and middlemen wherever you look. They're the ones who take the profit" (523). This is a principal that guides a great deal of the composition in *The Recognitions* and *J R,* from the slightest quotation to the deployments of plot and character. For what are the actions of a J R Vansant and a Recktall Brown, if not those of satanically masterful "middlemen"?

In fact, the satirist does not balk at bringing himself into this great flux. A figure named "Willie" makes several appearances in *The Recognitions,* disclosing to readers the very process of borrowings that are part of the novel's composition. In *J R,* Gaddis includes a page of bogus titles for pulp-fiction forthcoming from the J R Family of Companies, each title an anagram of *The Recognitions,* with an accompanying blurb lifted from actual 1955 reviews of the book (515–16). Again, one recalls Mr. Feddle, who scissors the titles from book reviews to present them as praise of his own rotten work.

At times the coinages may be even further disguised. Throughout *J R,* readers are dogged by the pied inscription of Greek letters that Schepperman, Jack's friend, suggested to the administrators running the school where everyone seems to work. I once thought the quotation derived from an obscure Hellenic source.[4] Instead, the letters form a delightful camouflage: behind "εβΦΜ ΣΑΟΗ ΑθθΦβΡ" (20) are Marx's famous words from his *Critique of the Gotha Programme*—"FROM EACH ACCORDING TO HIS ABILITY, TO EACH ACCORDING TO HIS NEEDS!" The tactic is Schepperman's way of overriding any objections to a communist epigraph. As a disguise, however, it constitutes an act of subversion that contrasts with the practices of a man like Recktall Brown, whose only sense of writing is to disguise one's plagiaries, because (as he says), "What hasn't been written before? You take something good, change it around a little and it's still good" (374). Elsewhere, he plans "a novel factory, a sort of assembly line" working in concert with "a public opinion board" that judges the content and style of the work (261). Schepperman's actions are those of an outsider (so outside that we never see him in *J R*); Brown's are those of the middleman, the man with the inside track on a closed course.

Thus, the languages of monetary and literary discourse collapse into one. But there is more. In Frank Sinisterra's underworld cant, counterfeit money is called "queer." This takes on special significance when Otto meets Sinisterra, thinking that he has at last reunited with his estranged father. In the ensuing mix-up, Otto receives a packet of forged twenties, "the queer," and describes himself as "a writer." This gains redoubled force when Sinisterra and others regard Otto as a homosexual: for writers, they say, are "always queer nowadays" (556). Otto is not gay, but he is a counterfeit. Characters who read the play, *The Vanity of Time,* recognize his plagiaries straight away, though they cannot pin down the source of his borrowings, which our outside perspective tells us is Wyatt, who even supplies Otto with the title when he recalls his father's sermon on William Law. So, in a way, it is Wyatt and his forebears who "father" Otto's writing, and when Otto becomes the character Gordon at the end of *The Recognitions,* "Gordon" being nothing but a concoction of Wyatt's talk, it is as if Otto continues the Gwyon line, completing the inward "turn of the screw." There is an especially significant sexual connection in these references. Otto frequently holds his play clasped between his legs; and the play is bound in leather, like the wallet he often checks. And when Frank Sinisterra passes him "the queer" beneath a table, Otto holds that bundle "clutched against his parts" (554). This conflation of sex, money, and the word runs throughout *The Recognitions* and reappears in *J R,* where it looms over Jack Gibbs' unsuccessful first attempt at making love to Amy Joubert, his (temporary) cure for writer's block, financial mismanagement, and sexual dysfunction.

Finally, these three motifs are subsumed within Judaeo-Christian signs of divinity. Using a brilliantly comical, extended simile, Gaddis ranges in *The Recognitions* over the history of procreation, from the time "before men knew of their part in generation, and regarded skirted women as autofructiferous," to the "discovery" of sexual generation and its accompanying displacement of the moon by a phallic sun, then to the "skirted priests" of the early church, when a "new religion which extolled the impotent man and the barren woman triumphed over a stupefied empire." This page-long survey tumbles at last toward a pair of young men exchanging confidences at a party: "So even now, under a potted palm with silver fronds, a youth making a solemn avowal held another youth by that part where early Hebrews placed their hands when taking oaths, for it represented Jahveh" (334). These two men belong to the same group of avant-gardists among whom Gaddis' lamb-of-God, Agnes Deigh, moves like a demivierge, "collecting members," as she puts it (203). Inside this world, to be "queer" is to participate in that vast, entropic "homogeneity" that governs every exchange. This is what is meant by counterfeiting.

Les Faux-Monnayeurs first set forward the idea that sexual, monetary, and literary exchanges form a startling homology. Hence Gide's complementary idea: that the modernist avant-gardes shape their attack on bourgeois culture by expropriating this same homology, only inverted — in sexual, monetary, and literary outlawry. Thus, Strouvilhou, an exemplar of the literary terrorist, jeers at the wealthy rake, Passavant: "I give you fair warning, if I edit a review, it will be in order to prick bladders — in order to demonetize fine feelings, and those promissory notes that go by the name of *words*." Yet Strouvilhou offers the young men to whom he stands as patron (just as Passavant stands as his) no kind of sanctuary once they become outsiders. The young men soon drift back to the safer but literally murderous regime of school. Bernard forgets the issue of his bastardy, returning at the last to his "father" Profitendieu and presumably also to some more actual "profit" than that signified in his name.

Gide's plot is a kind of archetype. In *The Eighteenth Brumaire of Louis Bonaparte,* Marx describes our habit of trying to shake off the nightmare of our forebears even as, on second thought, we turn back to borrow their coin. His well-known opening puts it this way:

> The tradition of all the dead generations weighs like a nightmare on the brain of the living. And just when they seem engaged in revolutionizing themselves and things, in creating something that has never yet existed, precisely in such periods of revolutionary crisis they anxiously conjure up the spirits of the past to their service and borrow from their names, battle cries and costumes in order to present the new scene of world history in this time-honored disguise and this borrowed language.[5]

In modernist literature, however, the currencies are no longer "borrowed." Languages are either taken in at a wholesale rate or stolen: Pound, of whom Wyndham Lewis wrote, "there is almost nowhere in the Past that he has not visited"; the Eliot of "Tradition and the Individual Talent," who urges his contemporaries to "procure the consciousness of the past" by any means. It was meant to seem heroic. Leaning into a felt collapse, the artist turns isolated moments of time into the *points d'appui* against which he tries to secure a "purchase."

One was supposed to get an image of the artist as Atlas. The critics have scarcely remarked it, but the fiction of William Gaddis insists that we redefine the context of such feats in terms of profit-mongering, boom-time technologies: not Atlas, then, but Charles Atlas.

For what was the modernist doctrine of the isolated moment but a behind-hand stroke of pseudoscience, an attempt to counter the invasion science had mounted on truth-values? Artists sought to forestall devaluations of their currencies through repertoires of pseudoscientific techniques, of which twelve-tone music, Duchamp's Large Glass, the "constructivism" of *Doktor Faustus,* the preoccupation with the past as a set of energized points, and formalist criticism may all be taken as models. I see an analogy between this Science/Art dichotomy and the dichotomy between Christianity and Art that Nietzsche remarks in his preface to *The Birth of Tragedy,* when he claims that "Christian teaching" expropriates truth wholly unto itself and relegates all of Art "to the realm of lies" and, we might add, of counterfeited performances. So perception is allowed to be divided up. Then it is locked up in mind-forged manacles.

This is exactly the cast of mind Thomas Pynchon satirizes in a character like Mr. E. W. A. Pointsman in *Gravity's Rainbow.* In *The Recognitions,* Gaddis is similarly disposed, though it takes nine hundred pages for Wyatt Gwyon finally to denounce the artistic habits of isolation: "With science you take things apart," he says, "then we can all do them." He denounces at the same time the "democratic" spirit of our common currencies, which "Get things nice and separated" (929). So Wyatt disavows the idea of consciousness as "a succession of particles passing separately" (60) that has afflicted him since he was a boy. The complementary recovery of his self-will—"Now at last to live deliberately," he says before exiting the novel—rings deeply of Bergson's *Time and Free Will.* His last words, "Yes, we'll simplify. Hear?" (960), look forward to Edward Bast's process of simplification in *J R.*

For a broader perspective here, it is tempting to read those great explainers of modernism, the French critics. Structural semiotics has shown how the generation of offspring, money, and texts cooperate under one dynastic rule. As early as *Writing Degree Zero* (1953), Barthes argued for the analogy between monetary and linguistic "currencies." In *S/Z* (1970), he develops the association in more detail, arguing for an outright collusion between auctorial control and patriarchy, linguistic and legal contracts, and literary and economic exchanges of property, all cooperating under the determinism of a reactionary culture. Against that, he projects the indeterminacy of "multivalent" orders, texts (like Gide's) that do not attribute and perhaps even mask quotations, do not respect paternity, origins, property, or propriety. Such works destroy that conventional demand for a "voice" betokening auctorial unity. The critics have neglected to notice it, but the satire Gaddis makes on the topic of "origins" in his first novel speaks to this break. And tracing his movement from the fringes of a determinist fiction, deeply into a realization of the entropy Barthes invokes, would be one way of graphing the twenty-year journey from *The Recognitions* to *J R*. Notice also a paradox: Gaddis' progress to the flux of voices in *J R*, beautifully anticipated in the cocktail party chapters of *The Recognitions*, is itself counterpointed in the progress of his protagonists, Wyatt intending to "simplify" and Bast creating at the last his univocal piece for cello.

In many ways, Gaddis has carried the anatomy of our monetized culture well beyond Barthes. Fredric Jameson, for instance, has said that among the *Tel Quel* group only Jean-Joseph Goux ever brought the analysis of currencies to its fullest expression. Yet even the piece Jameson mentions would make only a small-scale complement to Gaddis' vision. The Goux essay, "Numismatique: L'Or, Le Père, Le Phallus, et La Langue," shows the history of money as tightly harmonious with those of the *logos* and of sexuality.[6] These histories are mapped as a progress toward the abstract, then the conventional: in each case, from fetish to symbol to the "simple sign" of a currency. During this progress, as Goux demonstrates, the lexicons of spending, intercourse, writing, and divine revelation become hopelessly cross-referenced. One gets the impression that only Maxwell's demon could ever stand in the middle and sort them.

Gaddis will not sort, but he will supply principles of understanding. He will often recall Gresham's law: Bad currency drives out good. And if quotation was a principal mode of high modernism, quotation having been taken up as a program for loosening the word from history, releasing from the quotation unsuspected eloquences (recognitions) in the here and now, then the next logical step is totally to conventionalize the coinage. So the progress from fetish to symbol to common currency repeats itself in literature as a century of fiction moves from rituals of le mot juste, to venerating the ahistorical symbol a quotation makes, to proliferating currencies for their own sake. Extrapolating from there, one may suppose that—if Gresham was right—the next step would be to erase any difference between the real currency and the counterfeit.

With that erasure, satire is inevitable. As the last chapters of Melville's *The Confidence-Man* show, a virtual lack of "trust" is the darkest irony of all. Not even the so-called objectivity of ironic viewpoint can pull the writer back inside. "It is part of dissembling," wrote Wittgenstein near the close of his life, "to regard others as capable of dissembling."

As once with Melville, so Gaddis remains in the American standard purgatory between obscurity and critical respect. This is because his vision has committed him all along to strategies of irony, because his books are too big and demanding to succeed in college English courses, and because his novels bear little formal relation to anything else written in post-

war America. Most of all, it is because Gaddis rejects a literature that refers to only itself; yet, the admiration of self-reflexivity in fiction, and of
texts as "performances," are *the* critical standards of our time. But a Gaddis novel has a way of returning powerful echoes to this noisy, dissembling
culture; and many of those echoes bespeak the petty thefts on which the
fortune of modernism was raised, though its doctrines of plagiary and
quotation once were thrown like a gauntlet in the face of bourgeois culture. Now the doctrines are wholesale practice. I have heard a television
spokesman for Gus Mozart Volkswagen of Santa Barbara using botched
Tennyson ("To strive, to seek, to find, and never to yield") while trumpet-
ing the German quest for mechanical perfection. And I think it only right
that a watering hole called "The Bar," in Lexington, Kentucky, should tout
its ambience by expropriating the master of quotation, T. S. Eliot ("Do
you dare disturb the universe?" asks the adman, "Must you part your hair
behind?"). Not only fictional characters like Mr. Pivner and Edward Bast,
but all of us perform our lives amidst this noise.

Somehow one must get outside. If, as Gaddis claims in his recent
Harper's essay, "Entropy rears as a central preoccupation of our time,"[7]
then one underlying motive of his satires must be to crack the closed system in which the entropy goes its intractable way. Glibly to dismiss Gaddis' belief in the moral power of that possibility, as John Gardner does in
On Moral Fiction, is not to read very carefully the endings of these books.[8]
Wyatt's new alias, "Stephen," suggests that he is the only character to break
away from the heritage or curse of his name. Preparatory to his going outside, leaving the space of the novel, Wyatt comes full circle: Sinisterra,
who was responsible for Camilla Gwyon's death, is dead under ambiguous
circumstances. In his last scene, Stephen cups in his hands a small bird
that he frees, reversing the moment when, as a child, he had—in anticipa-
tion of the saint who supplies the name Stephen to Camilla—killed a wren
with a stone. In this sense, Stephen is the only character fully to redeem
the coin of his name. As for the bird, when Stephen opens his hands, it
flutters about the room in front of his latest canvases, as though warrant-
ing the artworks, which are no longer counterfeits of other artworks but
visions now of the outside: not mirrors, then, but windows. We are re-
minded of the argument Marx had to make so often, that not labor alone
but to an equal extent nature are the sources of use-values.

But compare Stephen's end to Stanley's. So afraid of expending himself
that he resists both baths and sexual contact, Stanley dies inside and alone,
playing the great mass he conceived as a perfected, self-contained design:
"every transition and movement in the pattern over and against itself and
within itself proof against time" (346). This work becomes so self-important

that *it* will literally "come through at the expense of everything" (p. 1020). It is, moreover, as though Stanley dies because he is driven to include every feasible voice in his work, even the "Devil's Interval," a low C from the instrument's longest pipe that vibrates, though Stanley does not recognize it himself, at the same frequency of the chugging ship's engine aboard the *Conte di Brescia,* which recalls Adamo da Brescia, the counterfeiter in Dante's *Inferno.* As if this weren't enough to damn him, Stanley plays this fatal note at an organ given to the Fenestrula chapel (note that the name suggests a "window") by an American industrialist, who installed the biggest instrument money could buy in a small and fragile building. At least one reader sees Stanley "soar in atonement" as the building falls around him.[9] I don't know how to read the ending except as the collapse of that modernist desire to shore up an imagined ruin; in other words, as a fierce satire against the modernist program and its masked conservatism, its hidden devotion to the Church of Money.

In *J R,* Edward Bast also leaves behind a self-nourishing entropy that, when it gets fully inside the person, leaves him mortally ill. In spite of that disease, he creates his finest work, and it is anything but a grandiose orchestration done to patronize some corporate fool. Instead, his piece for cello has value if only because a dying man named Isidore Duncan, of Zanesville, Ohio, happens to appreciate merely the idea of *doing* it, or (again) just "living it through" (956).

So it is not the use, but the uses of art as currency that trouble William Gaddis. The satire against institutionalized exchange rates powers both *J R* and *The Recognitions.* And if those works have not yet found the audience they deserve, perhaps it is because the system of controls operates less blatantly here than in cultures where artists work in the shadow of a totalitarian regime. Nevertheless, in his Nobel Address of 1980, the exiled Polish poet Czeslaw Milosz delivered an eloquent warning to the rest of us:

> There is, it seems, a hidden link between theories of literature as *ecriture,* of speech feeding on itself, and the growth of the totalitarian state. In any case, there is no reason why the state should not tolerate an activity that consists of creating "experimental" poems and prose, if those are conceived as autonomous systems of reference, enclosed within their own boundaries. Only if we assume that a poet constantly tries to liberate himself from borrowed styles in search of reality is he dangerous. In a room where people unanimously maintain a conspiracy of silence, one word of truth sounds like a pistol shot.[10]

One needn't buy the arguments of a John Gardner or a Gore Vidal to the effect that a Gaddis or a Pynchon must be read with their novels in one hand and some deconstructionist critic in the other. Good lord, their works are not "difficult" in that way at all! The whole point of a satire like *J R* or *The Recognitions* is to curb our demonic love of self-generating, self-contained works. Gaddis may challenge one's sense of reading, but only by imploring one to live dangerously again simply by going outside.

Notes

1. William Gaddis, *The Recognitions* (1955; reprint, New York: Avon Books, 1974), 613. Subsequent references to this work will be cited parenthetically in the text.

2. William Gaddis, *J R* (New York: Alfred A. Knopf, 1975), 244. Subsequent references to this work will be cited parenthetically in the text.

3. Bernard Benstock, "On William Gaddis: In Recognition of James Joyce," *Wisconsin Studies in Contemporary Literature* 6 (1965): 181–82.

4. See my essay, "Contra Naturam?: Usury in William Gaddis' *J R*," *Genre* 13 (1980): 101. Many thanks to William Gaddis for writing to point out his camouflage and the wildness of my guess.

5. Quoted in *Marx & Engels: Basic Writings on Politics & Philosophy,* ed. Lewis S. Fever (Garden City, N.Y.: Doubleday, 1959), 320.

6. Jean-Joseph Goux, "Numismatique: L'Or, Le Père, Le Phallus et La Langue," *Tel Quel* 35 (1968): 64–89; and 36 (1968): 54–74. For Jameson's comments, see his *Prison-House of Language* (Princeton: Princeton University Press, 1972), 180.

7. "The Rush for Second Place," April 1981, 35.

8. John Gardner, showing that he grasped neither the informing structure nor the satirical "morality" of *J R:* "Structure is the evolving sequence of dramatized events tending toward some understanding and assertion; that is, toward some meticulously qualified belief. What we see around us is, for the most part, dramatization without belief or else opinion untested by honest drama. William Gaddis has named the problem in *J R,* though he himself doesn't escape it: 'believing and shitting are two different things'" (*On Moral Fiction* [New York: Basic Books, 1978], 65–66).

9. I mean Joseph S. Salemi, who argues in his essay, "To Soar in Atonement: Art as Expiation in Gaddis's *The Recognitions,*" *Novel* 10 (1977), that "Art is the ultimate expiation" (136). One had better say: "Doing art work is a form of expiation."

10. Czeslaw Milosz, "The Nobel Lecture, 1980," *The New York Review of Books* 15 March 1981, p. 12.

12

The Paper Empires and Empirical Fictions of William Gaddis

Joel Dana Black

Like his contemporaries Thomas Pynchon and Carlos Fuentes in their most ambitious, encyclopedic enterprises to date, *Gravity's Rainbow* (1973) and *Terra Nostra* (1975), respectively, William Gaddis is clearly preoccupied in his most recent work, *J R* (1975), with the overwhelming specter of Empire. All three writers present sweeping visions of an Alexandrian Age, dominated by a vast corporate-political structure that to a great extent determines both the nonfictional discourse of social power-relations as well as the fictional discourse of the literary text itself. While Pynchon and Fuentes, however, discern in the debris of Empire an archaeology of concealed order, while they view history as the hidden agenda of a remote technocratic elite or heretical cult, at the core of Gaddis' revelation is nothing more nor less than a modern, snotty, sixth-grader pursuing an ostensibly innocent, socially sanctioned, but ultimately destructive, game plan. The corporate Empire of American big business itself provides the software, the endlessly proliferating coded messages and directives that Gaddis' sorcerer's apprentice quickly masters, and that enables him anonymously to throw the concealed levers and switches that operate the gigantic, Oz-like machine and bring its hardward to simulated life.

Gaddis' unlikely juvenile hero is the postmodern reincarnation of Mary Shelley's romantic monster in *Frankenstein*. J R is without an origin, without a childhood—in short, without a history. For precisely the same reasons, in other words, that Frankenstein's creation is monstrous, J R is also a monster; but also for those very reasons he is the product of his age, the child of his times, an orphan of the Empire. Bombarded with the media's

Reprinted from *The Review of Contemporary Fiction* 2, no. 2 (Summer 1982): 22–31, by permission of the author and publisher.

get-rich-quick-by-investing-in-America hype, J R takes it into his head to "play the market" as he would play any other children's game by investing at first in penny stocks. From the fliers advertising these stocks to the paper towels he uses to blow his incessantly runny nose (hoarding and playing with the paper wads afterwards), J R is surrounded by a manufactured world consisting of, and ordered and controlled by, paper. As his ragged portfolio blossoms with paper refuse, his holdings skyrocket almost overnight. J R takes this all in stride; he is never overwhelmed by his winnings, and in fact he is desperately unsatisfied. After all, it's still only a game, as even corporate presidents have told him:

> —I mean like when we went on that field trip where that Diamond Cable Company the president of it said if you're playing you might as well play to win but you can't just might as well, he came on skating the towel wad across the floor, gave it a slap shot with his instep. —You can't just play to play because the rules are only for if you're playing to win which that's the only rules there are.[1]

And much later he adds, "If you're playing anyway so you might as well play to win but I mean even when you win you have to keep playing!" "How am I supposed to stop everything!" J R asks privately (647), and his subordinates, who never know who their boss is, admire that negative entropy he seems to thrive on, which makes "every loss a profit" (522). This aloofness, this voracious desire to amass and acquire whatever the consequences, is stimulated by an inner emptiness, a value vacuum that finds eloquent expression in J R's favorite expletive: "Holy Shit!" And when the game J R is determined to play to win brings about the destruction of numberless businesses, fortunes, and lives, he still remains casually aloof. His game of monopoly does not finally interpenetrate successfully with the all-too-serious business world, nor is it redeemed by any idealized notion of truth. Instead, J R's game only creates havoc, even though his enterprising spirit is socially sanctioned.

In short, the character J R's lack of humor is responsible for the text *J R*'s black humor. The sixth-grade entrepreneur's paramount delusion is that he takes the game he plays to win in complete seriousness, but never with sufficient seriousness, because it always remains for him just a game. A memorable instance of the disastrous effects of such irresponsibility occurs when one of his subsidiary concerns, a toy company called Ray-X, supplies an African tribe with toy weapons that prove catastrophic (as one concerned investor learns) in a skirmish with a regime protected by private American business interests:

—Whole damn Malwi labor force decimated yes how the devil'd that happen, Dé's people supposed to annex it just heard they walked in these buggers meet them armed to the damn teeth Dé's bunch panic cut them down like flies go in to clean up find all they had's toys, pistols carbeens submachineguns rocket launchers every damn weapon you can think of plastic toys poor buggers. (709)

Gaddis' fiction is notably different from Cervantes' in this regard. Whereas Erich Auerbach argues that Cervantes finds "the order of reality in play,"[2] that Don Quixote's fantastic interpretations of the world somehow manage to interpenetrate successfully with a "real" state of affairs, no such coexistence of counterinterpretations is possible here. While Mambrino's barber pan may *also* appear to an eccentric individual as a helmet and while a group of windmills may be perceived by that individual as ferocious giants, there is no disagreement among *all* witnesses concerned that the Malwi labor force's arms *are* actually arms. In fact, this is precisely the problem: the weapons are taken for real arms when they are only *play*-weapons, and in *that* sense they are deceptive and ironically destructive. (A similar incident is recorded earlier in the work when a narcotics agent reconnoitering a public school shoots down a retarded child carrying a cap gun.) Cervantes' play is motivated by an initial hermeneutic disagreement among parties, each believing that its own *individual representation* of reality possesses exclusive validity. Gaddis' more "serious" play, in contrast, is the result of an assumed agreement among parties all too willing to suspend disbelief in an ultimate reality so long as the *collective representations*[3] that appear are not necessarily truthful but merely credible. Under the lax standards of the collectively credible, however, nearly everything is agreeable and almost nothing is incredible—i.e., empirically verifiable by a single individual. The problem in a world of collectively credible representations of reality is not the identification and verification of an object in the world, but the determination of its value as a plaything in an arbitrary but rigidly enforced game plan.

Such "serious" play has been admirably illustrated by news events in recent years. One may well ask after the mass suicides in Guyana whether we are now to regard grape Kool-Aid as a kid's soft drink or as a hard genocidal concoction. As with Gaddis' toy weapons, we are dealing with familiar, commonplace objects, innocent playthings (*Spielzeugen*), which, in the context of a slightly altered game plan, suddenly become the agents of horrendous catastrophe. Such calamities arise because modern, "serious" play no longer addresses itself either to the problem of empirically verifying what an object is in itself or of elucidating the function of that object within a larger context of social relations, but instead recognizes that whatever that object may in fact be—plaything (toy) or work-thing (tool, weapon, etcetera),[4] lightweight cap gun or heavy-duty artillery, Kool-Aid or cyanide—the same rules can credibly, if not honorably, govern its use, until the object's "actual," suppressed value erupts horrifically into view.

Credit and Credibility, as *J R* might alternatively have been called, may then designate what is responsible for the otherwise incredible fiction of J R's meteoric career as a profiteer. But both credit and credibility are in turn only valorized by the peculiar nature of the substance that J R operates both with and through paper. From the newsprint wherein he eyes the initial open invitations to purchase stock, to the letters he scrawls, to the shares and dividends he recovers, to the paper company he eventually acquires, to his misspelled directives, J R's empire is safely papered over with that malleable but essentially valueless medium (hence worthless stock is designated "wallpaper" until J R actually acquires a wallpaper company). In the end, it is the rules of the game that invest any paper with potentially overwhelming significance. All that is needed for this paper magic to work is the ready credibility of such "underwriters" as J R's opportunistic PR man, Dave Davidoff, who are willing captives of a discourse they take to be their own: "Believe anything I hear myself about paper" (513). And it is finally among his "ragged ribbons of newspaper, magazine pages torn jagged" (650) that J R narcissistically reads the press's eulogy of his success: "See then it tells about this whole paper empire see that's what it's called here Paper Empire" (651). Thus, the papers ultimately dub J R's achievement in their own image, anonymously spawning another message-unit into the world's discursive flow, which J R, deprived even of his own proper name, greedily clutches as his own.

It should be kept in mind, though, that the varieties of paper that J R masters and plays with *are* in fact paper—that is after all what makes it so easy for J R to grab hold of and to deal with his and others' fortunes —but they are also, among other things, money. And not *play*-money, except insofar as all money merits this description through its having any value at all. The seminal dialectic in *J R* between money and paper, value and worthlessness, meaning and nonsense, is dramatized in the reminiscences of two elderly sisters with which the book opens:

> —Money . . .? in a voice that rustled.
> —Paper, yes.
> —And we'd never seen it. Paper money.
> —We never saw paper money till we came east.

—It looked so strange the first time we saw it. Lifeless.
—You couldn't believe it was worth a thing.
—Not after Father jingling his change. (3)

In the very first two lines of the work, money is firmly identified with paper, but the isolated speaking voices, which, when joined by others, will constitute the entire choral text, are themselves disenfranchised—they *rustle* like paper because they are really no longer distinctive voices but have been devalued into the anonymous murmur of discourse. The attenuation of the "voice of money" from the jingle of silver to the rustle of paper currency is evoked elsewhere in the book, as in the scene where a youngster sells fifty dollars belonging to his father.

—He sold it.
—What do you mean he sold it.
—He sold it to some boys.
—He sold it?
—He didn't know, he thought the coins were better because the other's only paper. He sold the fives for a nickel and the ones for ten cents.
—Well why did he, my God, why did he . . .
—He thought the ones were better because they had George Washington.
—My God.
—But, but Nora what boys. Why didn't you stop him.
—I don't know Daddy just these boys, I wasn't even here. He got eighty-five cents, I helped him count, after. Mama . . .
—All right Nora that's enough, I told you to get ready for bed and pick up that toilet paper, it's all over the house. (314)

Gaddis' work is replete with instances of the destroyed illusion in which the assumed value of a collectively represented object is startlingly called into question through a confrontation of that object with its mimetic double. Unable to support such a sudden revelation of its duplicity, the doubled collective representation must immediately valorize (either) one of its aspects as the authentic object and the other as an inferior imitation, a play-object or game-piece. We have seen examples of this when what were taken to be guns were ruthlessly exposed as toys, or inversely, when what was assumed to be worthless paper turned out to be money. In another example, which explains the presence of toilet paper in the aforementioned scene, the harried mother cruelly demystifies her daughter Nora of another media-mediated illusion.

—Now what are you crying about.
—I'm a bride.
—Dressed up in toilet paper you're a bride?
—It's a bride dress. Daddy don't I look like a bride?
—Maybe it's something she saw on television, she . . . (311)

Similarly, J R's lightweight paper empire proves a credible and creditable substitute for an equally fictive but deadly serious and humorless hardcore corporate Empire. J R's enterprise actually succeeds in mimicking and challenging the corporate Empire as its mercurial double until the credit upon which J R's empire rests is revealed for what it quite evidently is: paper. J R's empire is a house of cards and the emperor has no clothes (although the forward-looking Davidoff does envision the corporate family "getting into paper clothes" [513]), as any child ought to know, and as the preadolescent J R knows all too well how to exploit for his own ends. For J R is the corporate sorcerer's apprentice, and no matter how unfounded or insubstantial his sorcery may be in itself, it becomes immeasurably powerful when subscribed to and "shared" by any number of willing believers. But the young emperor-sorcerer has so completely deceived himself, as well as Wall Street, that even when the latter realizes it has been defrauded (i.e., double-crossed) and so turns viciously on J R Corporation, its mastermind still fails to see anything wrong about his practices. He persists in his reckless ventures, unable to stop, convinced that his actions and intentions have always been sanctioned by the rules of the corporate game.

The problem, of course, is that J R is right: in terms of a conception of absolute truth, there is ultimately no difference between his operation and Wall Street's, between a game and an empire, between fiction and reality. It is only through the mystification of credibility that we are able to discriminate between the fictions that present themselves to us daily, arbitrarily crediting some and discrediting others, hypostatizing hype here and branding it hypocrisy there. For in an age of credibility—as opposed to an age of belief—one fiction will always try to conceal its fictional nature by attempting to dominate all the others as the supreme fiction of Truth.

In the story of the paper empire of J R, the ingenuous fraud-in-spite-of-himself, a number of issues are reworked from Gaddis' first and only other fiction, *The Recognitions,* a work of truly encyclopedic dimensions. Moreover, the protagonist of this work, the artist Wyatt Gwyon, and his minister father are themselves both disposed to encyclopedic undertakings; Gwyon *père* is an inveterate collector of bizarre cult objects: "He collected things, each of a holy intention in isolation, but pagan in the variety of his choice."[5] Gwyon *fils,* on the other hand, has accumulated innumerable books; in fact, both father and son are omnivorous readers, and the pages of *The Recognitions* are strewn with litanies of titles and passages of obscure texts the two have consumed. Wyatt's wife, Esther, is also bookish to an extent, but whereas she prefers "books out where everyone could see them, a sort of graphic index to the intricate labyrinth of her mind arrayed to impress the most casual guest. [. . .] Her husband, on the other hand, did not seem to care where his books were, so long as they were where he put them. That is to say, separate" (83). Insofar as it is possible to achieve the Gwyons' endeavor—to consider worldly objects in themselves, in isolation from the myriad allusions and imitations that surround them—an object may become (again) something ritualistic (a text may become a work, intertextuality may become tradition, literature may become scripture). Failing to achieve such sacred separateness, one risks reintroducing multiplicity and variety into the world; one reenters that infinitely proliferating, cross-referenced, encyclopedic world that is eminently profane, deceitful, and double-crossing. In the secular age of mechanical reproduction, the work of art is reduced to a substitutable intertext—it loses its aura (in the words of Walter Benjamin) or its rainbow (as Pynchon would say), because it has lost whatever gravity and whatever intrinsic centrality, solvency, validity it was formerly assumed to have possessed.

In this sense, all encyclopedic undertakings to disclose systematically some hidden central truth are doomed to failure. The encyclopedic pursuit of knowledge must rather recognize itself, as Jacques Derrida says in another context, as a zone "of *play,* that is to say, a field of infinite substitutions in the closure of a finite ensemble. Only because it is finite, that is to say, because instead of being an inexhaustible field . . . there is something missing from it: a center which arrests and grounds the play of substitutions."[6] And if, as one of Derrida's readers suggests, "Nietzsche's work is the unreconciled playground of . . . 'knowledge' and . . . forgetfulness,"[7] so *The Recognitions* presents its own encyclopedic enterprise as a playground of isolation and inundation upon which the central oppositions of Gaddis' text—originality and imitation, genuineness and forgery, the sacred and the profane—are dialectically dis-played.

Wyatt Gwyon is originally trained in the ministry to follow the profession of his father. As a child, he is drawn to art, however, and he is reprimanded by his stern Calvinistic aunt when he makes his first drawing. He is guilty of the sin of mimesis, i.e., of attempting to replace God in His creative role: "Our Lord is the only true creator," his aunt scolds him, "and only sinful people try to emulate Him" (34). A similar logic obsesses Wyatt in the secular world of art, and by first forging and then becoming a meticulous re-creator of Flemish masterpieces, he manages to avoid substituting himself in God's role as an original creator. Even if one refrains from condemning the romantic and postromantic cult of originality for its blasphemous presumption in identifying the creative act of the artist with that of God, the modern myth of originality may still be debunked, as Wyatt shows, purely on principles of postmodern aesthetics—that is, for taking itself so seriously and for neglecting the authentically creative, playful possibilities of endless repetition and imitation that are more in the line of true artistry. Wyatt learns, however, that (as in playing the market, as J R was to discover) playing God—even as a forger—is a serious, exhausting business. If the artist's primary imagination, according to Coleridge, is "a repetition in the finite mind of the eternal act of creation in the infinite I AM," the ingenuity of the con-artist may be said to involve the infinite substitution of himself in the role of creator of a finite number of always already original works of divine artifice. This, in turn, sets in motion a dizzying Calvinist nightmare of infinite debt and infinite loss. J R may for awhile appear to make "every loss a profit"; Wyatt may similarly appear to make every forgery an original. In both cases, however, entropy prevails in the long run: profit is finally (revealed as) loss, the original is ultimately (revealed as) a forgery. In the end, the practicing con-artist recognizes himself as the ever-present, fraudulent creator who wages a constant struggle with his demonic, repressed Other:

> As it has been, and apparently ever shall be, gods, superseded, become the devils in the system which supplants their reign, and stay on to make trouble for their successors, available, as they are, to a few for whom magic has not despaired, and been superseded by religion. (*The Recognitions,* 102)

Night after night, Wyatt struggles in secret with his demon originals. "It's this crazy Calvinist secrecy," his wife despairs (129). Even as a youth, Wyatt executed his forbidden re-creative performances in secret, desperately wanting to confess but having learned from his aunt "that there was no more hope for the damned than there was fear for the Elect"(35). The pathos of Wyatt Gwyon's artistic endeavor consists precisely in his recognition that the magic of "free," guiltless, postmodern artistic play entails a struggle and uncertain liberation from the Calvinist, anxiety-ridden legacy inherited by and from modernism with its "fearful subscription to a Hostility Who could afford no other gods before Him" (266).

Indeed, the recognition of the evil inherent in any symbolic endeavor, of the transgressive nature of all artistic creation, may be said to be a chief concern of twentieth-century Alexandrian fiction.[8] More precisely, authors such as Gaddis and Pynchon hark back to the gnostic perception of the pervasive difficulty involved in any attempt to return to origins and hence to be original. "A little cunning" such as Wyatt's estranged wife recommends to him, the mild deceit of nonmimetic textual play as advocated by a preponderance of postmodern writers and poststructuralist critics alike, will not be able to solve the immense problem of evil in the world, or to evade the *mimetic* nature of that problem. Man is always outwitted by the always prior, ever more cunning versions of himself whom he can only recognize as his gods. In fact, contemporary gnostic fiction seems to suggest that man's original sin resides precisely in the fact that his sins are *not* original but only cheap imitations of an original sin. To be evil is to be an imposter, a false copy, an *imitatio Christi,* a counterfeit of the inimitable Divine.

Unlike *The Recognitions, J R* seems to acknowledge the failure of all encyclopedic endeavors. One of the boy's many paper products is an encyclopedia of rather dubious merit: "Those are, oh yes that's a children's encyclopedia they're bringing out sir, it's doing extremely well even though it seems to be teeming with inaccuracies and a number of prominent educators have demanded its withdraw . . ." (693). Aside from J R, the work's most interesting character is a jack-of-all-trades named Jack Gibbs who originally sold encyclopedias to put himself through Harvard, and at one time tried to write a vast encyclopedic work on mechanization and the arts. Returning to his project after having abandoned it for years, Gibbs realizes the futility of his task: "He turned the pages more slowly, finally hunched toward the sill for the failing light 'must have thought I could, like Diderot good God how I ever thought I could do it . . .'" (588). It appears that in *J R,* Gaddis has concealed a critique of the ambitious encyclopedic enterprise that he himself had undertaken in his first work. Any attempt to compose a cultural encyclopedia implies that the author must fully have mastered his culture. An author guilty of such hubris will inevitably indulge in all sorts of distortions, omissions, and "teeming inaccuracies"; he will in the end produce not a neutral encyclopedia, but a power-crazed empire. Under such circumstances, it is perhaps best to avoid all encyclopedic pretenses and to design, playfully and deliberately, an empire—a paper empire. With this in mind, we can read *J R* as a fully realized playground where a "Diaspora of words" (*The Recognitions,* 85), a loose system of discursive exchanges, internally organizes itself as the cross section of an empire's rise and fall.[9]

In the saga of J R's financial empire, Gaddis abandons his earlier encyclopedic enterprise, and in so doing he comes very close to liberating his fiction (and one might even claim *all* fiction) from the nemesis of narrative, the Western mania for order and control. As a paper empire in its own right, *J R* is characterized by the fact that any shred of its discursive software may suddenly be invested with tremendous value and power because there is no longer any final repository of value in such an expansive and unbounded text. Perhaps nothing attests more vividly to this absence of authority than the work's greatest tour de force—the nearly total eclipse of the narrating persona as a responsible organizing consciousness or "umpire" in the work. Almost the entire text consists of recorded dialogue with virtually no narrative markings to identify the speaker in each case; even the few remaining "he said"—"she asked" conventions in *The Recognitions* have been discarded in *J R*. Characters can be recognized only by the idiosyncrasies of their speech; spoken discourse—not the characters speaking this discourse—enacts the essential nondramatic performance of the text. Without the narrative conventions—book and chapter divisions, section titles, and especially epigraphs—that characterized the earlier encyclopedic work, *J R* is, as nearly as possible, undifferentiated discourse whose movement appears to follow no consciously ordained direction other than the mindless free play of a disembodied principle of selection and attention.

I began this essay by distinguishing Gaddis' fictional simulation of Empire from related enactments by Pynchon and Fuentes. Such a contrast can be extended, if not accounted for, by pointing out these writers' reciprocal insights into the encyclopedic nature of discourse itself. Pynchon and Fuentes are both obsessed in their respective encyclopedic fictions by secular structures of control from *above,* left over intact from ancient sacred hegemonies and newly valorized through the occult legitimacy of scientific, economic, and ideological interest. Gaddis, on the contrary, is fascinated by the peculiarly American erosion and devaluation from *below* of formerly significant structures of exchange, whether it be in the realm of aesthetic, religious, or sexual experience. Moreover, while Pynchon and Fuentes suggest Empire indirectly so that its exact dimensions and extent are never completely known, Gaddis presents his version of Empire in a startlingly direct manner. Both in *The Recognitions* and *J R* there is no eerie, obsessive secret to be unearthed. The reader need not fear that the heart of Gaddis' Empire will ultimately be revealed as a yawning abyss presided over by some deadly technocratic elite, as in the case of Pynchon, or by a secret cult of heretical Magi, as in the case of Fuentes. Behind the scenes of Gaddis' Oz-like Empire is just a misguided, ambitious sixth-grader who has unwittingly taken advantage of the supreme irresponsibility of a system that allows its Howard Hugheses to operate with almost total anonymity. Indeed, this is the secret of J R's success:

—Like I mean this bond and stock stuff you don't see anybody you don't know anybody only in the mail and the telephone because that's how they do it nobody has to see anybody, you can be this here funny lookingest person that lives in a toilet someplace how do they know, I mean like all those guys at the Stock Exchange where they're selling all this stock to each other? They don't give a shit whose it is they're just selling it back and forth for some voice that told them on the phone why should they give a shit if you're a hundred and fifty all they . . . (172)

Gaddis delights in revealing the slow but inevitable process whereby all hypostatized values are gradually undermined, commercialized, mimicked, and debased through the massive assertion of popular interests—any vestige of an organizing, shaping narrative voice is ultimately drowned out by the inane jargon of the characters. Amidst this proliferation of competing strains of discourse derived from the codes of advertising, big business, politics, and public relations, how is it possible to discern a meta-discourse, a language in which a narrating persona can make itself heard?

It is this curious absence of any overriding, stabilizing speech in Gaddis' latest work that seems to give it such empirical authenticity. No single, identifiable consciousness appears to be in control. Yet so extensive and powerful is the Empire's controlling discourse on the minds of the individuals living under its dominion that any perspective of reality is predetermined. Spatial and temporal processes themselves are warped according to the Empire's centralized gravitational force, and historical transformation invariably accords with its discourse. Thus, if the Empire, its power and authority, is nothing but a monstrous cultural fiction, a nightmare from which the hapless individual (like Stephen Dedalus, the prisoner of another encyclopedic fiction) struggles to awake, we are compelled to acknowledge further that all empirical reality is no less a fiction, a fiction that is inseparable from the fiction of Empire for the reason that the very modality through which the world is experienced and known—the matrix of space, time, and history—is itself more or less regulated through the Empire's discursive control. For the individual living in an Empire, it is well-nigh impossible to get his historical bearings; and by the same principle, the reader of Gaddis' paper empire will find it similarly impossible to acquire absolute control of his narrative bearings. This resistance to understanding is not a weakness or failure in Gaddis' fiction; on the contrary, such unintelligible surrealism is intended not so much to defy comprehension as to resist control. Such resistance provides the saving grace through which Gaddis' paper empire and empirical fictions retain their own integrity and inviolability in the presence of the formidable pressures of the real Empire's all-too-real text.

Notes

1. William Gaddis, *J R* (New York: Alfred A. Knopf, 1975), 301. Subsequent references to this work will be cited parenthetically in the text.

2. Erich Auerbach, *Mimesis: The Representation of Reality in Western Literature,* trans. Willard R. Trask (1st ed, 1946; reprint, Princeton: Princeton University Press, 1953), 358. Earlier in his chapter on Cervantes, Auerbach writes that in *Don Quixote,* "reality willingly cooperates with a play which dresses it up differently every moment" (351).

3. I borrow this term from Owen Barfield, who discusses the collective nature of phenomenal representations in *Saving the Appearances: A Study in Idolatry* (New York: Harcourt, Brace & World, 1965).

4. Cf. Martin Heidegger's description of "Zeug" in *Being and Time,* trans. John Macquarrie and Edward Robinson (New York: Harper & Row, 1962), 95–107. Whereas the *Zeug,* or tool, is available, ready-to-hand (*zuhandene*), connected up in a world-totality of tools (*Zeugganzheit*), one may say that a toy or *Spielzeug* lacks any immediate practical function in the world and is instead available for *all* purposes.

5. William Gaddis, *The Recognitions* (New York: Harcourt, Brace & World, 1955), 16. Subsequent references to this work will be cited parenthetically in the text.

6. Jacques Derrida, *Writing and Difference,* translated with an introduction and additional notes by Alan Bass (Chicago: University of Chicago Press, 1978), 289.

7. Gayatri C. Spivak, "Translator's Preface" to her translation of Jacques Derrida's *Of Grammatology* (1974; reprint, Baltimore: Johns Hopkins University Press, 1976), xxxii.

8. Significant parallels may be found in Thomas Pynchon's *Gravity's Rainbow* (New York: Viking Press, 1973), as in the incident of Group Captain Basher St. Blaise's transgressive sighting of the Angel during his Palm Sunday bombing raid over the town of Lübeck: "But damn it, this was not a cloud" (151). In Carlos Fuentes' historical fantasy, *Terra Nostra* (trans. Margaret Sayers Peden [New York: Farrar, Straus & Giroux, 1976] 191f.), El Señor is oppressed by a blasphemous Italian painting depicting Christ without a halo. Like Wyatt Gwyon, El Señor is haunted by the gnostic recognition that the world is a mere copy or forgery of an original from which it is infinitely removed: "'We know only the last heaven, Guzmán, the most imperfect copy, the farthest removed from the original model although the closest to this earth we inhabit, and I fear that all the things of our earth are but the product of the creation closest to us but most distant from the Father who only indirectly created us, for first He created powerful angels who in turn created more and more inferior angels who in the end created us. We are the result of the uninterested caprice of a few bored angels who possessed only the strength and imagination necessary to invent human misery. But thus they fulfilled the secret design of the Creator: that man be what is farthest removed and least like the original Father.'" Not only does El Señor declare all man-made representations of God to be blasphemous, but he also brands as heresy the doctrine that man is himself the creation of God: "'What I wish is to purify totally the essence of God by freeing the Father Creator from the supreme sin, the creation of men; we cannot be His work, we cannot, no . . . Allow me to free God from the supreme sin that we attribute to Him: the creation of man.'"

9. Such a process of narrative construction recalls Gaddis' description in *The Recognitions* of Wyatt's artistic technique: "Over the emphatic drawing and the underpainting, translucent colors were fixed in intimate detail upon the established forms, colors added separately, unmixed on the palette, layer upon layer, constructed from within as necessity disposed these faces emptied in this perfect moment of the transient violence of life." (275)

13

Gaddis
A Tribune of the Fifties

FREDERICK R. KARL

In *The Recognitions* (1955), perhaps the novel of the fifties, William Gaddis makes counterfeiting his motif: for his characters, their activities, their emotional lives, and, ultimately, for the entire surrounding culture. His aim, as he continues it in *J R* (1975), is heuristic. But counterfeiting, we shall see, is not necessarily a purely negative form of expression; not always artificial or a form of plagiarism.[1] In some of its manifestations, it can lead to recognitions, especially in an era when "real things" are beyond attainment or themselves falsifications. Recognitions are related to Wordsworth's "spots of time," Joyce's epiphanies, religious revelations (the protagonist, Wyatt Gwyon, was once a seminarian), Proust's "privileged moments." They are moments of personal truth or acts of consciousness. When a person achieves a recognition, he has attained some connection between the universe and himself. Not to achieve a recognition is to remain unrealized or part of dead matter, unrecognized and unrecognizing; as, later, those impersonal creatures in Gaddis' *J R,* mutants attached only to "dummy corporations."

One reason Gaddis stresses Wyatt as an "avenging Christ" of sorts is to locate him in the historical tradition of those damned or cursed. Wyatt is not a Jesus figure, quite the opposite; for he lacks humility, charity, self-effacement. But he is a Christ, a Messiah to the Christians, or at least in his own mind. In Gaddis' treatment, he is more an avenging Messiah than one bringing salvation, but this is the result of Gaddis' blurring the lines between salvation and damnation. With a little twist of presentation, Wyatt could be a purely demonic force instead of a Christ. But the latter aspect wins out because he perceives himself as bringing a purifying and cleansing quality, a "recognition," to a society that has doomed itself with corruptive sophistication. They are all money changers in the temple, Christians and Jews alike; and his role is to clean them out with his work, his presence, his steely will. As an artist, even as a failed artist, he offers a peculiar integrity they all lack; and since integrity is a buffoonish quality in the fifties, Wyatt seems to us a failed Christ, an egomaniac out of phase with his historical era.

Halfway through this immense novel—almost a thousand pages, half a million words—a character named Otto says what serves as a motif for the novel and for the period after the war when it was written. It serves, also, as a theme for *J R*. Otto is a failed playwright, a young man striving for the truth within a context of plagiarism or counterfeiting. Unable to achieve recognition, he searches reflections of himself for the "real person," which would be an act of recognition. If he could attain that reality, then he would be able to write a valid play, instead of one full of borrowed feelings and language. He has glimpses of his plight:

—Like a story I heard once [. . .] a story about a forged painting. It was a forged Titian that somebody had painted over another old painting, when they scraped the forged Titian away they found some worthless old painting underneath it, the forger had used it because it was an old canvas. But then there was something under that worthless painting, and they scraped it off and underneath that they found a Titian, a real Titian that had been there all the time. It was as though when the forger was working, and he didn't know the original was underneath, I mean he didn't know he knew it, but it knew, I mean something knew. I mean, do you see what I mean? That underneath that the original is there, that the real . . . thing is there, and on the surface you . . . if you can only . . . see what I mean?[2]

How traditionally American—Emersonian, in fact!—and yet how applicable it is to the decade in which it appeared. Layers of untruth piled on, beneath it, somewhere, the real, while all the time we demand the forgery. We recall how in the fifties tags were used as forms of discourse— "cold war," "pinkos," "left-winger", "Red China," "McCarthyism", "Hiss," "Rosenbergs," "liberal intellectual," "egghead"—as though labels were a kind of totem. To repeat them was to reach for truth with a magic wand. We demeaned every experience and every response by means of a reductive vocabulary that transmitted only the artificial and factitious.

If this is granted, then *The Recognitions* becomes our archetypal experience for the fifties, a model or scenario for the way in which we saw and will continue to see ourselves. *J R* grows out of this like a chrysalis.

Rhetoric acts as if it were a palimpsest, layer after layer disguising the real or actual. Exaggeration, hyperbole, rhetorical trivia all pile paint upon the old master. The ambitious reach of the Gaddis novel, sweeping up vertically the American past and horizontally present-day America and Europe, permits us to see inclusively. It is the opposite of the slice-of-life fiction that characterized the fifties: Styron's *Lie Down in Darkness,* Bellow's *The Adventures of Augie March,* or Malamud's *The Assistant* and *A New Life.* The literary background of Gaddis recalls and goes well beyond Hawthorne, well beyond Joyce or the Joycean novel. His vast work is a kind of literary conglomerate: the entire American literary past, Hawthorne, of course, but also Emerson and Thoreau, the Melville of *The Confidence-Man,* Poe, and more Poe, Faulkner, Eliot; the Europeans—Dostoyevsky, Kafka, as well as Joyce and Céline. But these are only beginnings. Gaddis draws on extensive reading in and knowledge of religious literature, church fathers and historians, Latin works, church theologians, all sufficiently assimilated so that they can be regurgitated for parodic purposes. The point throughout is that every belief once sincerely held is now a subject of mockery, unless one has achieved a recognition.

Wyatt Gwyon, heir to a New England past, realizes that recognition of reality, actuality, truth itself, involves a commitment of self little short of obsessive. He is not a man of the 1950s, but a man misplaced in his time. He is surrounded by people who live at the level of forgery, who must relate every feeling to advertisements, publicity, exaggeration of self, and who, as a consequence, have removed themselves from "recognitions." Like Stephen Dedalus—the parallels are numerous and clearly pointed—he is moving on different levels of intensity and observation.[3] And like Stephen, he will prove his differences from the crowd by bringing forth with great personal suffering an art that distinguishes him from those who worship false idols. With this art, Wyatt will define his sense of "recognition." He is the most appropriate deliverer of the vision, for, like Stephen, he is as much divinity student as creator. Wyatt has forsaken his religious studies in order to pursue new shapes and forms, the churchly past giving way to the artistic present.

Yet Gaddis is pursuing a course different from Joyce's, although not less significant. Wyatt's own work, as a definition of himself, lacks meaning, until he finds he can express himself only through a relationship with the past and, in particular, with the Flemish masters of the fifteenth and sixteenth centuries: Memling, the van Eyck brothers, Roger van der Weyden, Hugo van der Goes, Thierry Bouts, Patinir; and including the Venetian, Titian. The Flemish masters, besides their religious themes, impressed Wyatt with their obsessive dedication to detail, their absolute devotion to fidelity of line and color. Each curve and shaping involved the sense of a world and universe; nothing was left to chance or coincidence. And their devotion seemed complete—no doubt, no removal of self, no narcissism. Instead of losing the subject in themselves, as in the narcissistic work of present-day creative artists, they lost themselves in their subject. If the 1950s were doubletalk and doublethink, labels that defaulted on thought, the Flemish masters were anchors in reality, in "recognitions."

So Wyatt, who must transform the religious passions of his father into forms in which he can believe, removes himself to the Flemish past. He finds his creative urge focused and shaped through his connection to a distinctive, identifiable art. Here, Gaddis expresses the originality of his motif, not only through technical experimentation with forms but through insight into how art can reflect the real, whereas contemporary discourse falsifies it. Wyatt is not a conventional forger of great art—not at all like van Meegeren, who forged Vermeers and supplied them to the market as originals. Wyatt does Flemish "originals." He paints pictures that his masters could have painted. By bringing together the styles, colors, and shapes of a particular master, he creates canvases that might have been done— pictures, in fact, that the masters were thought to have painted, but which have failed to turn up. He reconstitutes art history by discovering the work they did (but that has disappeared) and making them live in new shapes. As Valentine, a typically commercially oriented art critic, says, "His work is so good it has almost been taken for forgery."

Valentine, then, caustically justifies Wyatt's kind of art, not for the sake of the art, but for the market value it retains despite changes of taste and style:

> —Most forgeries last only for a few generations, because they're so carefully done in the taste of the period, a forged Rembrandt, for instance, confirms everything that that period sees in Rembrandt. Taste and style change, and the forgery is painfully obvious, dated, because the new period has discovered [. . .] him to be quite different. That is the curse any genuine article must endure. (230)

For Valentine, whenever one of Wyatt's "authentic forgeries" is questioned, the dealer's suspicions have nothing to do with art: the dealer really hopes to discredit the work and bring down the price. Every time the dealer guesses wrong, the market becomes that much better for the forgeries, since other dealers become reluctant to question them. Wyatt's forgeries, accordingly, enter a market in which the authentic article is really no different from the forgery. The dealer and purchaser connive with the seller and art critic, since all have everything to gain from putting across a forgery and little to lose from the discovery of one.

The complicity of market, purchaser, seller, and art critic closes Gaddis' trap around Wyatt. We are now about one-fifth through the novel, and the terms are set. Like a fish struggling in a net, Wyatt must find a way through or be pulled in. As readers of the 1950s, we are in the position of complicity, like the figures in Plato who seek reality in appearances. We have the power to seek out forgeries, or else we can acquiesce to imitation, insist on its authenticity at the expense of any "recognition" of the real or actual. If we assent to forgery frequently enough, we lose the definition of what is real, what is forged.

The intense interest Wyatt takes in eggs, especially the whites, is connected to his need to revitalize the old. Eggs are for him the key to an authentic painting base, but eggs are also a basic source of life, out of which older elements give living form to the new. By stressing the egg, Wyatt offers it as an aspect of recognitions, an adversary to counterfeiting.

All this, however, is too simplistic for Gaddis, too heuristic. For while Wyatt may be a forger, he is a man of a distinct and original vision, for which he will lie, even kill. The ferocious demon is internal, and one recalls Faulkner's Sutpen, who created his "Hundred" in order to define that demon. At the time of this conversation between Valentine and Recktall ("rectal") Brown, an art dealer, Wyatt is a fateful, Christ-like thirty-three, and we never lose sight of the religious dimension. With his forgeries or miracles, Wyatt will deliver us from the defilement of art, and the defilement of life beyond it.

The epigraph to part 1, chapter 7, compares Jesus Christ, who took upon Himself human nature in order to redeem mankind, to the artist, who must redeem us from those who defile creation. But Gaddis is not making the by now hackneyed plea for the superiority of the artist over life, but for the fixity of vision that rejects complicity, that marketplace notion of the real and actual. At stake, finally, is not solely art, but the quality of life, even when that life is itself based on counterfeiting. As in the religious parable, when the sinner achieves salvation, the less real here is more real, especially when those who market both do not care which is which.

Wyatt fulminates against reproductions because there is only *one* painting with its distinct aura, and the reproduction is a fake that cheapens the original, making the viewer think he is seeing something real, while the actual remains inaccessible to him. Reproduction, Wyatt indicates, is marketplace prostitution, in which the artist's vision is diluted by way of intervening methods.[4] His fanaticism brings from Valentine the rejoinder that "every piece you do is calumny on the artist you forge" (250). We are now at the crossroads for the American and the American artist: at that choice between mechanical reproductions (marketplace) and purity of the original (art), between the pristine order (Garden of Eden) and worldly rewards (earthly paradise). Wyatt's defense of what he does is a defense of "recognitions" themselves; a defense of his journey into the past for a reality that is singular and intense, undiluted by the mechanical detection tools of the modern critic:

> —Do you think I do these the way all other forging has been done? Pulling the fragments of ten paintings together and making one, or taking a . . . a Dürer and reversing the composition so that the man looks to the right instead of left, putting a beard on him from another portrait, and a hat, a different hat from another, so that they look at it and recognize Dürer there? No, it's . . . the recognitions go much deeper, much further back, and I . . . this . . . the X-ray tests, and ultraviolet and infrared, the experts with their photomicrography and . . . macrophotography, do you think that's all there is to it? Some of them aren't fools, they don't just look for a hat or a beard, or a style they can recognize, they look with memories that . . . go beyond themselves, that go back to . . . where mine goes. (250)

Wyatt has repositioned himself: "I'm a master painter in the Guild, in Flanders, do you see? [. . .] because I've taken the Guild oath, not for the critics, the experts [. . .] to use pure materials, to work in the sight of God . . ." (ibid.).

Wyatt is more than a crazy fool, only part Quixote, for his is more than a vision of what could be. He makes the vision happen, and his fidelity to the masters is so great he becomes a master, whereas his contemporaries remain forgers of taste, panderers to the market. A modern-day visionary, a Christ of aesthetics, he insists that the purity of his materials—the gold he uses, his pigments, his exquisite colors—suggests the nature of his art. Valentine says that while Wyatt paints "it's [his] own work," but what happens, he asks, when he attaches the signature? Wyatt admits he loses everything when that occurs; then he is, at the same moment alone, a forger. Valentine consoles him by saying that the sole thing he can be prosecuted for is the signature, whether Hugo van der Goes, or Patinir, or Hubert van Eyck, *that* forgery. The paintings are authentic: "The law doesn't care a damn for the painting. God isn't watching them" (251). Wyatt's greatest feat, he admits, would be to do a painting in the style of Hubert van Eyck, whose very existence as Jan van Eyck's older brother is in question. To paint a Hubert van Eyck, to document the painting, and prove not only that Hubert existed but that the painting is real—all this will fall on fertile ground, and the sole illegality would be the signature, not the painting.

Wyatt must live with this knowledge, that the moment he signs the painting and makes it valuable, at that moment he destroys the foundation of his art. The Faustian quality of his conflict is clear, and he follows it through by destroying everything, burning it, turning it into ashes, and then himself assuming the name Stephen Asche. He is the first Christian martyr, born out of the ashes of his own work. The paradoxes and ironies are those of the very nature of the American experience, the Fall implicit in the beauties and purities of the Garden.

Themes of forgery and counterfeiting underlie every aspect of the novel, including Gaddis' method of novel making. For a book of such great length (the size of three or four conventional novels), the author needed more than a conventional narrative; and the characteristic American picaresque (as in *Augie March* or *A New Life*), although appropriate to them, would have become untenable for a thousand pages—unless the entire book was parodic, as Barth's *The Sot-Weed Factor*. Gaddis devised two, really three, kinds of scenic development. The first involves the introduction of a character, unknown to the reader and, apparently, unconnected to the narrative, who then links up with someone we know from before. At the beginning of part 1, chapter 7, for example, we read: "That afternoon Fuller sat on a bench, his back turned to Central Park in December" (222). Since the novel is already so dense, we may feel we have missed Fuller's name in a previous passage, so confidently does Gaddis make the introduction. We remain unfocused until we catch Fuller's association with Recktall Brown, who has been discussed, however, only once before. That, too, is part of the plan: when an association is made, it hangs by a single reference.

Brown brings us eventually to Wyatt Gwyon, and to the forgeries that he is masterminding. But even when we meet Brown, along with Basil Valentine, the talk centers on a "he," who, we assume, is Wyatt. Once details flow in, we know it is "he," but not at first. The method, so far, creates immediate annoyance, especially since the tones and textures are also so ironic and paradoxical.

A second method that Gaddis employs, possibly as a carryover from Joyce and Faulkner, is to describe an entire episode without indicating the name or names of the characters, so that the reader must derive from the context who is involved. This method, incidentally, as well as several others compatible with it, is employed even more extensively in *J R* twenty years later. In a scene in which Reverend Gwyon is never named, we find Wyatt returning to the New England town of his forebears, where Gwyon has gone mad, has been moved to a private institution, and finally has died. Dick, the new minister, visits Wyatt's father in the institution, where he is not recognized by the older man. Gwyon is reduced to ashes—which turn up later in Spain in loaves, which the son eats—while the new minister prepares his sermon for the following Sunday curled up with copies of the *Reader's Digest.* No names, and Reverend Gwyon passes through his agony and madness without coming to us as an identified person, only as a substance, ashes at that.

The final part 3 of the novel, one-quarter of its length, incorporates both methods: unnamed characters and characters who seem to have little connection to what preceded. In addition, scenes are themselves so placed that they appear unassociated with people we have met. We have, then, actually three unknowns. Modernism with a vengeance! Because we may try out several alternate possibilities before we hit upon the "right one," we reconstruct many kinds of sequences. And in places, even the most careful reader cannot be certain of each character, event, scene.

Some of this Gaddis may have gained from Joyce, or from Eliot's modulations in *The Waste Land,* but he differs from Joyce—I have in mind chiefly *Ulysses*—in essential ways. The narrative line of *Ulysses* is frequently secondary to what occurs along the way; discourse and digressions are at least as important as anything that happens. Part of the modernity of *Ulysses* was just this seeming indifference to narrative thrust. Voices are themselves thematic, language its own object. But *The Recognitions* has a strong narrative drive; it is not a secondary item, nor can it be ignored while we pursue method. A good deal does happen, including all kinds of forgery and counterfeiting, some conspiratorial work (Basil Valentine is a secret agent of sorts), even murder, and the exile of the main character, himself a murderer. What Gaddis has done is to locate his narrative under layers of disguise and deception, finding there in plot line the equivalent of counterfeiting. Like that Titian itself, which lies under layers of paint, Gaddis' narrative awaits someone willing to peel away coats that falsify and corrupt.

Since the theme of the book is forgery, the motif recognitions, Gaddis' aim is clearly to defamiliarize the familiar so as to force us to experience it freshly. Thus, every kind of scene—even if as familiar as cocktail party scenarios—gains fresh tonal varieties from the method of presentation.

Overlapping with the three methods mentioned above is Gaddis' theory of indeterminacy. There is a kind of scenic development in which the description trails off; the set-in situation is not resolved in any way, and the character or characters simply vanish, either permanently, or else to turn up in another way. We experience a novelistic sense of inconclusiveness, built into it as part of the fragmentation, of characters trailing in and out, the cutting and montage we find in films. This is organic: the novel is made up of numerous incomplete stories whose conclusions are never to be seen or defined.

For example: a man named Sinisterra ("sinister land") is a parallel forger to Wyatt. His forgeries, however, are standard types; he is not original in his creations but is a counterfeiter of existing forms, the American $20 bill, for instance. He runs through the lower criminal world as Wyatt does through the higher criminal world of art, artists, art dealers, and the wealthy. In both worlds, the aim is, literally, to make money. Sinisterra's first appearance in the novel occurs on page 5 in a fleeting reference amidst a good deal of frenetic authorial maneuvering. It becomes a typical Gaddis ploy.

His early importance is this: Reverend Gwyon and his wife, Camilla, parents of Wyatt, sail for Spain on the *Purdue Victory.* Camilla develops acute appendicitis and is operated upon by a so-called ship's surgeon, Sinisterra. She dies under the knife, and, as it turns out, Sinisterra is not a doctor, but a counterfeiter traveling under (his own) forged papers. In his defense, he offers evidence that he had once aided a vivisectionist in Tampa. He now leaves the scene, to reappear almost five hundred pages later in chapter 5 of part 2, the *Purgatorio* of our *Commedia.*[5] When we meet him, he appears in the standard Gaddis manner, apparently a new character who will, somehow, be connected to the others.

The epigraph for this chapter is the order from Abraham Lincoln's treasurer "to the director of the Mint" to declare the "Trust of our people in God" on our national coins. The mint was charged to prepare a device with a "motto expressing in the fewest and tersest words possible, this national recognition" (487). The word *recognition,* the presence of a counterfeiter, the large role of Sinisterra (the "killer" of Wyatt's mother) all point up Gaddis' ironies. The world as conspiracy, while not born here, is given sustenance and shape. This is not only high comedy, but high politics.

Sinisterra's chief reading is the *National Counterfeit Detector,* a publication devoted to describing the latest gaffes in counterfeiting. Since he values his art as much as Wyatt, he becomes more disturbed by poor evaluations of his work than by the prison sentence he serves. While Wyatt strives to achieve a perfect "Jesus figure," Sinisterra aims at a perfect Jackson portrait on the $20 bill. As we follow Sinisterra's intense career, we focus on the "real Jackson" much more attentively than we would without the counterfeit president; forgery energizes what the real deadens. By way of Sinisterra, Gaddis enters American history and finds forgery establishing its own culture, including bank issues of money made on fictitious banks, banks that backed fictitious or worthless notes. That world based on forgery fills Sinisterra with extreme pride:

Behind him lay the Protocols of the Elders of Zion; and the magnanimous grant of Constantine, though that emperor was some five centuries dead when the spirit of his generosity prevailed through forgers in Rome, to bequeath all of western Europe to the Papacy. Behind him lay decrees, land grants, and wills, whose art of composition became a regular branch of the monastic industry, busy as those monks in the Middle Ages were keeping a-kindle the light of knowledge which they had helped to extinguish everywhere else. Behind lay Polycrates, who minted gold-coated lead corins in his own kingdom of Samos; and Solon, who decreed death for such originality in his. Canute severed guilty hands; and England . . . removed not only hands but eyes. (494)

Sinisterra holds on to his edition of Bicknell's *Counterfeit Detector* as proudly as a noted surgeon may exhibit a copy of Galen's *Anatomy*. His ideology parallels that of the other characters: Otto, the failed playwright, who plagiarizes; Esme, Wyatt's model, whose poems move in and out of plagiarism; the art dealers and critics, as well as buyers and sellers, already mentioned as panderers to the marketplace. His counterfeiting extends even to his parental role, for Sinisterra plays the false father to Otto and then, later, as Mr. Yák, a Rumanian, takes a paternal role with Wyatt, returning him to his original name, Stephen, and adding Asche. At this time, Sinisterra is characteristically trying to sell off a corpse as an ancient Eygptian mummy.

In a further extension of the forgery, while playing the false father to Otto (who hasn't seen his father since childhood), Sinisterra gives him a large bundle of beautifully printed $20 bills. The innocent Otto spreads them, even to his real father (a Mr. Pivner) and, of course, to his circle of artificial, partying friends. When the print on the bills runs, Otto and Pivner are identified with the forgery and caught. The bills pass through society by way of people with counterfeit feelings, an entire society a ready marketplace.

About halfway through (that is, after about two hundred and fifty thousand words), Gaddis increasingly comes to favor a modified stream-of-consciousness narrative without authorial intrusion. While avoiding the breakup of language the true method calls for, Gaddis nevertheless slips narrative into individual consciousness to the extent that consciousness is nearly all. There is no intervening narrator until near the end, when he provides some exposition of events. By chapter 3 of part 3, with identification of characters left entirely to the reader—characters are merely voices—the end has circled around to the beginning. At the start of the novel, Reverend Gwyon and his wife made their ill-fated voyage to Spain

and met Sinisterra as the bogus ship doctor; now, Wyatt having burned
his paintings and rejected his forgeries, has fled to Spain, a murderer. There,
he meets Sinisterra, now Mr. Yák, whose aim, as we have mentioned, is
to prepare and sell a corpse done up as an ancient Egyptian mummy. The
chapter is aptly titled "The Last Turn of the Screw."

Like Stephen and Bloom in *Ulysses,* the two meet oddly. By this time,
Wyatt is ready to become Stephen, the name originally destined for him;
and Sinisterra adds Asche on Stephen's false papers. As Stephen Asche,
Wyatt, the forger and murderer who once sought recognitions in counterfeit paintings, attempts rebirth. Obsessed with failure, pursued by demons,
compulsively seeking some form of truth, Wyatt-Stephen has returned to
Spain to seek his mother's grave, unaware, of course, that the man offering him aid is the ship doctor who butchered her. Further, because of a
mixup with his father's ashes, Stephen does not know that the loaves he
eats contain mixed in with the flour those very ashes, an act of true communion. Not only is he eating the wafer, he is consuming the actual body,
this act of cannibalism indeed recognition of the real.

All these efforts at the real and actual on Wyatt-Stephen's part, however,
occur under a mantle of deception, disguise, and forgery. Yák circles around
like the Great Mother because he needs Wyatt's skill in preparing the
mummy, which he hopes will be his consummate swindle. Sinisterra thinks
he can win over Stephen by asserting he, too, is a craftsman and an artist;
he insists he has fallen, not because he is a bum or has stabbed someone,
but because "they" were jealous of his work. Wyatt is now so strung out
that it is questionable if he even hears Sinisterra. Having put all his energies into creating great Flemish "originals," an effort to transcend his contemporaries' inconsequence and technical deficiencies, he drifts, a battered
Orpheus, or perhaps an avatar of 1950s "Beats."

The structural tension in the novel lies in that play between great energy
and great passivity; between a surface of growth and development and the
sense of nihilistic weariness, enervation, exhaustion, what could in fact
be considered twin aspects of the American fifties. This tension can be
spatially expressed. We note the great stress on traveling: Wyatt's frenzied
movement from New England to New York, then to Europe, accompanied
by the frenzied movements of the other characters. Even those who go
nowhere move to and fro like Michelangelo, consuming space at cocktail
parties. As against this, however, is the almost overwhelming desire to rest
or drop out. In fifties fiction, we have such a conflicting range of titles—
"Lie Down" or "Flee the," become an "Invisible" or "Underground" Man,
or go "On the Road," or else have "Adventures of" and gain a "New Life."
In swings of movement and passivity, we locate the contradictions of peo-

ple who must get there so they can rest or disappear, or who become passive in the hope of gaining energy for a new foray.

In this respect, Gaddis' novel is archetypal. We can see how Pynchon, with his idea of the yo-yoing effect, is indebted to him; that expenditure of circular energy. We can, in turn, perceive how Gaddis sought in Hawthorne and Poe those intense inner energies that war with passivity, for this tension connects to larger American themes and paradoxes. Sweeps of limitless space and time run up against degeneration, entropy, paralysis, and withdrawal, As Gaddis shows here and later in *J R,* American affirmation is "against"—a value system erected on negativism and nihilism. The reason is that American attitudes are predicated on the Edenic myth and Fall, and Gaddis, accordingly, plays on faith gained and lost, like a yo-yo.

That desire to hide oneself, so evident in Wyatt, is the result of complications that work at the extremes: either easy acceptance and celebrity, which means a form of death; or desperate, often hopeless opposition, which leads to a different kind of personal ruin. Every form of success—and Wyatt is an outstanding success as a forger, as an "original" counterfeiter—must be a form of death. This is a profoundly political idea, the American equivalent of European ideologies. That attack *Life* made on the contemporary American novel in September 1955—the year of *The Recognitions*—went further than a misunderstanding of the fictional process; it was based on political outrage that the novelist had rejected those easy resolutions that, *Life* assumed, made up the good life and that the novelist saw as forms of death. The "good life" for Wyatt, as for art critics and dealers, would have been a continued exploitation of his talent for original counterfeits and his silence in the face of external demands made upon him. Success, in *Life*'s terms, was assured: the counterfeit was the real. Gaddis, however, insisted on a more layered sense of the counterfeit: that while it could falsify on one hand and still seek truth on the other, a more intense truth lay within, beyond the reach of all aspects of counterfeiting. The working out is extremely complex and requires the close reasoning of intricate scenes and dense structuring, not a flat statement of direction.

We are at that point when the novel as a genre had to respond or else succumb to its own success. There began in the fifties the growing awareness that even the novel—a traditionally stable, solid presence—was insufficient as a reflection of reality; that, as Tony Tanner comments, "American writers seem . . . to have felt how tenuous, arbitrary, and even illusory are the verbal constructs which men call descriptions of reality."[6] There was the need to seek more radical forms so as to keep pace with or mirror the phantasmagoria called up by science and technology, what we find in

Gaddis and Barth now, Pynchon, McElroy, and Barthelme later, Hawkes earlier.

Counterfeiting and invisibility work well with nearly any of these fictional developments. Tuned in as the American novelist has been to energy and linear development of character, counterfeiting and invisibility present a tension: counterfeiting, the use of imitative form and derivative life; invisibility, a negation of spatiality and vitality, a substitute of darkness for light, innerness for movement. The twin themes allow for that curious disaffection we discover in our novelists of the fifties and sixties. That is, they may seem dark or black or Gothic—whether Barth, Mailer, Southern, Roth, Heller, Pynchon, or Barthelme—but all too frequently they slip away from the ultimate nature of their observations to resolve or slide off to areas of life that offer more dynamics than counterfeiting or invisibility allows. Such novelists flirt with the disintegration implicit in their themes, while fascinated with energy and movement. The point, except for a few, seems to be: counterfeiting and invisibility accommodate their personal attitudes, but movement and energy preempt their ideology. Even those who recognize the trap, such as Roth and Malamud, possibly Mailer, blur the full adversariness of their experience and compromise the paralytic implications of their material.

Perhaps the novel of the fifties except for *The Recognitions,* which blurs least, is *Invisible Man.* Counterfeiting and invisibility control Ellison's vision, just as narcissism, circuitry, and memories define his main character. We see how Ellison combines paralysis and enervation with typical American themes, building his tensions between traditional ideas of space and energy and the particularities of his narrator's experiences, which suggest exhaustion and stasis, self-examination and narcissism. He has blended the American sense of things, in Emerson, Whitman, Melville, Twain, and Wright, even Hawthorne, with the European—Dostoyevsky and Kafka, among others—to give us a sense of the period, in the same way Gaddis was working along a blend of Hawthorne and Kafka to produce a "counterfeit decade."

Once these observations are made, Ellison and Gaddis part ways, for the former, however ironically, is more concerned with growth and development, characteristics firmly in the *Bildungsroman* tradition. Gaddis moves into the more doomed part of the American tradition, associated with Melville's Ahab, Hawthorne's fated figures, Poe's nightmarish characters and scenes. Ellison foresaw enervation, but also the potentiality of growth. Gaddis identifies with the doom that lies beneath enervation. The images in the final sections of *The Recognitions* are of an incoherent Wyatt, a pilgrimage of doomed figures to Rome, a lunatic Otto, and Sinisterra with his counterfeit Egyptian mummy. Widely dispersed geographically, they are all circumscribed by the final scene of the novel. Stanley, an imitational composer, enters a church in Fenestrula, sees a gigantic organ, and indicates to a priest who understands no English that he intends to play it. When Stanley pulls out two particular keys, the priest puts them back, with the warning, in an Italian that Stanley cannot comprehend, that the church is so old the vibrations from the bass keys could be dangerous: "Per favore non bassi . . . e non strane combinazioni di note, capisce . . .'"

Like the poor reader with no Italian, Stanley understands nothing of the warning and rolls out the deepest possible sound of the bass pipes. "Everything moved, and even falling, soared in atonement. He was the only person caught in the collapse, and afterward, most of his work was recovered too, and it is still spoken of, when it is noted, with high regard, though seldom played" (956). The apocalypse has arrived, with an explanation in Italian; and this experience of Stanley's, personally doomed, while his counterfeit work soars in atonement, is a perfect expression of Henry Adams' virgin and dynamo: the machine crushes, the Virgin saves. Gaddis' vision, both hilarious and doom filled, goes much further than Ellison's toward a reading of the 1950s, even the entire postwar era.

When he returned to fiction in the 1970s, with the monumentally conceived *J R* (1975), his world is a thriving, writhing, buzzing nightmare, a continuation of fifties counterfeit and postwar forgery. The key here is the method: interrupted conversation, incomplete lines of thought, a shorthand language—language that no longer serves its traditional functions. Gaddis has tried to put gesture and expression into the written word. But it is, also, the language we feed into computers, set phrases programmed for rapidity, where our interest lies only in the printout.

The walls that come tumbling down at the finale of *The Recognitions,* Gaddis' *Götterdammerung,* lead, fittingly enough, into an early part of *J R,* which presents a school production of *Das Rheingold,* with J R himself as the dwarfish Alberich. But Gaddis' Wagnerian model does not lead to the death of the gods or to human love, but to another kind of god, which is business, high finance. *Das Rheingold* accommodates the prologue of this immensely long novel, since gold, geld, capitalism are forms of paradise or nightmare for all who enter.

We recall Alberich's key speech to Woton and Loge in *Das Rheingold,* and we need only substitute J R, the school performer who becomes Alberich. Wagner's dwarf:

> I will capture all you godly folk!
> As I have renounced love,
> so all things living

shall renounce it;
lured by gold
you shall ever lust for gold alone;
Oh blissful heights
in happy meditation
you lull yourselves;
you immortal dwellers in luxury
despise the black goblins!
Beware, beware!
For once you people serve
my might
your pretty women,
who spurn my wooing,
the dwarf shall force to his pleasure,
though love smiles not on him. . . . Beware!
Beware of the dark legion
when the Nibelung treasure shall rise
out of the silent depths into the light of day![8]

The content, once extracted, is familiar: the business of America is business; but Gaddis has found a form, a language as well as focus for his view of postwar America. Many devices from *The Recognitions* remain. The withholding of vital information is crucial, for the retention of material creates a pressure on the reader comparable to that of water, dammed, suddenly let go. We are caught, in part, in a guessing game, in a suspense drama, and in a purely dramatic action. Postponement, as in drama, is the key; we push against unknowns.

That device in isolation does not convey Gaddis' method. Along with Hawkes, Barth, Pynchon, Barthelme, Gaddis tried to parallel or even improve upon the major moderns in creating "voices." The withholding of information recalls Faulkner, in particular *Absalom, Absalom!*, perhaps *The Sound and the Fury*. The Faulknerian presence (and behind that, Joycean) is, in fact, everywhere, in phrasing, in interrupted speech that suggests great unspoken depths, and in broad verbal wit. Intermixed with the incomplete or withheld information strategy is an analogous device, also familiar from Faulkner: the unidentified speaker. The beginning of *J R* is one of the most deliberately confusing in literature:

—Money . . . ? in a voice that rustled.
—Paper, yes.
—And we'd never seen it. Paper money.
—We never saw paper money till we came east.
—It looked so strange the first time we saw it. Lifeless.[9]

This continues for pages, with names slipped in that mean nothing, the speakers unidentified: rocky excrescences for which there is no mountain. The reader struggles not only for identification of the speakers, or for the information, but for some thread of argument that connects these discrete pieces of material. Long before recognition is forthcoming, the scene, we discover suddenly, has shifted to a school, where the main part of the plot eventually settles. Without warning, different speakers appear. Words and voices, however, seem disembodied. Location, direction, content are unclear. Compared with *J R*, *The Recognitions* is almost traditional.

The scene becomes fixed on a musical performance, *Das Rheingold*, with a shadowy schoolboy as the dwarfish Alberich, our J R, a twentieth-century Huck Finn. But the J R or Junior of the title rarely comes into clear focus. He is a sixth-grader, and a full-faced portrait, Gaddis realized, would be of little interest. Moving in shadows, however, he can be a giant, the mastermind of a vast corporate enterprise, something it takes us hundreds of pages to identify. In those early school scenes, we know him only as Alberich, in an opera concerned with the Gold of the Rhine. Since the opening lines were fixed on paper money—that is, stocks and shares—we begin to perceive a theme, although unassociated with any particular characters. The theme, then, rather than characters, will dominate the novel. Characters are subsumed into process. Just as in *Das Rheingold*, the Gold of the Rhine will dominate the opera and entire *Ring*, so money will open and close the cycles of *J R*.

In its largest sense, this is a novel about education, school systems, places of learning, locations where the young are acclimated to the values of America. In this large sense, the school that J R attends is a replica of America, and behind the school system are all the values that feed into education and that make it and America the way they are. As a novel about education, *J R* reaches out toward the more traditional *Bildungsroman,* the novel about the apprenticeship of a young person to life; and to the picaresque, the narrative about a rogue or outsider who, moving on the margins of society, seeks his way in. In Gaddis' school, instruction has shifted from blackboard and books to field trips and television snippets. Education is based on media events; instruction is by way of experience. It is fitting that the teachers and school board are nearly all dedicated to other activities; that education is their excuse for excursions into money-making schemes. In this respect *J R* is not anomalous, but the perfect product of the school system. The symbol for schools now is the field trip; television is the language of the classroom. Money is the motif, counterfeiting the ideology.

This is still only a crude description of the novel. Paramount is the use of interrupted speech, in what approximates a contemporary lingo. About seventy-five thousand words into the novel, we have our first clear indication of what is going to be significant. The unidentified J R says to Mr. Bast, the music coach,

> —You what I was thinking on the train hey? he came on righting his load, hurrying alongside—like I have this thing which what it is is it's this selling outfit where what you do is you send in and they send you all these different shoes which you get to wear them around so people can see them, you know? See that's how you sell them, see? I mean not the ones you're wearing right off your feet but like you take their order and then you make this commission, you know? Like it says you can make a hundred dollars a week in your spare time and you get to wear these shoes around too, you want me to find it? (133)

This is one of J R's few long speeches, and it is interspersed with interrupted sentences, a printout or shorthand method. The long sequences are fluid and of a conversational ordinariness that is remarkable. Gaddis' execution is merciless; more than satirical, the style strikes at the heart of every type of communication. Later, a radio plays because the turnoff knob cannot be reached. It catches our attention in small bursts, then relinquishes; and our speech patterns are similar. People listen, then stop, then are caught up in their own speech, interrupt, are interrupted, and the cycle renews itself on human self-indulgence. We hear, ultimately, only our own thought patterns, which we attempt to relocate in a language that is strangled before it reaches fulfillment. Counterfeit thoughts become part of an oral tradition.

Incomplete speech is the language of money-making. The director of the school operation, Whiteback, also heads a bank; and all school business is interrupted by his telephone that signals bank business. The educational plant, and the language interred in it, is intermixed at every level with the world of the bank. A financial scheme advanced, in fact, is to advertise in textbooks items that would be suitable to the needs of the reader; for example, deodorant tampons in advanced algebra or French III. Within this frame of reference, the sixth-grader, J R, is carrying out a function with words he can barely pronounce, no less understand: to do the work of the banks and make money. We bank while we learn.

Obstacles for the audience of this Americanized *Das Rheingold* are overwhelming. Gaddis is so unbending, and, one may add, obsessive, that the reader is almost forgotten. Nevertheless, there are scenes that are among the most hilarious in American fiction. This may be a doom-filled vision, but it is also one of tremendous comedic value. We can cite the Marx Brothers scenario for the Ninety-sixth–Street apartment that is the financial hub, with mail pouring in; Bast trying to write music for a "zoo movie"; the hippie, Rhoda, protesting that the scene is too far out even for her; water cascading from a broken sink and then a broken tub faucet; a radio playing somewhere beneath the books, the books themselves identified only by "III GRIN-LOC"; the proliferation of "Wise Potato Chips Hoppin' with Flavor"; volumes of *Textile World, Forest Industries, Supervisory Management* strewn everywhere—all this as part of the financial empire J R has been building by way of telephone and the mails. This is incomparable comedy, although for the reader to reach it, he must come through a verbal and narrative obstacle course.

Gaddis is, in a sense, carrying on an extended, obsessively detailed dialogue with himself; he is the programmer, and he receives the printout. All voices echo, a true universe of words, a parallel phenomenon to *Gravity's Rainbow.* The chief conduits for all information are the telephone and the mails. In no novel has there been so much fed into the telephone, so that we can say this is a "telephonic novel," or a "postal novel," part of that Tristero system outlined in Pynchon's *The Crying of Lot 49.* Essentially, these are tools of obsession: placing calls, needing phone booths, making change for the call, and then gathering information without appearing. J R is a small, impersonal figure, in fact only a voice (often disguised) or a signature on a printed form requesting free goods.

The idea behind the novel is remarkable: that with the telephone and the mails, money can be made by any marginal operator, by a sixth-grader, through a self-perpetuating system. The basis of J R's fortune is a shipment of one million surplus navy forks. The goods of the world are simply recycled: the forks, originally ordered by the navy, were produced for the navy and then dumped by the navy as detritus, only to be picked up by J R through the mails, started through the system once again, becoming the basis for further deals, all of which involve recycled materials, paper deals, penny stocks, goods that, having become unfashionable or dysfunctional, are then returned into fashion. J R is the new generation of entrepreneur, and his fortune will result from his intuition that goods shuffling through the system become themselves the touchstones of wealth; movement, not production, is necessary. Without money or visible goods, J R is worth millions.

Gaddis stresses the depersonalization of money-making as part of the wasteland in which people operate and thrive.[10] The subject is familiar, but the point of attack is original. The structural equivalent of the theme is hundreds of thousands of words of dialogue, Gaddis' demonic way with

conversational gambits: interrupted speech, run-together names and statements, broken-off phrases and barely uttered words, an oral shorthand.
As in *The Recognitions,* we must pick up speakers from the situation and
their words; but here the torrent of language pouring over us makes identification more difficult. In terms of language, Gaddis has tried to do for
the oral American idiom what Joyce did for written English — rediscover
it as a literary voice, defamiliarize it so it seems fresh. His is the poetry,
flow, and rhythm of routine speech, as much code as communication.

> —Oh JR I . . .
> —Oh, hi Mrs Joubert . . . as quickly gone behind the glass panels clat-
> tering closed on the first ring. —Hello . . . ? pencil stub, paper scraps sur-
> facing —this is him speaking yes, I'll accept it . . . portfolio jammed up
> against a knee —hello? Yes hi, boy it's a good thing you called hey I . . . where
> just now at the hotel? Did you [. . .] no what kind of full uniform, you mean
> with a gun and all . . . ? No but . . . no but sure I know we got this here
> hotel suite so you could partly use it to play the . . . (464)

As a legatee of modernism, Gaddis appears to omit the reader's needs,
demonstrating a good deal of hostility, as if the latter were an excrescence.
One of the qualities of modernism is to squeeze out the reader, making
it appear that only the artwork itself exists, dissociated, as it were, from
an audience. Gaddis plays on this technique, but he also provides a mag-
net for the reader in his use of language. His language is a kind of subtext
in that while it functions to communicate necessary bits of narrative information, its real function is to move beyond information into gray areas
where speech is merely sound, a noise medium like background music or
street traffic. Thus, for Gaddis, the language of the novel is syllables, voices,
arrangements even more so than communication. The subtextual aspects
of words is almost the same as gesture, in the way we use movement to
comment when language fails.

For scenic development, Gaddis works with a very complicated montage: not simply shifting within a scene, or shifting from brief scene to
brief scene, but moving from one long segment to another without any
shading in or sense of direction. This fits his sense of modern communication, as aborted phraseology, undigested bits of information, false data
purveyed as fact. It conveys, as well, his detestation of contemporary drift,
lack of commitment, whether work, art, or even self. It is a true response
to the vapidity one felt in the postwar years, when high finance *was* good
for America and the life of the mind was considered counterfeit.

Since the goal is seamlessness and flow, there is considerable and conscious overlap of data. Gaddis' game is a form of suspense based on incompletion and interruption, sudden shiftings of locale from school to bank to investment office to apartment in a verbiage that permits no clear definition or demarcation. This is a suspenseful story without crime or traditional criminals, and the reader must play along for clues. Since so much is a compulsion *not* to give, the reader desperately scrambles for what is given, like the tension we experience in crime stories. Our role is to be shaped by data.

As a corollary of education, Gaddis is concerned with crime: the crime of the decade, century, American history itself. For him, the deepest crime, whether in the counterfeiting process of the earlier novel or the financial recycling of the later, is individual loss of recognition, actuality, perception of the real, if that can ever be determined. It may be impossible to achieve recognition, but to forgo the possibility is to collapse and subvert the individual.

A good example of a young man trying to attain perception and definition is Edward Bast. A serious composer in the contemporary mode, he is first seen directing and conducting a school performance of *Das Rheingold*. Yet despite his aspirations, Bast, whose name can be "enough" or "bastard," finds himself drawn into J R's financial schemes. He also becomes drawn into composing "animal music" for a zoo movie, a scheme intermixed with financial shenanigans by a man named Crawley. Like Whiteback, who blends education with banking, Crawley moves back and forth effortlessly between financial deals and his "zoo movie." Bast is caught between, drawn toward finance, which he cannot comprehend, and yet intent on music, which he tries to compose amidst the clutter of the Ninety-sixth–Street apartment. Music, his kind, would help define him, whereas J R's schemes and Crawley's offer suck him in. Unable to resist, he begins to float toward his own kind of doom, loss of recognition of himself and of what is outside.

One peculiarity of the novel is that the titular figure is really not a character in the narrative. As we suggested above, J R hovers but is not a presence—somewhat like the Holy Ghost floating over Wyatt in *The Recognitions*. He is the catalyst for the financial empire that develops around the mail drop at Ninety-sixth Street, but the novel functions almost entirely without his appearance. We note the Joycean conceit: a Ulysses of the title who is absent from the book, and whose presence must be extrapolated from his opposite, Bloom, a kind of negative analogy. J R becomes, on his smaller scale, a mythical figure—the J R of legend rather than the J R moving in the novel. Only "Hey Mister" signals he is there.

One of his very few solid presences comes late in the novel, about two-

thirds through, and, characteristically, J R is on the telephone. He is speaking to Bast, but not as a sixth-grader or an eleven-year-old. Here he is completely the corporate manager, the financial plunger, the man who has
studied the market, futures, pork bellies, and margins. He has all the lingo
of finance, although parts of it confuse him. He turns to his sixth-grade
teacher, Mrs Joubert, for further instruction: "Like now we already learned
about the stock market and all with this here our share of America? See
so now if we bought some of these futures like if we got in these here bellies and learned the . . ." (472–73). He asks, further, about "hedged com-
modities" and wonders if it is possible to "hedge in these futures"—all
questions that she, as the "expert" in finance, cannot answer. J R sees
millionaires wherever he looks; he is obsessed with the ideology of money
and money-making, pointing to water-fountain millionaires, lightbulb millionaires, even locker millionaires, while Mrs Joubert tries to make him
see the evening, the sky, the wind, the moon. But J R is intent on his own
mission and fails to gain recognition.

We could, possibly, characterize the novel as "Some Inversions of
Pastoral," perceiving it as an antipastoral. If J R is our contemporary Huck
Finn, then *J R* is Gaddis' parody of what we, a pastoral nation, have be-
come. Both novels end with the voice of the protagonist heading out for
"new territory." Huck is running to open space, where he can breathe;
J R is seeking to exploit a new money-making scheme. J R denies pastoral—
that is, natural truth—in every scene where he appears. The composer,
Bast, attempts to demonstrate to the youngster the wonder that lies in
Bach and Wagner: "There's such a thing as as, as intangible assets" (655),
but J R has closed off this experience, which is the quality of pastoral.
For Gaddis, pastoral is everything that exists outside systems in areas of
value judgment; it has the mysteries Thoreau attributed to the depths of
his pond.

Implied in this parodying of finance is the parody of technology and
science, what we see contemporaneously in Pynchon's *Gravity's Rainbow.*
Gaddis works at several levels, describing devices such as an electric letter
opener that is a devastating weapon; an electric tie rack arranged by color,
with a pushbutton selector; a "Steak-watcher," which computes the time
necessary for cooking steaks and chops. Science parodies itself as it tries
to develop a "Frigicom":

—Dateline New York, Frigicom, comma, a process now being developed to
solve the noise pollution problem comma may one day take the place of
records comma books comma even personal letters in our daily lives comma,

according to a report released jointly today by the Department of Defense and Ray hypen X Corporation comma a member of the caps J R Family of Companies period new paragraph. The still secret Frigicom process is attracting the attention of our major cities as the latest scientific breakthrough promising noise elimination by the placement of absorbent screens at what are called quote shard intervals unquote in noise polluted areas period operating at faster hyphen sound speeds comma a complex process employing liquid nitrogen will be used to convert the noise shards comma as they are known comma at temperatures so low they may be handled with comparative ease by trained personnel immediately upon emission before the noise element is released into the atmosphere period. (527)

The translation: sounds can be frozen into a solid state.

Since all is flow, whether sound, water, conversation, a radio playing, publicity and advertising, or characters and scenes themselves, there is no external order. Once caught in J R's international money schemes, the characters have no lives except what the flow determines. As a novelist who carries the fifties into the seventies, Gaddis is linked with Pynchon and Barthelme, writers who have constructed their universe almost entirely of words and whose basic theme is counterfeiting. To these, we can add Nabokov, in *Ada,* as well as the earlier *Pale Fire.* Behind them is Borges, and parallel is Barth. For all, their verbal constructs are not solely connected to a more experimental phase in the arts — although that may be present — but to a distinct reaction to fifties and sixties political and social themes. That stress on verbal constructs is not withdrawal from statement, but statement itself. Fiction has become an intensification of a verbal universe. Gaddis and Pynchon, in particular, do not use language to enter an interior world where all is self, narcissism, or indulgence, but as a way of exploring the outer reaches of language where it blurs into disorder. Their verbal construct is not a hiding behind words as a shield, but the forcing of words outward where language and things merge into each other.

The distinction is important, for it separates Gaddis and Pynchon as wordmen from Barthelme and Nabokov. The latter two are following in the Joycean tradition of internalizing experience, shunning the external, and locating activity by way of words that point inward. Barthelme does this and at the same time disbelieves in it, whereas Nabokov pursues it for the sheer exuberance of his own versatility, especially in the fruitcake-like *Ada.* All is performance.

Gaddis and Pynchon are very much social and political novelists, quite concerned with the external world, whether America as a corporate empire in *J R* or as part of a multinational cartel in *Gravity's Rainbow.* Their barrages of words, like Pynchon's rockets, are centrifugal, not centripetal, forces. The impersonality of *J R* results from Gaddis' construction of a huge "outer world," with an existence of its own; in that world, which spans two decades, we find an entire value system, not a retreat from it. Similarly, in *Gravity's Rainbow,* we discover that language works to thrust us into energy and movement, toward a confrontation not with lassitude and enervation but with infinitude.

For both Gaddis and Pynchon, the corporate empire embodies tremendous energy. Once created, it takes on a vitality and vibrancy that is cataclysmic. The key image is Pynchon's *thrust* and *thrusting,* sexual as well as financial, athletic as well as martial; the method based on exuberance. Both may parody finance, capitalism, the corporation, but they see in that a form of existence that gives real meaning to individual lives. While it may, in its multiplicity and energies, bury the individual, it also engages him. Edward Bast may reject the financial dealings of J R, but he comes alive in that chaotic, nightmarish Ninety-sixth-Street apartment. And J R, that schoolboy, grows into an energetic, resourceful giant once he attaches himself to high finance. The personal source may be greed or desire for power, but the process is vital.

Barthelme and Nabokov, to whom we could add Barth, are exuberant wordmen of exhaustion and enervation; they play not only with the death of the novel but with the death of feeling itself by constructing verbal analogies to the state of dying. Nabokov's work is almost always the end of something; and Barthelme has worked a similar vein: the death of the fairy tale in *Snow White,* the death of the father and an age of paternalism, the death of communication at cocktail parties, the death of writing and painting, the death of verbal communication itself.

Gaddis and Pynchon, however, limn the contours of energy even when their goals are satire and parody. *The Recognitions,* a more formal work, is roughly equivalent in Gaddis' career to *V.* in Pynchon's, published eight years later. In both novels, the expression of the fifties and early sixties created a certain amount of exhaustion—the feeling that we noted of "the end of." Their novels of the seventies are a different matter, however, a recovery from malaise, an exuberance that may be a partial extension of the sixties, and a direction for the American novel so outside the realist-naturalist tradition that the critic can point to a revitalized fiction.

Notwithstanding, they are not congruous. Gaddis works outward from a tiny base, the rooms of an apartment, a school office, or a telephone booth. Small voices are emitted from cramped quarters. Although he sweeps beyond to a country, *J R* rests on the tip of an inverted pyramid. Pynchon, of course, has taken the immensity of the universe for his province and uses rocketry as a way of exploring it; he follows Melville's dictum that great themes require immense subjects. Pynchon gets at suffocation of the individual by way of spatial immensity; Gaddis by way of Kafka's enclosed space. Gaddis has remained a man of the fifties, working outward from what could have been enervating enclosures, whereas Pynchon is very much a writer of the sixties, extending into spaciousness, having assimilated the previous decade and its freedom of movement.

We have, fortunately, I believe, entered another modernist phase. This phase did not begin in the sixties, but in long novels that, in Gaddis' case, reach back to the late forties, continue into the fifties for their ideological base and textures, pick up again in the sixties with the gestation of *J R*, and continue into the early seventies when the novel was completed. For almost a thirty-year period Gaddis has been developing two works displaying an American form of modernism. *J R*, in particular, has affinities to the other major developments in the arts. The electronic sounds of new music, for example, lead directly into the telephonic nature of the novel. The reliance there on sounds alone, in new sequences, or in seemingly random patterns, finds its parallel in the nature of media communication, a polyphony of voices that explodes into different and contrasting levels of meaning. The loss of melodic line in modern serial music finds still another parallel in the interrupted speech patterns of *J R*. In art, in particular, the laid-on paint we associate with Jackson Pollock, or the stress on linear arrangements and field of vision of the action painters can be found in both *The Recognitions* and *J R*, although more recognizably in the latter. Pop art, whose development paralleled the gestation and writing of *J R* (itself a pop title), informs the novel at every turn, with the apartment on Ninety-sixth–Street a repository of the junk objects, a Warhol factory that nourishes pop culture.

When J R speaks of there being no inside ("How could I be inside, there isn't any inside!"), he turns his vision of America into a gigantic mail-order firm: America as Sears or Montgomery Ward. When everything in that world crosses and crisscrosses, when all goods are in constant movement, then process is substance and there is, indeed, no inside. This is a witty view of America—the quintessential 1950s, the years of Eisenhower and American financial recovery; and it is by no means entirely destructive, since, as balance, Gaddis provides Bast's music and Mrs Joubert's sense of nature. Art and nature are still "out there," although not inside. We may only indistinctly and intermittently see that world "beyond," but it has alternate meanings, and it can be internalized if we achieve recognitions.

Notes

1. When Pynchon picks up the theme in *V.*, counterfeiting becomes "stencilized," Herbert Stencil's programmed existence. But *V.* is a novel of the sixties, when anything not natural was deemed unnatural. Pynchon's allegiance to Gaddis' *The Recognitions* is clear throughout his entire career, and one result of that adherence is that *Gravity's Rainbow* and *J R*, which appeared within two years of each other, should be read as tandem novels defining the postwar era.

2. *The Recognitions* (1955; reprint, Cleveland and New York: The World Publishing Co., Meridian Fiction, 1962), 450–51. Subsequent references to this work will be cited parenthetically in the text.

3. While Gaddis has himself disavowed any direct influence from Joyce, Stephen is *there* as a presence and Joyce is there in uses of language.

4. We find a parallel argument in Walter Benjamin's "The Work of Art in the Age of Mechanical Reproduction," which Gaddis may have been familiar with. Benjamin quotes Valéry to the effect that new techniques in reproduction of art will alter our entire perception of the Beautiful, affecting artistic invention itself, changing how we view matter, time, and space. Benjamin's argument is that a work of art depends on its *aura*—that is, "its presence in time and space, its unique existence at the place where it happens to be." Wyatt's defense of his particular kind of forgery, whereby he produces a painting that falls within an existing canon, echoes Benjamin's conception of the *aura*, which makes each work of art unique in the face of mechanical reproduction. This *aura*, as Benjamin uses the word, means that the work of art controls or determines its history during the entire time of its existence. Changes in its physical condition, movement among owners, increase or decrease in its sales price all have no effect on the essential work. It is that very control over the work that Wyatt wishes, one reason why he rejects original work in the present era, where reproduction and other mechanical forms have preempted the *aura* of a master. At the time Gaddis wrote *The Recognitions*, controversy over originals, reproductions, and availability was created by André Malraux's contention that art now belonged to everyone, that museums no longer had walls. In this view, reproduction is the ultimate egalitarianism, not to be despised but applauded.

5. Dante placed counterfeiters in Bolgia Ten of Circle Eight of Malebolge. The falsifier of money is a "sinner of the third class," whose body is loathsome and racked by thirst. All he is capable of is abuse. The archetypal counterfeiter for Dante was Adamo da Brescia, who falsified the Florentine florin by making it of twenty-one-rather than twenty-four-carat gold, thus precipitating a currency crisis. Sinisterra aims lower.

6. Tony Tanner, *City of Words: American Fiction, 1950–1970* (New York: Harper & Row, 1971), 27.

7. *J R* won the National Book Award for the best novel of 1975 and then sank into oblivion.

8. Libretto for Solti *Ring*, 26.

9. *J R* (New York: Alfred A. Knopf, 1975), 3. Subsequent references to this work will be cited parenthetically in the text.

10. Although the sources for a book like *J R* are America itself, nevertheless one perceives parallels to the Brecht-Weill opera, *The Rise and Fall of the City of Mahagonny*. The capital crime in Mahagonny is poverty, whereas wealth, acquired in whatever manner, rules. In a sense, this is the other side of Puritanism, a parodic view of earthly wealth as symbolic of the heavenly riches yet to come—a view Gaddis in both novels could accommodate.

Bibliography

Works by William Gaddis

BOOKS

The Recognitions

New York: Harcourt, Brace & Company, 1955; 2d printing (May 1964) by Harcourt, Brace & World.

Toronto: George J. McLeod, 1955.

Cleveland and New York: World (Meridian Fiction), 1962.

London: MacGibbon & Key Ltd., 1962.

(*Le perizie*). Translated by V. Mantovani. Milan: Mondadori, 1967.

New York: Harcourt, Brace & World (Harvest Books), 1970.

(*Les Reconnaissances*). Translated by Jean Lambert. Paris: Gallimard, 1973.

New York: Avon (Bard Books), 1974.

J R

New York: Alfred A. Knopf, 1975.

London: Jonathan Cape, 1976.

CONTRIBUTIONS TO BOOKS

"Les Chemin des Anes." In *New World Writing,* edited by Arabel J. Porter et al., 210–22. New York: New American Library, [April] 1952.

"From *The Recognitions.*" In *Writers in Revolt,* edited by Richard Seaver, Terry Southern, and Alexander Trocchi, 225–49. New York: Frederick Fell, 1963. Reprint, New York: Berkley, 1965.

[Self-portrait.] In *Self-Portrait: Book People Picture Themselves*. From the collection of Burt Britton, New York: Random House, 1976, 9. Reprinted in *New York Times Book Review,* 5 December 1976, 96.

Contributions to Periodicals

Harvard Lampoon

"As Lampy Sees Them." 1 October 1943, 26–27 (theater and cinema reviews, co-written by Leon A. Harris).

"The Addict." 1 October 1943, 28–29 (short story).

"De Provincialitate." 1 October 1943, 37 (short essay on Boston as opposed to New York City).

"Paradise Revisited: A Play." 1 October 1943, 48, 50.

"Sic Transit Gloria . . ." 19 November 1943, 62–63 (parody of an adventure story).

"A Thought for Thursday." 19 November 1943, 63 (a thanksgiving for Harvard life).

"Nautical Nomenclature." 19 November 1943, 68 (short essay on the christening of ships).

"Les Jours Heureux." 19 November 1943, 68 (on Radcliffe).

"Banyan Day in the Wax Works." 10 December 1943, 84 (mock record reviews).

"I Want You for Christmas." 10 December 1943, 88–89 (short story).

"A Tear for Alma." 10 December 1943, 89 (poem).

"The Kid in Upper Five." 10 December 1943, 96 (short story).

"Christmas List." 10 December 1943, 112 (humorous "suggestions for the whole family").

"Dogfish Defunct." 14 January 1944, 1 (poem).

[Untitled poem beginning "Lost my faith in whiskey"]. 14 January 1944, 6.

[Untitled poem beginning "Once came upon a quiet college town"]. 11 February 1944, 7.

"The Book of John." 11 February 1944, 34 (biblical pastiche).

"Books." 11 February 1944, 40–41, 45 (book reviews of William Shipway's *The Campanalogia* [1816], the *Vatsayana*, Lawrence's *Lady Chatterley's Lover,* and Bartlett's *Familiar Quotations* [11th ed., 1937]).

[Untitled joke.] 1 April 1944, 70.

[Untitled poem beginning "'The time has come,' the Ibis said"]. 15 May 1944, 79.

"Suffer the Little Children." 15 May 1944, 80–81 (short story).

"Lasting Values in a World Gone Mad." 15 May 1944, 84 (poem).

"Unmöglich Apgar." 15 May 1944, 85 (on perpetual calendars).

"Let's Go to Press." 15 May 1944, 89 (short story).

"Lampy's Crossword Puzzle Department." 15 May 1944, 93.

"Lampy's Crib Notes for Psychology Majors." 20 June 1944, 106.

"Non Disputandum." 20 June 1944, 112 (poem).

"God Bless Our Still." 20 June 1944, 116 (short story).

"Lampy's Language Crutch: La Belle Dame Sans Merci—or, The Beautiful Lady Who Forgot to Say Thank You." 20 October 1944, 28 (a comically literal translation of a French selection).

"The Descent of Man, or Sparta on The Charles." 20 October 1944, 32–33 (short story).

"Old Wive's [*sic*] Tale: A Play in the Elizabethan Manner." 30 November 1944, 58, 65.

"A Psychometic Study of the Effects of Nourishment." 30 November 1944, 59–60 ("Harvard horribilia—the dining hall").

"Mordred." January 1945, 108 (short story).

"Tripanosomiasis in B Flat." January 1945, 116 (poem).

[Reprint of untitled poem, "Once came upon a quiet college town"]. February 1945, 31.

[Reprint of "The Book of John"]. February 1945, 40, 48.

Other Periodicals

"'Stop Player. Joke No. 4.'" *Atlantic Monthly,* July 1951, 92–93. Reprinted in Moore: *Reader's Guide* (see below), 299–301.

"J. R. or the Boy Inside." *Dutton Review,* no. 1, 1970, 5–68.

"Untitled Fragment from Another Damned, Thick, Square Book." *Antaeus* 13/14 (Spring/Summer 1974): 98–105.

"Nobody Grew but the Business." *Harper's,* June 1975, 47–54, 59–66.

"In the Zone." *New York Times,* 13 March 1978, p. 21. Reprinted in Moore's *Reader's Guide,* 301–4.

"The Rush for Second Place." *Harper's,* April 1981, 31–39.

Works about William Gaddis
(excluding those reprinted in this volume)

CRITICISM

Aldridge, John W. *The American Novel and the Way We Live Now.* New York and London: Oxford University Press, 1983, 46–52, 148. A revision of his excellent review of *J R* in the *Saturday Review,* 4 October 1975, 27–30.

Bakker, J. "The End of Individualism." *Dutch Quarterly Review of Anglo-American Letters* 7 (1977): 286–304. A Marxist examination of the relationship between man and community in *The Recognitions* and Pynchon's *Gravity's Rainbow,* concluding Wyatt's final "recognition" is "that the self is dispensable, and that reality resides in the people, the community, in humanity, in the species."

Balazy, Teresa. "A Recognition of *The Recognitions.*" In *Traditions in the Twentieth Century American Literature.* Edited by Marta Sienicka. Poznań, Poland: Adam Mickiewicz University Press, 1981, 23–33. A fine examination of "the tension between the religious and the aesthetic" in *The Recognitions* and its iconography. Though somewhat awkwardly written, it sparkles with many insights.

Banning, Charles Leslie. "William Gaddis's *J R*: The Organization of Chaos and the Chaos of Organization." *Paunch* 42/43 (December 1975): 153–65. An essay-review of Gaddis' second novel with an emphasis on its thematic continuity with his first.

Benstock, Bernard. "On William Gaddis: In Recognition of James Joyce." *Wisconsin Studies in Contemporary Literature* 6 (Summer 1965): 177–89. An ingenious case for the influence of Joyce's *Portrait* and *Ulysses* on *The Recognitions* — neither of which Gaddis claims he has ever read.

Bishop, Ferman. *William Gaddis.* Boston: G. K. Hall, Twayne United States Authors Series, forthcoming.

Boccia, Michael. "–What Did You Say Mister Gaddis? Form in William Gaddis's *J R.*" *Review of Contemporary Fiction* 2, no. 2 (Summer 1982): 40–44. A discussion of the demands made on the reader by Gaddis' second novel, with analogies from Norbert Wiener's work on information theory.

Bouchouk, Monique. "Un long voyage sur la Terre Vaine: Les Reconnaissances de William Gaddis." *Caliban XII* (L'université de Toulouse-Le Mirail) n.s. 11 (1975): 3–15. An introduction for French readers. Mme. Bouchouk places *The Recognitions* in various literary traditions — Continental as well as American — and concludes that the novel is, like *Ulysses,* both a culmination of and a departure from literary tradition.

Durand, Régis. "On Conversing: In/On Writing." *Sub-Stance,* no. 27 (1980): 47–51. Includes a brief discussion of Gaddis' use of dialogue in *J R.*

Eckley, Grace. "Exorcising the Demon Forgery, or the Forging of Pure Gold in Gaddis's *Recognitions.*" In *Literature and the Occult.* Edited by Luanne Frank. Arlington: University of Texas, 1977, 125–36. An unfocused essay marred by factual errors, misreadings, and assorted irrelevancies. Though not totally without value, it is to be approached with caution.

Green, Jack [pseud.] "fire the bastards!" (parts 1–3). *newspaper,* nos. 12–14 (24 February, 25 August, 10 November 1962): 1–76. A lively history of *The Recognitions'* critical reception 1955–62 and a reassessment of the novel's worth; 70–76 contain a full bibliography of all reviews and material pertaining to *The Recognitions* to 1962.

Gregson, David E. "*The Recognitions.*" In *Survey of Contemporary Literature.* Rev. ed. Edited by Frank N. Magill. Englewood Cliffs: Salem Press, 1977, vol. 9: 6275–79. A useful outline of the novel's basic elements.

Guzlowski, John Z. "Hollow Gestures and Empty Words: Inconsequential Action and Dialogue in Recent American Novels." *Markham Review* 12 (Winter 1983): 21–26. The second half of this article discusses the noise factor in the dialogue of *J R.*

———. "Masks and Maskings in Hawkes, Gaddis, Barth, and Pynchon." *Journal of Evolutionary Psychology* 4 (Fall 1983): 214–26. Includes a brief discussion of young J R's imprisonment in "a world where money talks while the inner self remains speechless."

———. "No More Sea Changes: Hawkes, Pynchon, Gaddis, and Barth." *Critique* 23, no. 2 (Winter 1981–82): 48–60. On sea symbolism in *The Recognitions* (53–57).

Koenig, Peter William. "Recognizing Gaddis' *Recognitions.*" *Contemporary Literature* 16 (Winter 1975): 61–72. A general description of the novel and its critical reception, with several valuable quotations from Gaddis' manuscript materials.

Kuehl, John, and Steven Moore. "An Interview with William Gaddis." *Review of Contemporary Fiction* 2, no. 2 (Summer 1982): 4–6.

Lathrop, Kathleen L. "Comic-Ironic Parallels in William Gaddis's *The Recognitions.*" *Review of Contemporary Fiction* 2, no. 2 (Summer 1982): 32–40. An examination of the juxtaposition of comic and serious elements in Gaddis' first novel.

LeClair, Thomas. "Missing Writers." *Horizon,* October 1981, 48–52. The final page discusses Gaddis' reclusiveness and features several quotations by Gaddis on his art.

———. "William Gaddis, *J R,* & the Art of Excess." *Modern Fiction Studies* 27 (Winter 1981–82): 587–600. A brilliant examination of the excessive nature of Gaddis' work and the waste motif in his second novel.

McNamara, Eugene. "The Post-Modern American Novel." *Queen's Quarterly* 69 (Summer 1962): 265–75. Includes Gaddis as one of four writers who are "creating works which are original in a radical sense."

Madden, David. "William Gaddis." In *American Novelists Since World War II.* Edited by Jeffrey Hellerman and Richard Layman. Dictionary of Literary Biography, vol. 2. Detroit: Gale Research, 1978, 162–70. A serviceable introduction enhanced by Jill Krementz's photograph of Gaddis and reproductions of two pages from the manuscript of *J R.*

———. "William Gaddis's *The Recognitions.*" In *Rediscoveries.* Edited by David Madden. New York: Crown, 1971, 291–304. A useful overview of the novel's major themes, characters, and stylistic devices.

Malmgren, Carl D. "William Gaddis's *J R*: The Novel of Babel." *Review of Contemporary Fiction* 2, no. 2 (Summer 1982): 7–12. On the functions of dialogue in Gaddis' second novel.

Martin, Stephen-Paul. "Vulnerability and Aggression: Characters and Objects in *The Recognitions*." *Review of Contemporary Fiction* 2, no. 2 (Summer 1982): 45–50. On the aggressive nature of the physical universe and the characters' susceptibility to it.

Miuamoto, Yokichi. "Rainichi shita William Gaddis: Yomu Tanoshisha to Kaku Tanoshisha" [William Gaddis Visits Japan: The Pleasures of Reading and Writing]. *Eigo Seinen* 122 (1 December 1976): 404–6. A report on the two-week lecture tour of Japan made by Gaddis in September 1976, with some comments by Gaddis on his work.

Moore, Steven. "Additional Sources for William Gaddis' *The Recognitions*." *American Notes & Queries,* in press.

———. "Chronological Difficulties in the Novels of William Gaddis." *Critique* 22, no. 1 (1980): 79–91. An attempt to fix the time schemes and historical backgrounds of both novels.

———. "'Parallel, Not Series': Thomas Pynchon and William Gaddis." *Pynchon Notes* 11 (February 1983): 6–26. An examination of the question of influence, with remarks on thematic similarities between the two writers' work.

———. *A Reader's Guide to William Gaddis's "The Recognitions."* Lincoln and London: University of Nebraska Press, 1982. An introduction and set of annotations to the novel.

Safer, Elaine B. "The Allusive Mode, the Absurd and Black Humor in William Gaddis's *The Recognitions*." *Studies in American Humor* n.s. 1 (October 1982): 103–18. Examines Gaddis' ironic use of literary allusion and the absurdist vision that results.

Sawyer, Tom. "False Gold to Forge: The Forger Behind Wyatt Gwyon." *Review of Contemporary Fiction* 2, no. 2 (Summer 1982): 50–54. On Han van Meegeren, the Dutch forger whose career Gaddis adapted for that of his protagonist.

———. "*J R*: The Narrative of Entropy." *International Fiction Review* 10, no. 2 (Summer 1983): 117–22.

Schaber, Steven C. "*J R*." In *Masterplots 1976 Annual.* Edited by Frank N. Magill. Englewood Cliffs: Salem Press, 1977, 151–53. A useful outline of the novel's basic elements.

Stark, John. "William Gaddis: Just Recognition." *Hollins Critic* 14, no. 2 (April 1977): 1–12. A general introduction to Gaddis' two novels, better on the second. Though marred by a number of factual errors and especially misattributed quotations, it is useful in underscoring *The Recognitions'* debt to Dante's *Inferno* and the Clementine *Recognitions*.

Strehle Klemtner, Susan. "'For a Very Small Audience': The Fiction of William Gaddis." *Critique* 19, no. 3 (1978): 61–73. Like Stark's article above, a general introduction to both novels, and likewise better on the second.

Tanner, Tony. *City of Words: American Fiction 1950–1970.* New York: Harper & Row, 1971, 393–400. The British critic sees the novel as an imitation of *Ulysses* and concludes that Wyatt's final acts of "restoration" indicate a rejection of art altogether as a hindrance to reality—two points that could easily be challenged. Tanner reworked some of these arguments for his review of the Avon *Recognitions* in the *New York Times Book Review,* 14 July 1974, 27–28.

Thielemans, Johan. "Gaddis and the Novel of Entropy." *TREMA* [Travaux et Recherches sur le Monde Anglophone] 2 (1977): 97–107. An excellent study of communication in *J R.*

Weisenburger, Steven. "Contra Naturam?: Usury in William Gaddis's *J R.*" *Genre* 13 (Spring 1980): 93–109. Reprinted in *Money Talks: Language and Lucre in American Fiction.* Edited by Roy R. Male. Norman: University of Oklahoma Press, 1981. An instructive look at some of the fields of reference operative in *J R,* Weisenburger's examination of Wagnerian references is excellent, but his discussion of Empedocles is hobbled by his misunderstanding of the Greek inscription, for which see Matanle's essay reprinted in this volume.

Werner, Craig Hansen. *Paradoxical Resolutions: American Fiction Since James Joyce.* Urbana: University of Illinois Press, 1982, 165–81. Following in the wake of Benstock ("who guided me through the writing of the early drafts"), Werner discusses Gaddis' (nonexistent) debt to Joyce and exposes what he regards as shortcomings in *The Recognitions.*

DISSERTATIONS

Banning, Charles Leslie. "The Time of Our Time: William Gaddis, John Hawkes and Thomas Pynchon." Ph.D. diss., State University of New York at Buffalo, 1977. *Dissertation Abstracts International* [*DAI* hereafter] 38 (March 1978): 5471–72.

Braha, Elliot. "Menippean Form in *Gravity's Rainbow* and in Other Contemporary American Texts." Ph.D. diss., Columbia University, 1979. *DAI* 40 (July 1979): 255–56.

Brownson, Robert Charles. "Techniques of Reference, Allusion, and Quotation in Thomas Mann's *Doktor Faustus* and William Gaddis's *The Recognitions.*" Ph.D. diss., University of Colorado, 1976. *DAI* 37 (June 1977): 7733.

Cunningham, Don Rodger. "Cabala to Entropy: Existentialist Attitudes and the Gnostic Vision in William Gaddis's *The Recognitions* and Julio Cortazar's *Rayuela.*" Ph.D. diss., Indiana University, 1980. *DAI* 41 (July 1980): 236.

Fuchs, Miriam. "'Persistent Pattern and Significant Form': The Conceptual and Formal Impact of *The Waste Land* on Selected Anti-Realistic American Novels." Ph.D. diss., New York University, 1979. *DAI* 40 (September 1979): 1467.

Guzlowski, John Zbigniew. "The Assault on Character in the Novels of Thomas Pynchon, John Barth, John Hawkes, and William Gaddis." Ph.D. diss., Purdue University, 1980. *DAI* 41 (December 1980): 2604–5.

Hegarty, George. "Gaddis's *Recognitions*: The Major Theme." D.A. diss., Drake University, 1978. *DAI* 39 (February 1979): 4948.

Koenig, Peter William. "'Splinters from the Yew Tree': A Critical Study of William Gaddis' *The Recognitions.*" Ph.D. diss., New York University, 1971. *DAI* 33 (September 1972): 1172.

Matanle, Stephen Hayward. "Love and Strife in William Gaddis' *J R.*" Ph.D. diss., American University, 1980. *DAI* 41 (September 1980): 1058.

Miller, David Edwin. "Complex Business: Realism and the Study of Businessmen in Four Contemporary Novels." Ph.D. diss., Duke University, 1982. *DAI* 44 (July 1983): 169–70.

Minkoff, Robert L. "Down, Then Out: A Reading of William Gaddis's *The Recognitions.*" Ph.D. diss., Cornell University, 1976. *DAI* 38 (September 1977): 1393.

Morton, Marjorie. "The Orchestration of Chaos: The Context and Structure of the Novels of William Gaddis." Ph.D. diss., McGill University (Canada), 1981. *DAI* 42 (October 1981): 1637.

Simmon, Scott Allan. "The *Ulysses* Tradition: Open and Closed Form in the Novels of James Joyce, William Gaddis, and Thomas Pynchon." Ph.D. diss., University of California at Davis, 1979. *DAI* 40 (April 1980): 5441.

Stonehill, Brian. "Art Displaying Art: Self-Consciousness in Novels of Joyce, Nabokov, Gaddis, and Pynchon." Ph.D. diss., University of Chicago, 1978. No *DAI* listing.

Thompson, Gary Lee. "Fictive Models: Carlyle's *Sartor Resartus,* Melville's *The Confidence-Man,* Gaddis's *The Recognitions,* and Pynchon's *Gravity's Rainbow.*" Ph.D. diss., Rice University, 1979. *DAI* 40 (September 1979): 1462.

Contributors

JOEL DANA BLACK teaches Comparative Literature at the University of Georgia. Besides his studies of the postmodernist fiction of William Gaddis and Thomas Pynchon, he has written about the philosophical and cultural background of Anglo-German Romanticism. Professor Black's articles have appeared in *Comparative Literature, Boundary 2, The New York Literary Forum, Poetics Today,* and *The Review of Contemporary Fiction.* He has completed a book on model-theory in art, science, and culture.

MIRIAM FUCHS is head of the English department at Elizabeth Seton College. Her work in modern literature includes articles on Hart Crane (*Book Forum*), Djuna Barnes (*The Hollins Critic*), *Nightwood* (*Literature and Medicine*), and Coleman Dowell (*The Review of Contemporary Fiction*).

FREDERICK R. KARL, Professor of English at New York University, is the author of *Joseph Conrad: The Three Lives* and numerous articles and books on the novel, including *A Reader's Guide to Joseph Conrad, The Contemporary English Novel,* and *The Adversary Literature.* He is editor of the Collected Letters of Joseph Conrad and co-editor of the first volume, *Letters, 1861–1897.* His encyclopedic study, *American Fictions: 1940/1980,* was published by Harper & Row.

CHRISTOPHER KNIGHT is a lecturer at the University of Texas-Austin. He is presently writing a book that examines the empiricism of Gertrude Stein, Ernest Hemingway, William Carlos Williams, and Marianne Moore.

DAVID KOENIG, author of the pioneering dissertation, "'Splinters from the Yew Tree': A Critical Study of William Gaddis' *The Recognitions,*" teaches at Oakton Community College. He was a Fulbright Lecturer in Germany during 1974. Winner of several prizes for poetry, Professor Koenig is the director of a post-Holocaust poetry project.

JOHN KUEHL, Professor of English at New York University, is the author/editor of several books, including *The Apprentice Fiction of F. Scott Fitzgerald, 1909–1917*; *Write and Rewrite: A Study of the Creative Process*; *Dear Scott/Dear Max: The Fitzgerald-Perkins Correspondence*; and *John Hawkes and the Craft of Conflict*. His articles, reviews, and interviews have appeared in many scholarly journals.

JOHN LEVERENCE administers the Emmy Awards for the Academy of Television Arts & Sciences. His interest in Gaddis dates from graduate school days at the University of Chicago and Bowling Green State University.

STEPHEN H. MATANLE is an Assistant Professor of English at the University of Baltimore.

STEVEN MOORE, who is in the doctoral program at the University of Denver, has contributed to *A Wake Newslitter, Critique, Pynchon Notes,* and *The Review of Contemporary Fiction*. The University of Nebraska Press published his *A Reader's Guide to William Gaddis's "The Recognitions"* in 1982.

JOSEPH S. SALEMI teaches English at Pace University. Although his specialization is in Renaissance literature, he writes on a wide range of scholarly subjects. His articles have appeared in *Novel, Chaucer Review, Allegorica, Blake Quarterly,* and *Maledicta*. He has also published many translations from the Roman lyric poets. Currently, Professor Salemi is at work on an edition of the *Facetiae* of Poggio Bracciolini, the fifteenth-century humanist scholar.

JOHN SEELYE, Alumni Distinguished Professor, Department of English, University of North Carolina, Chapel Hill, is the author of *Prophetic Waters: The River in Early American Literature, The Kid* (a novel), *Dirty Tricks* (a novel), and *Mark Twain in the Movies*. Professor Seelye is General Editor of the Penguin American Library.

SUSAN STREHLE, an Associate Professor of English at the State University of New York at Binghamton, has published articles on Gaddis, Barth, Heller, Gardner, Nabokov, Pynchon, and Fowles in such journals as *Critique, Modern Fiction Studies, The Journal of Narrative Technique,* and *Contemporary Literature*. She is presently working on a book exploring representations of the new physical reality in several contemporary authors, including Gaddis.

JOHAN THIELEMANS teaches American literature at the Higher Institute for Translators and Interpreters in Ghent, Belgium. A regular contributor to the Third Programme of the Belgian radio, he has interviewed a number of leading American writers. Mr. Thielemans is co-editor of a drama magazine.

STEVEN WEISENBURGER, of the Department of English at the University of Kentucky, has published essays on Nathanael West, Flannery O'Connor, Thomas Pynchon, and William Gaddis. He has finished a complete set of annotations to *Gravity's Rainbow* and is now writing a book on American fictional satire.

IN RECOGNITION OF WILLIAM GADDIS

was composed in 10-point Digital Compugraphic Sabon and leaded two points
with display type in Sabon
by Metricomp;
printed by sheet-fed offset on 55-pound, acid-free Glatfelter Antique Cream,
Smythe-sewn and bound over binder's boards in Joanna Arrestox B,
by Maple-Vail Book Manufacturing Group, Inc.;
and published by

SYRACUSE UNIVERSITY PRESS
SYRACUSE, NEW YORK 13210